By Gospel Alone

By Gospel Alone

A Historical, Doctrinal, and Pastoral Counseling
Perspective on the Primacy of the Gospel

DAVID MENENDEZ

WIPF & STOCK · Eugene, Oregon

BY GOSPEL ALONE
A Historical, Doctrinal, and Pastoral Counseling Perspective
on the Primacy of the Gospel

Copyright © 2018 David Menendez. All rights reserved. Except for brief quotations in critical publications or reviews, no part of this book may be reproduced in any manner without prior written permission from the publisher. Write: Permissions, Wipf and Stock Publishers, 199 W. 8th Ave., Suite 3, Eugene, OR 97401.

Wipf & Stock
An Imprint of Wipf and Stock Publishers
199 W. 8th Ave., Suite 3
Eugene, OR 97401

www.wipfandstock.com

PAPERBACK ISBN: 978-1-5326-5487-9
HARDCOVER ISBN: 978-1-5326-5488-6
EBOOK ISBN: 978-1-5326-5489-3

Manufactured in the U.S.A.

Contents

Chapter 1: Introduction: Why the Need of Christ as the Gift for All of Life | 1

Chapter 2: How Free Can a Free Gift Be? Its Point of Origin, the Biblical Gospel | 13

Chapter 3: How Does a Free Gift Become No Longer Free? Lost in Shipping, Early Corruption | 24

Chapter 4: How Is a Free Gift Kept No Longer Free? Lost in Transit, Ongoing Seeds of Corruption | 36

Chapter 5: How Is a Free Gift Further Lost by High Middle Ages Handling? | 45

Chapter 6: How Can a Free Gift Be Recovered? Lost and Found | 60

Chapter 7: How Is a Free Gift "Mixed Up" in Reception? Sorting Out Reformed Abuse and Confusion | 82

Chapter 8: A Redemptive Cognitive-Relational Narrative Framework to Pastoral Counseling: In Search of Christ-Centered Applications to Counseling Psychology in Christian Practice | 114

Chapter 9: A Romans Catechism with Counseling Vignettes and Implications within the RCRN Framework | 130

Chapter 10: Concluding Thoughts to Keep the "Package" Going | 178

Bibliography | 189

Vita | 193

CHAPTER 1

Introduction

Why the Need of Christ as
the Gift for All of Life

THE PRESENT WORK PURSUES an apologetic plea on behalf of the gospel. It would seem to many that the gospel is doing just fine, and we need to concentrate on other very pressing and important issues such as missions, evangelism, social justice, and moral transformation and change, just to name a few. But it will be our argument that no matter how good it may be with the gospel, and how many other pressing issues may exist, the church must continually articulate the gospel as the ever pressing need of the day. And by gospel we mean the doctrine of Christ's perfect God-pleasing life as empowered by the Spirit under the law, in order to be the Father's incarnate Lamb of God who takes away sin by his atoning reconciling death, for the justification of sinners by faith alone without their works, merits, or obedience before God. It is the doctrine of faith, grace, and Christ alone in order to be thus received and embraced by the lavish, abundant, and unconditional loving mercy of the triune God. Furthermore, we want to show that the gospel provides a very practical framework to live in communion with God and with one another. It is indispensable for living, and for living such a life as it is daily delivered by God unto us sinners in the communication and apprehension of the gospel as undeserved and unconditional, yet efficacious and transforming gift.

Mankind was not created to live by their own self-made resources, performance, and identification. Actually, life and all that we enjoy in it that is good comes to us as gift, a gift from our creator, from God. This is one key and foundational biblical insight, namely, that all the good we have should go by the name of gift, and that such gifts come from above. My esteemed colleague Pastor Ken Jones, cohost of the *White Horse Inn* for twenty years and contributor to *Tabletalk* publications among others, often reminds us[1] how it was a feature of God's original creation to have man created to worship God in a Sabbath day of rest, and thus Adam and Eve are welcomed in covenant after everything else has been created. They receive gifts from God in creation and ought to worship and honor God in gratitude and faithfulness. This is not the grace of redemption but the gifts and goodness of creation by which Adam, our representative head, should have kept covenant with God. Such goodness and gifts in the original creation or works covenant anticipate the future display of further and richer goodness in God, who will not only create but also redeem a fallen creation through the ultimate gift of the Son, Christ Jesus, the last Adam, and our representative head for new creation through grace.

The Reformed confessions generally recognize this reality, even more so in the grace and goodness of redemption, with its concomitant spiritual implications. The Heidelberg Catechism, just to name one, recognizes that we should be asking God for his gifts through prayer, and that those who receive such gifts should offer themselves to God as an offering of gratitude.[2] If this is so, then, human life in relationship with God should be essentially about recognizing the goodness and benevolence of the gift-Giver, and consequentially, about putting them to use in a wise, grateful, and graceful manner.[3] Thus, the idea of our work, vocation, and productivity should never be separated from the essential posture of being a gift-receiver, a gift-shapen and gift-sharing creature, and thus, and only thus, a human creature. This, in a few words, is the essence of true religion, of a true way of relating to God and his creation. Furthermore, this is also the way of true meaning and delight in life. Let us agree to call this *gift living*.

Sadly, we humans have bought a big lie: It's the lie that we can make ourselves, that we don't need gifts from above or from outside, but rather, have in ourselves the necessary resources to perform, achieve, and accomplish the good we want. Lane and Tripp explain this unfortunate human characteristic in light of God's gift, particularly in Christ: "In human relationships, each person contributes some strengths and gifts, but that is not

---

1. Pastor Ken Jones is currently involved with the author and two other pastors (Jose Prado and Aldo Leon from Miami) as cohost of *Saints and Sinners*, a radio program and podcast located in the Miami area.

2. See Heidelberg Catechism, questions 43 and 116.

3. For a thorough study of the significance of gift anthropologically and historically, particularly in the contemporary context of the New Testament, see Barclay, *Paul and the Gift*.

true in this case. Paul had placed his confidence in the assets of his own achievements, pedigree, and morality . . . he wrongly put his confidence in a resume of his own making."[4] Then, the personalized diagnosis as they immediately add, "We can do the same thing. We can put our confidence in our performance and obedience rather than recognizing them as gifts and strengths that should lead to gratitude." When this is the case, man is not a receiver and a shapen, dependent being, but a god-like creature that is able to carve out his own identity, his own reality, and, hence, his own meaning and satisfaction in life. We are what we do, what we decide to be, or what we rise to become. In short, mankind's distorted self-view in the world has to do with finding in themselves the way to redemption. This calls for action on their part—whether it be: liberation from absolute moral standards or strict adherence to them, escaping the world or improving the world, rejecting worldly pleasures and pursuits or embracing them, pursuing science or favoring religious creeds and experience, pursuing philosophical speculation or just practical pragmatic living, or any combination thereof; the end of it all is to arrive at some form of self-made, self-discovered, self-justified existence. And by self we are not just saying individually, but singling out the essence of mankind's pursuits, both, individually as well as collectively. Let us agree to call this *work living*.

In the above, we have tried to offer a view of things through an existential lens. We can, and we will, also, describe things from a theological lens. The Bible does both. It addresses the plight of mankind and interprets the creature in their human quest vis-à-vis the knowledge of God. In other words, the study of God, or of theology, always takes place intersecting or, better yet, within the story of creation and redemption. We cannot know God in a vacuum; we know him in the human story, and that is the way God has wanted to be known, namely, in his self-disclosure in the human redemptive narrative, and this revelation takes the form of the cross.[5] God reveals himself and speaks to the existential plight of mankind in "cross" language. God's actions for and in creation through the cross disclose who he is and who mankind is in light of such revelation. Forde cites Luther in a passage from the Psalms worth quoting in its entirety around the same time of the Heidelberg Disputation:

---

4. See Lane and Tripp, *How People Change*, 57.

5. For a penetrating analysis of such a concept, see Forde, *On Being a Theologian of the Cross*.

> In the kingdom of his humanity and his flesh, in which we live by faith, he makes us of the same form as himself and crucifies us by making us true humans instead of unhappy and proud Gods: humans, that is, in their misery and their sin. Because in Adam we mounted up towards equality with God, he descended to be like us, to bring us back to knowledge of himself. That is the sacrament of the incarnation. That is the kingdom of faith in which the cross of Christ holds sway, which sets at naught the divinity for which we perversely strive and restores the despised weakness of the flesh which we have perversely abandoned.[6]

Apart from such actions, God remains hidden and inscrutable. And that is precisely the Bible, the story of God's actions for and in creation that ultimately leads to Christ, the epitome and end goal of such actions. Christ's incarnation, identification with sinners, humiliation, death, and resurrection is God's ultimate and final self-disclosure for and in creation. Thus, if we are going to know anything about ourselves, our world, our lives, we must know Christ. And to know Christ is to know the essence of human living, of God acting in and for creation. God, in Christ, reveals and interprets the essence of our existence, or, what we have already named *gift living*.

Some folks would object to such an existential approach to theology with the objection that man is not the center of things, but God. That the way to glorify God is to make him the center of our theological endeavors and practice. Such a view would contend that God does not live for us, but that we should live for him; that God does not revolve around our human needs, but that we should push through and beyond our needs to concentrate in our service of him. One of the ways in which this contention is made is to say that *we should not live to be happy, but to be holy*. While one must agree with the premise that God is to be glorified, not the creature, and certainly to be viewed at the center of all things, not man, we would argue that the total implication of such a contention as presented above is not biblical and, actually, amounts to *work living*, rather than *gift living*. Let us explain: simply put, mankind cannot serve God except out of the recognition and praise of the faithful and benevolent supply of God's provision. This means that God is always the server while the creature always the receiver of such service. God is glorified in this arrangement because he is highlighted as the gift-giver for all of life. He alone is to be indispensable, needed, wanted, desired, prized, cherished, and marveled at. This he

---

6. See Forde, *On Being a Theologian of the Cross*, 14, citing Luther from WA 5.128.31–129.4. Lenker 1:204.

does by serving the creature, by supplying creation with all the riches of his goodness and beauty, by exalting himself as the ultimate good and need of the creature, by acting decidedly, irrevocably, and unilaterally in favor of sinful man, by acting in Christ as *the gift for all of life*.

Gift living as opposed to work living revolves around the premise that God's atoning and substitutionary work in Christ received by faith is able not only to justify sinners, but also transform them to love God and serve neighbor. This transformation or being conformed to the image of Christ constitutes what some have called the process of sanctification.[7] We aim to advance the premise in this work that both justification and the process of sanctification that ensues are the monergistic work of God whereby, through faith, the justified believer also grows in the fruits thereof. Many have advanced theories of sanctification that, while they rightfully make justification the starting and foundational point, yet fail to see its ongoing centrality. They distinguish justification and sanctification so sharply as to sever the ongoing significance of justification for sanctification. The ensuing approach is one where the centrality of Christ as the fountainhead of all good fruit and work in sanctification is replaced by a combination or cooperation of our works, efforts, and disciplines with the help of the Spirit. While, in the best of cases, much is made of the Spirit and dependence on Christ for sanctification, there is a practical failure to highlight the role of the gospel and faith in such pursuits.[8] This work does not deny the need for effort and perseverance in the Christian life but argues for the centrality of the gospel promise, and hence of faith, as the way not only to be justified but also to bear the fruits of sanctification. Everything is gifted of God through faith. Such a view necessitates the proper distinction between the law and the gospel, and the proper role for each clearly enunciated and demonstrated. We would argue that it is a failure to do so that has made for much of the confusion and problems that has existed in the body of Christ when it comes to the topic of sanctification.

If we recognize that God must always, in keeping with his holy nature, demand of the creature total conformity to his character and will as revealed in the law, but that we always fail to live up and conform ourselves to such

---

7. See Reformed confessions and catechisms for a treatment of the topic where sanctification is viewed as a subsequent process of growth in personal righteousness or obedience, for example, Westminster Confession, ch. 13.

8. See Bridges, *Discipline of Grace*. Other notable examples, in our estimation, lacking gospel centrality and law/gospel distinction are: Piper, *Future Grace*; and, MacArthur, *Gospel According to Jesus*.

perfect standards, then we can appreciate the grace of God in receiving us through the gift of faith apart from our works of righteousness (Ephesians 2:8–9 and Titus 3:5–7). So, one could say: on the one hand, there are works of righteousness as defined by the law, which demands total submission, surrender, commitment, and obedience in love involving all of one's being—namely, intellect, affections, and will; on the other hand, we have the lack of the above, and in its place faith or trust that despite our lack, or rather on account of our lack, God receives as the instrument or channel to grant us everything by way of gift, namely, Christ. Thus, the way of salvation is the gift of Christ with all that he is for us without our works, but only with our lack—nay, because of our lack. Christ's forgiveness, wisdom, holiness, sanctification, and everything he possesses God bestows upon sinners on their simple faith or trust that all their lack is swallowed up in all of Christ's abundance. Luther opens up his Heidelberg Disputation with the foregoing understanding expressed in thesis 1: "The law of God, the most salutary doctrine of life, cannot advance humans on their way to righteousness, but rather hinders them"; and then begins to conclude with thesis 26: "The law says, 'do this,' and it is never done. Grace says, 'believe in this,' and everything is already done."[9] These statements certainly could be said to be the bookends of the case we aim to make in this work, namely, that the righteous shall live by a faith that confesses what we always lack in us, as exposed by the law, but always possess in Christ as promised in the gospel. Such a faith or gift living supplies, motivates, and energizes the Christian along the way of his practical, ongoing, or progressive sanctification.

We have seen two errors that need addressing with manifold implications for the faith. These errors are two sides of the same coin issuing from the lack of a proper distinction between law and gospel as briefly sketched above. Correspondingly, there are two cases that can be highlighted as notable examples of such problems: one, the case where the sinner is called to salvation, to Christ's gift conditioned upon their full commitment or total surrender unto discipleship, and only upon this full surrender can one claim to be such and by extension to be saved, as is the case of John MacArthur's teaching—let's call this the front-end works living approach; the other, a case where much is made of faith alone in the front-end but unravels into a future or back-end works living approach where a final justification on the basis of works is awaited. In both cases, salvation and the gospel that proclaims it are conditioned upon some kind of law obedience together

---

9. Forde, *On Being a Theologian of the Cross*, 23, 107.

with faith. And in both cases disciples must look to the signs and evidence of their full surrender in obedience as the ultimate proof of their salvation. This salvation does not fully come to those who fully lack, but only to those who fully begin to get better or those who have fully attempted to do so along the way with something to show for it. We shall interact with these authors later, but the following two quotes may provide some initial stimulation for our subsequent discussion. MacArthur asserts,

> He demanded that people deny themselves completely. He required their implicit obedience. He instructed them to be ready to die for Him. He called for them to relinquish all their normal priorities—including family, friends, personal plans, ambitions, and everything else in this world. Their whole lives were explicitly and irrevocably placed under His authority. His lordship was total and nonnegotiable. Those were His terms, and would-be disciples who tried to dictate different terms were always turned away (Luke 9:59–9–62) . . . Yielding completely to Christ's lordship is that vital an element of true saving faith, and therefore the proclamation of His lordship is an absolutely necessary component of the true gospel.[10]

Then Piper:

> Picture salvation as a house that you live in. It provides you with protection. It is stocked with food and drink that will last forever. It never decays or crumbles. Its windows open onto vistas of glory. God built it at great cost to himself and to his Son, and he gave it to you. The "purchase" agreement is called a "new covenant." The terms read: "This house shall become and remain yours if you will receive it as gift and take delight in the Father and the Son as they inhabit the house with you. You shall not profane the house of God by sheltering other gods nor turn your heart away after other treasures . . . 'True faith embraces Christ in whatever ways the Scriptures hold him out to poor sinners.' This "embracing" is one kind of love to Christ—that kind that treasures him above all things.[11]

Needless to say, there is much good in the writings and lives of these two authors. Given their wide public acceptance and the nuanced nature of their arguments, it becomes more of a challenge to refute them. However, because the errors they espouse strike a potentially deadly blow to the heart of the gospel—in other words, it is not secondary or lesser matters

---

10. MacArthur, *Gospel According to Jesus*, 32, 36.
11. Piper, *Future Grace*, 42, 159.

at stake, but the very gospel itself—they must be confronted. Implicit in this confrontation is a larger criticism of an offshoot or strands of the Reformed tradition with the potential to damage the gospel of Christ. The danger we shall constantly be warning of consists in turning gift living into works living; this we shall contend happens in many subtle ways, but the end result is always the same, namely, the Christian life as gift—as Christ for us, his work and righteousness as our righteousness and perfect standing before God—gets obscured by an emphasis on transformation, works, or progressive sanctification.

One of the most subtle ways this happens is when gift living is subsumed into "transformation" living, where faith is not distinguished from the fruits thereof so that to have faith is to be transformed, to love, to obey, to be holy in practice. An example of this "transformation" of faith into a practical "doing" can be seen in Barclay's work *Paul and the Gift*; while this contemporary author has so much to offer in so many levels and writes with a tremendous erudition and penetrating insight, his view of faith arguably suffers from the "transformation syndrome," which as noted harkens back to a lack of proper distinction between law and gospel. Barclay makes a brilliantly nuanced argument that speaks of living by the Christ gift, yet, upon closer examination, we contend the Christ gift Barclay conceives is framed in terms of the transformation Christ in us has produced.[12] Barclay writes,

> . . . the saving gift has already been given in Christ, without regard to worth, and that God considers "righteous" those whose new lives evidenced in faith, have been generated from the Christ event . . . faith is the evidence that one's life is incorporated into the *saving, transformative dynamic* of the Christ *event* [italics mine], which is nothing less than the death of the self (2:19) and the emergence of a new life more properly described as "Christ in me" (2:20). "Torah-practice" and "faith in Christ" are in one sense parallel: they are both evidenced in human lives and could be taken as

---

12. See chapter 12 in Barclay, *Paul and the Gift*, 351, for a full discussion of the Christ gift in the community of believers as a recalibration of norms—faith as an expression of new life springing from the Christ event; rather than just trust that by Christ's person and work, definitely his forgiveness and righteousness, I stand accepted without works or transformation unto love as prescribed in the law. While Barclay evidently tries to correct some aspects of NPP teachings, his effort to extricate himself from the law as a way of living and being accepted by God does not succeed in our estimation because he turns faith into law keeping in Christ, no matter how many other words and semantics are used to disclaim it and "upend" everything from the Christ event.

grounds for being considered "righteous." But faith in Christ is not just an alternative orientation or a different pattern of life: it is the mode of a new life, suspended from an event that has created what is humanly impossible, life out of death (2:19–20). God considers this "righteous" not because faith is a superior disposition, but because faith in Christ is the expression of a life derived from the Christ-event, a new creation (6:15) that has been released from the power of "the present evil age" (1:4). We do not have to imagine here a "transfer" of the "righteousness of Christ," effected through a believer's union with Christ. It is enough to say that God recognizes as "righteous" those who indicate by faith in Christ, that the Christ-event has become the ground of their being.[13]

Barclay shines in his brilliant effort to vindicate the absolutely new thing or new life in Christ Christians have as opposed to the law or Torah-keeping. He insightfully recognizes that even Luther had reference to participation in Christ in relation to justification.[14] On this basis, he makes a very intelligent case for the Christian life as gift with faith being the practical "habitus" of such gift. However, as we shall continue to argue, gift living is compromised when our practical living, transformation, "habitus," obedience, love, welcome and acceptance of others, or progressive sanctification, whichever way is chosen to call it, is made the ultimate thing,[15] or the confirming final verdict of our justification and/or acceptance before God. This, in various ways, will be the substance of our objections to a problem we see recurring through the history of Christianity and doctrine. We would like to somehow offer a very brief sketch or plotting of its varied manifestations at different stages in the history of Christianity, with greater focus in the Reformed as an intramural discussion or criticism to our own tradition. Once again, we shall contend that a failure to properly, not only distinguish between law and gospel in preaching and teaching, but to hear and receive Christ daily for us as crucified and risen for our daily dying and rising with him through faith can compromise the witness of our Savior both to our souls and to others. We aim to provide a brief sketch of this gospel threat running through the historical edifice of Christianity.

---

13. Barclay, *Paul and the Gift*, 378–79.
14. See Barclay, *Paul and the Gift*, 379 n. 75.
15. See Barclay, *Paul and the Gift*, 504f. on the concept of "habitus" for further illumination of Barclay's view of the Christian life as a gift that cannot be separated from its ongoing practice.

We shall see throughout the brief historical survey and sampling of Part I that there has always existed a tension, and even more, an outright conflict between approaches to the Christian life that are more law-based versus gospel-based. There has always been through history an attempt to highjack the free gospel of God's grace and subject it to ethical demands. We would love to promote a view of sanctification or growth in the Christian life that never commits the error of conditioning the grace of God in the gospel to any demands for law and holiness obedience. Rather, we want to argue for the fruits of sanctification as always the consequence or the results of our increasing apprehension of the unconditional love of God in Christ for us sinners. This involves an understanding that faith and repentance are the means or instrumentation, apart from works, through which God works in us to conform us to Christ; that this process is fitted or resourced through repentance and faith, which is another way of saying through, specifically, looking or keeping our eyes on Christ, his person and work—to wit, the gospel.

Furthermore, this present work seeks to highlight the aforementioned truth that Christ is the gift for all of life vis-à-vis the glory of God, namely, that gift living is the way to glorify God. We shall contend that God has created our existence to enter it through the gift of the Christ event, and thus show us what it truly means to be human vis-à-vis Christ's incarnation to redeem; what it truly means for the creature to be creature and for God to be God. To find in such revelation that all theology points to an anthropology of *gift living*, of living out of an identity that flows from the person and work of Christ for us. We aim to offer a criticism of all theology that aims to corrupt *gift living* in favor of *work living*; in other words, to denounce all attempts by mankind to erect a monument to themselves rather than a monument to God; because in erecting a monument to God we find our secure place of shelter and peace, the tabernacle where God dwells with mankind as our eternal felicity and blessing. We would like to point the theological endeavor into a practical path where the gospel, in distinction from the law, empowers the creature to truly embark on a path of God-exalting, creature-healing *gift living*.

We shall do so by tracking in Part I how this *gift living* in Christ is revealed in the Bible as the hub and core of its message, as well as how it came to be corrupted throughout history. This biblical attempt to highlight the gospel in the context of history, we contend, is always a necessary endeavor because *gift living* has been, and will always be under fire and assault by work living, as Paul insightfully and pictorially explains in Galatians, where the enslaved and enslaving Jerusalem always seeks to persecute the free Jerusalem from above. Chapter 2 will look at the Pauline argument in Romans that advances a gift for those who are not and never will be worthy of such, in the context of some contemporary conceptualization and practice of gift giving and virtue that backgrounds Paul. Chapter 3 will begin to provide an interaction with early historical witnesses subsequent to the apostles and into the Middle Ages with the purpose of showing how the gift nature of the gospel was "lost" in transit. In chapter 4 we shall continue this interaction with Middle Ages witnesses to show the ongoing seeds of corruption that plagued the gospel. Chapter 5 will focus on the High Period of the Middles Ages to bring closure to our brief historical sketch of how gospel corruption evolved. Chapter 6 examines in what ways the Lutheran Reformation managed to recover the "lost in transit" gift, highlighting the crucial distinction between law and gospel, and its implications for faith and works, repentance and its fruits; at this point, we shall continue to provide for the theological and biblical arguments for the practice of grace or *gift living*. Chapter 7 will begin to provide an intramural criticism of Reformed views on sanctification that arguably endanger the free, apart-from-works nature of the gospel and gift living. In this chapter other samples from history will be provided showing diversity within the Reformed camp that can be contrasted in search for voices that speak with greater clarity on the gospel and must be used as better models of what gospel apologetics and preaching may look like. Again, the distinction between law and gospel and its vital implications will be fleshed out as well as pursuing clarification on the topic of repentance. This chapter will engage in dialogue with contemporary preachers, teachers, and their doctrines and practice of grace in light of recent controversies on the issues of law, gospel, and sanctification.

In Part II, we want to elucidate what this gift living sounds and looks like from an exegetical analysis of a key portion of Scripture on the subject as found in the book of Romans, particularly chapters 1–8. We shall do so through an integration of theology and psychology in pastoral contexts of discipleship and counseling, although we will present a stand-alone hermeneutical section for these chapters. In chapter 8 we will provide some counseling and psychological theoretical principles and background pertinent for what could be called gospel-centered counseling. We shall be presenting real-life counseling vignettes that will be informed by the theology of Romans 1–8, and the counseling psychological implications that arise from it. In the spirit of Reformed traditions, we shall craft catechetical instruments for both the theological and counseling applications of the chapters on Romans that may help better inform, edify, and equip the body of Christ on their sanctification journey. The above shall be fleshed out in chapters 8–10. We aim to be careful in the integration of practical biblical counseling with counseling psychology by noting in every case what insights psychology uses that it has derived from Scripture, and even natural law, and/or the common grace that God has afforded humanity in his redemption story. When necessary we will offer on-point criticisms of some counseling and/or psychological practices or premises that are not compatible with Christianity or with life as God has ordained and revealed it to us.

The contributions we aim to produce lie in the freshness and usefulness of hermeneutical and counseling catechetical instruction that centers on the gospel. While Reformed confessions and catechisms have been largely focused and built within a "loci communes" framework, our approach seeks to provide catechetical instruction that is constructed and focused along hermeneutical and counseling lines. The result should hopefully be a tool of theological reflection and instruction that is, at the same time, laser-like focused on the detailed handling of Scripture for the application of gospel or *gift living* in very specific real-life situations. We hope to remind the body of Christ that the means of grace are designed to lead us back to the cross, back to the gospel. Going forward in the Christian life can never be done without our eyes firmly fixed in Christ and who we are in him through his death and the imputation of his righteousness. We hope to delineate in such theological and counseling tools that the Christian life proceeds along the lines of a daily dying and rising in Christ through faith. Furthermore, that this is not a works venture, but a faith venture where our primary task lies in keeping our eyes on our alien righteousness, in looking outside of us to the cross, to our death and resurrection in Christ as victoriously and gloriously proclaimed in the gospel. This is Christ, the gift for all of life!

CHAPTER 2

How Free Can a Free Gift Be?

Its Point of Origin, the Biblical Gospel

THE QUESTION WE ARE asking now goes to the heart of whether the gift of God of salvation in Christ is one that does not have regard to any merits or fittingness in the human recipient. We see Paul in the book of Romans making the case that God justifies the ungodly without any reference at all to anything meritorious or worthy in them for such a gift. This is a question on which much will depend. Either God grants grace upon those who are absolutely unworthy and lack any conditions of worthiness for such a gift, or God may be called gracious indeed but not without the wisdom and justice of carefully ascribing his gifts where they belong, namely, upon those that prove themselves a fitting match for the gracious but just allocation of his benefits. Does God ever place any conditions of worthiness or fittingness for the receiving and maintaining of his gifts, namely, his favor and acceptance? Does he ever look to any conditions of worthiness in the sinner through obedience or anything else in them to qualify them as fitting or worthy of his gift? Sadly, opinions and practices abound that condition the grace of God and his acceptance or justification of man for eternity on something in man. These opinions run the wide spectrum from those that believe, in varying degrees, that God helps those who make the best of, or cooperate with, the grace of God; to those who believe that man receives everything from God, but yet God will justify man through some infusion of virtue and grace God gives them in order to make them acceptable before him. Our focus in this present paper will mainly be on the latter group since such a view has abounded among the Reformed and presents itself in subtle ways that are often hard to discern, but yet easily spreads the poison of a compromised gospel.

The biblical answer is that God accepts sinners without any conditions of worthiness or fittingness in them, or as Paul says in Romans 4:6, ". . . the blessing of the one to whom God counts righteousness apart from works." In this chapter, Paul appears to develop an antithesis between works and faith in order to demonstrate that God's gift of righteousness to the one who believes is not based on any conditions of worth or merit whatsoever. Hence, Paul writes in 4:4–5, "Now to the one who works, his wages are not counted as a gift but as his due. And to the one who does not work but believes in him who justifies the ungodly, his faith his counted as righteousness." If this is the case, then one must establish as a principle that God accepts sinners without any works of the law, any obedience of works, or anything in them that could be construed by God as a worthy condition they have met for acceptance. Not at all; the free gift in Christ Jesus lies precisely in the fact that they bring nothing to the table of spiritual worth or merit that would cause God to qualify them as worthy in any sense. They bring nothing at all and God accepts them through faith in Christ; the instrumentality of faith highlights the gratuitous nature of the gift because faith being opposed to works stands for lack of worthiness or merit on the part of the sinner.

In Romans 3:24 Paul explains that we are justified freely by God's grace, or by his grace as a gift, which may strike us as an odd expression since it may cause someone to ask, how free can his grace be? Again, the view has existed through history that although we are justified by the grace of God, this grace does not necessarily disregard conditions of worth that mankind must meet, even if those conditions are considered meritorious or worthy only because God has ordained to accept such rather than their being meritorious in themselves.[1] In other words, God does not owe the grace of justification to anyone, but he will grant it upon the sinner's worthy cooperation or use of it. Another variation lies in God granting man the virtues of grace that man will in turn demonstrate through their works for God's acceptance. In both cases, though in different ways, mankind and his works of virtue, whether just inspired and stimulated by God or simply infused into their souls to activate virtuous living, the variable that carries the weight and ensures their

---

1. See McGrath, *Iustitia Dei*, as well as McGrath, *Intellectual Origins of the European Reformation*, for a thorough analysis of different accepted theological strands that allowed for human cooperation and some "kind" of merit as a condition for justification, e.g., via moderna right before the Reformation in addition to the widely known outright Pelagian and semi-Pelagian views of earlier times.

ultimate acceptance before God is mankind's works, their obedience, their own *in-them* kind of righteousness.

Consequently, it does not matter how much anyone may want to add and talk about faith in these approaches, how much anyone may claim that this is all done in faith or by faith; the reality is that faith ends up justifying because of its obeying quality, which makes for the essence of what faith is. The implications are manifold. First, no longer is faith opposed to works for acceptance before God as in the biblical antithesis, but now faith must have or include works for this justification or acceptance to be complete or final, because faith on its own, without works, is not sufficient to stand before God. Second, God's only instrument of justification in Paul's view, namely faith, is no longer a mere receiving posture from the sinner, but it actually provides something meritorious in some way, something fitting or worthy of the God whose favor and acceptance we seek. Now, in addition to the merits of Christ, we must meet God with something of worth in ourselves or of our own doing for his acceptance. And, third, the gift of God's grace is no longer totally free or independent of anything we bring, but actually conditioned to our contribution or cooperation with his grace; hence, the gift is no longer a free gift. In Seneca's moral essays on benefits we can see the conceptual framework for the dynamics and workings of gift giving around the time of Christ, which may help shed further light on the nature of this free grace or free gift that Paul talks about: "For it follows that, if they [gifts] are ill placed, they are ill acknowledged, and when we complain of their not being returned, it is too late; for they were lost at the time they were given" (*De Beneficiis* I.1.1). The glaring implication stands out that those who receive gifts, while receiving from the liberality of the giver, yet receive because thy are a rather fitting and good place to bestow gifts, as Seneca complains about wasteful giving:

> Nor is it surprising that among all our many and great vices, none is so common as ingratitude. This I observe results from several causes. The first is, that we do not pick out those who are worthy of receiving our gift. Yet when we are about to open an account with anyone, we are careful to inquire into the means and manner of life of our debtor; we do not sow seed in worn-out and unproductive soil; but our benefits we give, or rather throw away without any discrimination. (*De Beneficiis* I.1.2)

And then the conclusion:

> The benefit that is a delight to have received . . . is one that reason delivers to those who are worthy, not the one that chance and irrational impulse carry no matter where. (I.15.3)[2]

Dr. Linebaugh offers some reflections on the nature and implications of Greco-Roman notions of gift giving related to the above quotes, which further illuminate Paul's free gift and its radical nature for its contemporaries: "this discerning benefaction in no way disqualifies the graciousness—the giftness—of the gift. On the contrary, a gift is defined as such precisely as it is rationally extended to a fitting recipient."[3] Hence, some type of merit or fittingness on the part of the recipient does not disqualify gift giving but actually requires it for it not to be wasted. Another contemporary witness that contains similar views is found in the Wisdom of Solomon, where he who "has not acted unlawfully or meditated wickedness against the Lord will receive the exquisite gift of grace in return for his steadfastness" (3:14); and, "Wisdom will not enter a fraudulent mind, nor make a home in a body mortgaged to sin" (1:4) because wisdom "seeks out those who are worthy of her" (6:16).[4] Paul surely had such ideas in his mental landscape as he wrote by the Spirit. These ideas have grace and wisdom indeed as gifts of God, but gift to the worthy, deserving, and meritorious in some kind of sense, even if it does not rise to the exact level of righteousness God demands; there must be at least some suitability between the gift and the recipient. Dr. Linebaugh very succinctly highlights this interacting with Wisdom thus: "This condition of suitability can be variously met by requesting (7.7; 8.21; 9.1–1–18), loving (6.12, 17; 8.2), honouring (6.21), serving (10.9), desiring (6.13, 17, 20, 8.2) and seeking (6.12; 8.2, 18) Wisdom."[5] Here we clearly see the notion that God considers something in the recipient as the fitting or worthy basis for God's bestowal of his grace or gift, in this case wisdom. Granted, their in-them virtue does not constitute grounds for deserving what God is about to give them, but while not deserving, they are definitely the right or appropriate match for God to make them objects of his gracing or gifting. Dr. Linebaugh elaborates on the implications:

> But again, as emphasized above, while it is the worthy who are saved, it is Wisdom who saves (9.18). Wisdom's repeated insistence on the suitability of the human recipient of divine grace

---

2. Seneca, *Moral Essays*, vol. 3 trans. John W. Basore.
3. Linebaugh, *God, Grace, and Righteousness*, 51.
4. Winston, *Wisdom of Solomon*.
5. Linebaugh, *God, Grace, and Righteousness*, 50.

is not indicative of notions of human earning. On the contrary, though Solomon was good . . . his obtainment of the *Xapis* of Wisdom required an act of genuine giving . . . His goodness made him a "fitting" recipient of the divine gift, but the gift remains a gift—a rational bestowal of divine Wisdom to one who corresponds to an appropriate standard of pre-conditional worth. In this theological context, an act of grace or a divine gift is an unearned-non-contractual, voluntary-though explainable-fitting, congruous-benefaction.[6]

There is another witness from history that we could add to the wisdom that makes man virtuous, and thus worthy by their works, or in this case, by habit. We are talking about Aristotle's ethics who wrote his treatises over three centuries prior to Christ, and, undoubtedly, was also a factor in the conglomerate of ideas that made up the Greco-Roman world. Paul F. M. Zahl, in his work *2000 Years of Amazing Grace*, writes, "The Protestant reformers . . . rejected Aristotle. They contended that Aristotle's book, *Nicomachean Ethics*, asserted a view of the good by which a human being was the sum of his works. Luther observed, rightly, that Aristotle taught justification by works rather than justification by Grace."[7] Aristotle in his ethics says things like: "moral virtue comes about as a result of habit . . . we are adapted by nature to receive them, and are made perfect by habit . . . we become just by doing just acts, temperate by doing temperate acts, brave by doing brave acts."[8] Zahl concludes, "There is no question that Aristotle's ancient ethics proposed a view of the achieved good that is entirely contradictory to Paul's notion of God's Grace." The gift for all of life that Paul contends for stands in direct opposition to the wisdom heritage received by the era that saw the glorious but alien message of grace dawn upon them in Christ. The mind of natural mankind has been trained, not only by its natural disposition in the natural law written in their hearts, but also by the philosophical and religious wisdom of centuries, to think contrary to God's grace in Christ.

In light of such great intellectual hurdles, it must be the duty of pastors and everyone teaching Christian doctrine to focus on breaking this Gordian knot that keeps people from being able to discern the true gospel. This is why we argue for the centrality of Christ and his grace in preaching.

---

6. Ibid.
7. Zahl, *2000 Years of Amazing Grace*, 214.
8. Aristotle, *Nicomachean Ethics*, book 2.1.

It should suffice to know that the Bible directs us to do so; however, the intellectual context in which we live, particularly in America, is such that a performance-and-virtue-based identity does not recede easily to the preaching of the gospel. Rather, it seeks to co-opt the gospel and enlist it as yet another tool in the arsenal of building virtue, worth, and rewards on the basis of what we do, on the basis of works living. While God has provided ways or means of grace to keep communicating to us our identity of grace in Christ, our flesh, our natural sinful desires and inclinations, takes the holy law of God and any directives or imperatives, for that matter, and turns them into a way of either paralyzing us through guilt and shame at our failure or deceiving us by the pride of growth in virtue and good works. Perhaps Zahl sums it all up in a very succinct paragraph in his book *Grace in Practice*, where he asserts about the nature of law or works living, "Law is true. It is also impotent and counterproductive. It produces its opposite."[9] Lane and Tripp also point in a different direction away from our performance and unto our identity in Christ as the grounds for our lives,:"We see that our lives do not consist only in what we have, how we feel, or what we have accomplished, but in who we are in Christ. This enables us to stand where we would once have fallen down."[10]

The issue at hand is that true Christianity is based on embracing an identity that is for us but outside of us. We are in Christ, in his perfect work outside of us, which he accomplished on our behalf. It is Christ's obedience, godliness, virtues, and faithfulness to the Father in love that provides the grounds for our forgiveness without any merits whatsoever. God only accepts full and perfect merit or righteousness because of his perfection. We can only approach God in the fullness or perfection of righteousness, in the covenant keeping of his law. We cannot appear before God as covenant breakers; to appear before him with only a certain amount of merit or worth in our efforts to conform to his moral demands according to his character would be to appear as covenant breakers. God must condemn covenant breakers, law transgressors, sinners who do not conform to his moral character. This is what the preaching of the law so ably and fittingly accomplishes. Paul explains by citing Old Testament Scripture: "For all who rely on works of the law are under a curse; for it is written, 'Cursed be everyone who does not abide by all things written in the Book of the Law, and do them.' Now it is evident that no one is justified before God by the law, for

---

9. Zahl, *Grace in Practice*.
10. Lane and Tripp, *How People Change*, 61.

'The righteous shall live by faith.' But the law is not of faith, rather 'The one who does them shall live by them.'" Thus, the law condemns and consigns to nothing but curse every effort, work, and striving that we perform under it because we never truly obey it but are always breaking it. Many are perplexed at this state of affairs, thinking that the law was given for us to fulfill, or at least do our best efforts under it for some kind of congruous merit, as we have already observed. However, Paul again answers what the purpose of the law was in Romans 3:19–20: "Now we know that whatever the law says it speaks to those who are under the law, so that every mouth may be stopped and the whole world may be held accountable to God. For by works of the law no human being will be justified in his sight, since through the law comes knowledge of sin."

Thus, the law is a mouth stopper; it eliminates the boasting of our flesh. It is not the means for self-improvement but the means for self-"disprovement." Through the law, the Adamic fallen nature we have inherited, or the flesh, gets denounced as guilty, condemned, and dead. The law reveals and exposes the curse of our flesh that must be killed vis-à-vis the holiness of God, hence, the shameful death of the cross. The cross, then becomes God's no to man's yes in Adam. What does Adam (old nature) seek? To provide a rationale to justify their existence vis-à-vis God's judgment. God through his law says to fallen man, "You cannot," but our old Adam insists in responding, "Just command and I will." Simon J. Gathercole, in *Where Is Boasting?*, makes a case for the boasting of the Jews upon the basis of their obedience to God's commandments within the law covenant. The author exposes such a boast with reference to Second Temple Jewish literature to bolster his Romans thesis:

> . . . we have seen that confidence before God and obedience are inextricably entwined in texts such as the Assumption of Moses, Baruch, the Damascus Document, the Wisdom of Solomon, and 2 Baruch. In the first, the statement that Israel has never broken the commandments is succeeded by the verdict that the commandments are the basis of the strength of Taxo and sons. In CD 7, the covenant is the basis of confidence for those who obey the commandments. In the Wisdom of Solomon, there is an expression of confidence that God will always be with his people, to which the author responds by declaring that they will never sin . . . he also describes this state as a historical reality: "for neither has the evil intent of human art misled us" (15:4). Similarly, the

author of 2 Baruch notes that "we know that we do not fail as long as we keep your statutes."[11]

Gathercole exposes the Jewish boasting as one that not only relies on their privileged elected position within the covenant of the Law: "... the relationship between obedience and reliance on the Law in the texts above might be better described as reliance on the law *presupposing or including* obedience to it. It is against this background of Paul's indictment of the Jewish nation as sinful that he proceeds to talk of the justification of ungodly Jews and gentiles . . ." He contends that Paul's interlocutor in the opening chapters of Romans "needs to be persuaded of Israel's sinfulness in the course of 2:1–5; 2:21–24; and 3:10–20. This idea is not a shared assumption since the interlocutor thinks of himself as obedient to the covenant." It is this stubbornness of the flesh in not submitting to God's "You can't" that God will always root out and expose because the free gift must be received freely indeed. If Christ as the gift for all of life is thus announced and thus received, then human boasting has been crucified; this is God's way to bring sinners through death and unto life by the message of the gospel.

Interestingly, the recent trends on Paul known as the New Perspective, which Gathercole and others have so ably addressed and convincingly questioned, if not outright refuted,[12] provide a rationale to talk about justification in a way that softens the original Reformation's cutting edge of sola fide.[13] This rationale, we would argue, undermines Paul's contention, as we have already noted, that man is justified before God without regard to any works, merits, or obedience. Yet, this is precisely what is trending among many evangelicals as well as the Reformed. While it is not in the scope of this paper to delve deeply into the New Perspective (NP), we believe its assumptions as well as some of its implications have found resonance among many. Such resonance goes along the lines of arguing for a gift that does not

---

11. Gathercole, *Where Is Boasting?*, 203

12. For detailed interaction with NPP, see Johnson and Waters, *By Faith Alone*; and, Waters, *Justification and the New Perspectives on Paul*. Gathercole, *Where Is Boasting?* also provides a powerful critique of NPP even though this current paper will not fully agree with its positions, especially on final justification.

13. For a critique of NPP more in line with this paper's position when it comes to justification and faith, see Westerholm, *Justification Reconsidered*. The author provides, in our view, a clear validation of sola fide evidenced in his refutation of a final justification based on works, as well as an affinity for the language of imputation. He appears more sympathetic to the Lutheran classical view with minor modifications. We shall come back to this author in subsequent chapters.

negate the necessity of works or obedience on the part of the sinner for justification before God, hence, in our view, divesting the gift from its absolute freeness. Federal Vision proponents as well as prominent or popular voices among what could be generally labeled as Reformed seem influenced, or at least compatible, with some of NP's implications.[14]

It would seem, and we contend, that the gospel is often compromised even by involving good aspects of our Christian faith such as the transforming work of the Spirit. In other words, even in those that reject justification by works of Torah or of the law, an attempt can be perceived to enlist the good "works'" or fruit of the Spirit as condition or instrumentality in our justification, even if just at the end. Somehow, Christ and his work alone do not suffice for a righteousness that God accepts alone. Authors such as Barclay and Gathercole, whom we have cited positively in their renunciation of Torah, however, allow for the role of our obedience, our transformation—admittedly, Spirit transformation—to figure in the ultimate equation of faith unto justification; works find a way of inserting themselves either into what faith is or as playing a role in final justification. Their separation from Torah does not separate the gospel from works deemed necessary for justification, so that other pertinent questions could be framed regarding justification thus: Is one justified by the works of the Spirit? Did Christ die and rise so that one would be justified by the work or works of the Spirit in us inclusive of both faith and love? Are we justified by the indwelling Spirit who now helps us in the fulfilling of the law by faith through grace? Is grace given us so that we by his Spirit through faith may now fulfill the law and thus be justified? Barclay, unlike Luther, does not believe that "'works' or 'working' signifies a faulty soteriology" because, as he goes on to explain, "Not by works of the law' means, quite concretely, 'not by the practice of the Torah." The author concludes that "Paul makes it clear that faith also involves action (5:6), arising from and made possible by the Christ-gift (2:20), and that in such action eternal life remains at stake (5:21; 6:8)."[15] In Gathercole we find a similar reticence to embrace Luther's raw sola fide:

---

14. For a thorough interaction with Federal Vision theology from a traditional Reformed perspective, see Waters, *Federal Vision and Covenant Theology*. We would argue that even among those critical of NPP there exists a view of Christian justification that includes obedience and not just faith, or at least that redefines faith to include obedience or transformation.

15. See Barclay, *Paul and the Gift*, 375 and 406, respectively. In chapter 12 the author describes faith as a "habitus" that involves working according to the recalibrated norms or allegiance unto the Christ event.

> This does not permit a return tout simple to Lutheran theology (while God does initially 'justify the ungodly,' the indwelling Christ and the Spirit enables obedience that culminates in final justification), but neither is the New Perspective's interpretation adequate . . . Paul is operating with two somewhat distinct perspectives on justification: the first occupying initial justification and the justification of the ungodly ('to the one who does not work') and the second referring to God's final vindication of the one who has done good . . .[16]

Thus, we see that in the best of cases, although there may be an understanding that Torah is not the way of righteousness, another way may be suggested that rejects Torah works but embraces Spirit works as part of the criteria for God's acceptance. It becomes justification by the gift or "gifting" of the Spirit as it relates to the enablement to do good works, rather than the gift of Christ, his work and person for us without works. Such a discussion will be further elaborated on in chapters 5 and 6, as we advance a little more on our historical survey. But suffice it to say for now that the language of final justification, of fulfilling the law by the Spirit, of Christ-oriented and -empowered works or working by love, the emphasis on such works for salvation assurance, the language of repentance as a beginning of obedience, as well as a language of covenant obedience for the believer in Christ that blurs the lines between the covenant of works and the covenant of grace, and the lack of distinction between law and gospel, are among the maladies we seek to correct. When the gospel that announces an absolute free gift for all of life from beginning to end is allowed to be encumbered by such additions, not only is the salvation point of entry obscured, but its continuation or life process is also deeply affected with manifold adverse ramifications for our Christian lives. If salvation is not so absolutely free, then our walk in this journey of life shall proceed with heavy fetters of bondage that neither please God nor further our spiritual service to him and community. If we are freely justified by the work and covenant keeping of another without regards to our works or obedience, the rest of our Christian lives will be one lived in light of such an amazing reality, or as Forde would say, "sanctification would be a process of getting used to our justification." We would never get past our justification; its glorious truth as a free gift without any conditions of obedience will become the center of any endeavor and efforts in our Christian walk.

---

16. Gathercole, *Where Is Boasting?*, 264–65.

Consequently, we will argue that sanctification, conceived as the process of bearing obedient fruit to God and neighbor in the true spirit of the law, is also by grace alone through faith alone as in justification. It is here that we seek another correction, especially among the Reformed, who seem content to speak of justification by grace and faith alone, but then want to argue that sanctification or bearing fruit of obedience involves a synergistic cooperation with God where our works must be added to our faith. While we acknowledge that God uses means of grace in the life of the believer, and even more that the Christian life will involve effort and struggle, we negate that any combination of faith and works is the proper dynamics to explain this process. We want to unequivocally make the case that faith is the walk of the Christian. Faith means always looking to Christ, to his gospel, whence the energy, motivation, and power are always derived. Furthermore, the means of grace are not works we do or add to the gospel, but, basically, the channels that God will use to keep speaking gospel truth to our lives, namely, conduits of gospel forgiveness, absolution, and love talk upon hearing the law. But before we elaborate on these concerns, we want to keep tracking with this free gift through history to get somewhat of a better grasp as to how this gift is always in danger of being lost or distorted in transit.

CHAPTER 3

How Does a Free Gift Become No Longer Free?

Lost in Shipping, Early Corruption

We now turn our attention to what happens right out of the gate of Christian history. Other authors have shown the best that the church fathers have to offer in terms of anticipating and articulating, although very imperfectly in our perspective, the biblical doctrines of justification, forgiveness, and the free mercy of God.[1] We agree that early fathers like Irenaeus, Chrysostom, Ambrose, Ambrosiaster, and later Augustine, to name a few, present worthy examples of the grace and mercy of God in justification apart from the merits of law and works as they view such. It's not like the language of forgiveness, mercy, and justification has totally disappeared from the landscape, much less the church or even the apprehension of gospel truth as basic and obscured as it may have been. However, it is our contention that such enunciations, even in the best of cases, are surrounded by much that militates against a clear articulation and transmission of the pure gospel Paul taught as delineated in the preceding chapter. Our purpose is to offer a pungent critique of the fathers in light of a pure enunciation of gospel truth as we espouse in this paper.

Principally, we contend that no works of any kind, whether of law or of the Spirit by faith, including any consideration of their merit, worth, or virtue, ever counts before God for the saving and final acceptance of justification. We affirm an acceptation before God that only has regard to the perfect atoning sacrifice and righteousness of Christ for our standing before God now as well as at the end. Hence, we will highlight that seemingly for

---

1. See chapters 2 and 3 in McCormack, ed. *Justification in Perspective*, for a more tempered and favorable view of the period in terms of its justification doctrine.

the fathers not an imputed righteousness by faith alone sufficed for present and final justification as we contend, but an infused righteousness of grace wherein virtues, works, and a certain merit of love must be required as well. We will fully support throughout this paper the many good works and virtues that may and do accompany our salvation in varying degrees along our sanctification journey, but flatly denounce any attempts at including them, at any point, as part of the instrument, conditions, or criteria for acceptance before God.

We want to provide a brief examination and survey of what was the general tenor and tone of the writings of those that succeeded the apostles in the following decades and centuries into the Middle Ages. What one can see, when looking at the history of Christianity in light of what happens to the free gift contained in the gospel, is nothing short of, arguably, a distortion in our estimation. While the language shall remain Christian, the substance of that language is far from what Paul taught about the free forgiveness and freedom from under the law, about a justification before God freely without works. One would think, given the importance of the Pauline letters and their emphasis on grace as the life of faith lived on the basis of Christ's death and resurrection for our salvation, that such a theme would find echoes in the writings of subsequent generations like the Apostolic Fathers, but that is not generally the case. There is no distinction for the most part between law and gospel, which turns their Christianity into a new law, a way of salvation by obedience. Of the way of grace, of free gift apart from works, of an acceptance before God on the basis of unconditional love, of the way of faith on the death and resurrection of Christ as the basis for our righteousness, of the confession of sinners who continue to sin yet find unremitting kindness and absolution in the person and work of Christ, we see little with crystal clarity and unequivocal precision.

Rather, what we see is a strong moral emphasis in the direction of legalism colored by mystical and philosophical tendencies in most cases. While the language, as we will see, uses Christian phraseology and references, glaringly distorted are teachings that would emphasis Pauline themes of justification by faith alone, or freedom from the law's condemnation to serve under grace without fear, or union with Christ in terms of the destruction of the body of sin by the death and resurrection of Christ; absent are the pure notions of legal imputation, of our assurance by faith in our sanctified position and identity in Christ as beloved children. Arthur Cushman McGiffert, a scholar of old, provided the following assessment about this initial period, with which we concur wholeheartedly: "It was as a law that these Christians chiefly thought of Christianity. Of Paul's notion of Christian liberty there is no trace in their writings . . . he that obeys the law will inherit eternal life; he that disobeys it will suffer eternal punishment . . . the keeping of the law was the indispensable and sufficient condition of salvation. Upon this all were agreed."[2] Justo L. Gonzalez, another scholar in the area of historical studies, provides a similar assessment: ". . . in their total theological outlook, one senses a distance between the Christianity of the New Testament—especially that of Paul—and that of the Apostolic Fathers. References to Paul and the other apostles are frequent; but in spite of this the new faith becomes more and more a new law, and the doctrine of God's gracious justification becomes a doctrine of grace that helps us act justly."[3] This is the constant danger that the free gift and gift living are susceptible to, given our weakness, namely, to turn the grace of God ever so subtly from a focus on a mercy, forgiveness, and rescue we get from outside, from another, in spite of our sins, to a power in us to help us deal with that sin and gain mastery over it.

Consequently, the liberation and power of forgiveness is turned into the liberation and power of ethics, of moral living and personal obedience. Grace, then, never gets a chance to stand on its own grounds because it must be defined by its effects, by its fruits, by what it accomplishes or enables us to work. Thus, grace is first and foremost the power for right living, the personal enablement and resourcing of our souls to meet God's ethical demands. While we affirm that grace does empower believers for obedience and ethical living, we do not wish to do away with what we believe to be the essence of grace, of free gift, or *gift living*, namely, that those who are not worthy and never in compliance inherently—by their own obedience and merits—with God's moral demands, yet get to enjoy and bask in God's full acceptance and favor in Christ; and herein lies its power. Thus, grace is not forgiveness and power but, rather, the power of forgiveness. It is only if grace is allowed to be shown for what it is, on its own, that its power shall be made to feel upon those who receive it and live in its light. It is only if forgiveness, which God freely gives because of his mercy and liberality in Christ, is allowed to stand as the center or the defining core for what grace is, that we will discover a power to live in a broken world where much cannot be fixed, but only forgiven; much healing, even if not

---

2. McGiffert, *History of Christian Thought*, 1:69.
3. Gonzalez, *History of Christian Thought*, 95–96.

fixing, may result from that. The Bible supports this definitional space for grace when it teaches that it is grace that leads to moral change, to a different life: "For the grace of God has appeared bringing salvation for all people, training us to renounce ungodliness and worldly passions, and to live self-controlled, upright, and godly lives in the present age waiting for our blessed hope..." (Titus 2:11–13a). We must notice that grace is the one that does the training or teaching, thus grace in the passage screams out for its own definitional and, even more, core and central role. Our obedience is the consequent or result from such training in grace; the training and its fruits must be distinguished.

With this in mind, let us enjoy, or rather endure, the distorted scenery that lies all along the historical journey into the Middle Ages when it comes to clarity in the handling and reception of this precious, yet fragile because of our weakness, free gift. One must start right at the time of the apostles; it is clear to see that during their lifetime they had to contend with those who preached "another" gospel, as Paul would denounce them. To fail to see this struggle in the writings of the apostles themselves is to be blind to a core component of our Christian apologetic endeavors. When Christians fail to see how it is the gospel that the enemy throws under attack daily with all kinds of scheming assaults, they can be easily distracted and thrown into confusion themselves about the nature of their struggle. Paul when writing to the Philippians claims that he has been "put here for the defense of the gospel," and later in the same letter warns the readers, "Look out for the dogs, look out for the evil doers, look out for those who mutilate the flesh. For we are the circumcision, who worship by the Spirit of God and glory in Christ Jesus and put no confidence in the flesh" (1:16b, 3:2–3). This struggle is so easily missed amid other important emphases the apostles make, such as: service, good works, vocation, family, civility, evangelism, etc. However, it is our contention that the important must never take the place of what is central because, as it is the case, the important always flows derivatively from what is central. The gospel must be restored to its centrality amid all other important concerns; the gospel is not to be balanced with other doctrines or matters of importance, but should be firmly entrenched as the core or hub upon which everything else hinges or depends.

It is clear that Paul, the preacher of grace and gift living, is engaged throughout his ministry in a battle that keeps resurfacing along the way, now in Galatia, then in Macedonia, on again in Asia Minor. It seems that this battle was one emerging in every territory Paul covered with the gospel. No one else like Paul was so painfully aware of such a conflict since he was counted among those in the opposition before his conversion. The conflict is between Judaism and the gospel. Francis Watson explains, "Paul stresses in Phil.3:6 that his zeal for the law had once led him to persecute the church; there could hardly be a clearer proof that Judaism and the gospel are irreconcilable . . . it is impossible to have both at once, and the latter is infinitely preferable."[4] It is worth letting Watson explain very aptly and succinctly, in his own words, what lay at the heart of this conflict theologically as well as sociologically:

> It seems that the Judaizers claimed that the promises of salvation were originally given to Abraham and to his seed, and that the seed of Abraham are those who are circumcised and who have submitted to the requirements of the law; that is the theological basis for their demand that the Galatians be circumcised. Thus, their understanding of Christ is set in the framework of the religious traditions of the Jewish community as a whole; for them, although no longer for Paul, Jesus is still the Jewish Messiah.[5]

It is interesting, then, to see how the apostle Paul inextricably ties theology and community, knowledge about God and ways of living in community before God in light of the gospel. Gospel truth translates into gift living in community, which means we no longer associate on the basis of any distinctive on the flesh, such as genitalia mutilation, because our distinctive or identity lies with the Spirit. Watson insightfully addresses this shocking language of Paul in Philippians 3, explaining that "he tells his Gentile converts that circumcision, the rite of entry into the Jewish community, is simply castration, mutilation and phallus worship, and such charges were probably the stock-in-trade of Gentile mockery of Judaism."[6] Paul, then, shifts his converts pastorally to their place of assurance before God and fellowship with one another, the identity of the Spirit. And the Spirit's identity is one of faith, an identity before God and one another that does not look to our own righteousness under the law, or shall we say, inherently in us, in our own "enfleshed" works under the law, but solely to the righteousness of Christ, God's own "enfleshed" work, namely, Christ's incarnation for the living and dying of the cross as proclaimed in the gospel. Believers are those, like Paul, that boast before God and rejoice with one another as

---

4. Watson, *Paul, Judaism and the Gentiles*, 77.
5. Watson, *Paul, Judaism and the Gentiles*, 69–70.
6. Watson, *Paul, Judaism and the Gentiles*, 76.

the community of sinners who confess their sin; those who call themselves sinners, in order to confess the love they have received in the Savior for sinners, for law breakers. It is this confession that, according to the elderly John in the opening of his first letter, that both forms and identifies the Christian community as those who walk in the light and keep the truth, those that live in the empowering light and love of *gift living*.

One has to wonder whether the Apostolic Fathers and most of the church into and throughout the Middle Ages acquired what could be called the "Judaizing" syndrome. By this syndrome let us now understand a way of relating to God and to one another in community that looks to our *"Christianizing"* marks in the flesh as the defining identity, namely, *works living*. These *"Christianizing"* marks, as we shall begin to see in our historical survey, could be said to be: right knowledge or enlightenment, as in the case of the Gnostics; good philosophy and conduct, as in the case of the philosopher apologists; law obedience and strict requirements for repentance, church membership, and moral living, as in the case of the rigorists; divinization or participation with the divine for spiritual elevation and transformation, as in the case of the more mystically and sacramentally inclined; or, simply, unquestionable compliance to the ecclesiastical structures and authority figures for those interested in preserving the unity and integrity of the church established and bequeathed by the forebears. Whatever variations or combinations of the foregoing *"Christianizing"* marks used in the subsequent centuries of the history of the Christian church, they were, we contend, illegitimate and fleshly ways to establish identity and community before God and one another; it was tantamount to *works living* as opposed to the gospel, or *gift living*.

Sadly, the church in this period seems to have lost track of the gift and succumbed to the attacks so subtly employed by the enemy to turn the gospel and our *gift living* into something primarily that we must do rather than what God has done in Christ for us; something we must finish, complete, or improve upon within ourselves rather than the—outside of us, for us, already finished and completed—work of God in Christ for sinners. Our following survey will not be necessarily chronological or comprehensive in its presentation, given that we only aim at capturing the essence of the attack or struggle with the gospel that always, not only throughout this period, characterizes the life of the church. Our beginning samples shall examine some portions of the writings of *The Didache* and *The Shepherd of Hermas* as illustrative of the moralism and legalism that began to take shape early into the second century. Let us begin with *The Shepherd* in order to discern how ethical concepts and repentance are so emphasized in a way that actually destroys the gospel of grace. In the Mandates, the second and lengthiest section of the work, we hear the following: ". . . 'I have heard, sir,' said I, 'from some teachers, that there is no other repentance except that which took place when we went down into the water and obtained the remission of our former sins.' He said to me, 'You have heard rightly, for so it is. One who has received remission of sins ought never sin again, but live in purity . . .'" And thus, repentance is turned into a sacrament that administers grace, and this grace translates functionally into purity of life never to sin again. The Shepherd, in his own merciful way, allows for one repentance after the initial receiving of grace unto purity of life: ". . . he declared, 'after this great and holy calling, if a man be tempted by the devil and sin, he has one repentance. But if he sin and repent repeatedly – repentance is of little value to a man, and with difficulty he will live.'" One has to appreciate the concession made here in the interest of mercy and comfort for the sinner with hope of restoration; however, it falls far short of biblical repentance and its implications are devastating for the gospel as the following response demonstrates. "I said to him, 'I am made to live again by hearing these things from you so accurately; for now I know that if I do not again add to my sins, I shall be saved.' 'You shall be saved,' he said, 'and everyone who will do these things.'"[7]

One can see clearly from the foregoing dialogue that something has drastically gone wrong from the biblical language of grace and even the renewal of the Christian walk in sanctification anchored in the indicatives of grace. The gospel of grace has been turned into the law of commandments that the penitent sinner must observe and keep for their salvation after forgiveness of sins. Another portion from *The Shepherd* continues to bear this out:

> And [the shepherd] answered me and said: "As many," he said, "as repent with their whole heart and purify themselves of all the wickedness mentioned before, and no longer add anything to their former sins, – they shall receive from the Lord a healing for their former sins, provided they are not double-minded in regard to these commandments; and they shall live to God. But as many," he

---

7. Jurgens, *Faith of the Early Fathers*, 1:35.

continued, "as add to their sins and live in the lusts of this world – they shall condemn themselves to death."[8]

We see that grace is made tantamount to obedience of the commandments, and it is on the basis of this obedience that forgiveness and salvation are assured to the repentant obedient sinner. It seems like repentance and obedience, grace and law, faith and works, can be made to be coterminous in meaning. We shall later elucidate the implications of such comingling or confusion of terms and concepts, as well as provide a clearer path with law and gospel distinctives where grace is not nullified but rather affirmed and made to work as the gift that empowers for all of life.

Another influential witness from the early period is *The Didache*. On this document Justo L. Gonzalez offers the following evaluation:

> From the point of view of the history of Christian thought the *Didache* is important above all as an expression of the moralism that very early took possession of some theological currents. At times, this seems to become mere legalism. Thus, for example, the distinction between "hypocrites" and Christians is based principally on their different days of fast or on the fact that Christians repeat the Lord's prayer three times a day.[9]

Furthermore, the document cites the way of the commandments as the way of life. "There are two ways, one of life and one of death: and great is the difference between the two ways. The way of life is this: first, you shall love God, who created you; second, your neighbor as yourself. Whatever you would not wish to be done to you, do not do to another . . . You shall not abandon the commandments of the Lord; but you shall keep what you have received, adding nothing to it nor taking anything away."[10] While the emphasis on right conduct and God's commandments is laudable, it is the failure or silence on any comprehensive articulation of the gospel as the free gift of grace in Christ that stands out very conspicuously. The way to recognize false prophets does not come by way of recognizing the gospel teaching, but by the following evidence: "if he remains for three days, he is a false prophet. When an apostle goes forth, let him take only enough bread to last until he reach his night's lodging. If he ask for money he is a false prophet." It is the behavior that is accentuated and emphasized at the

---

8. Jurgens, *Faith of the Early Fathers*, 1:36.
9. Gonzalez, *History of Christian Thought*, 70.
10. Jurgens, *Faith of the Early Fathers*, 1:1–2.

exclusion it seems of the doctrine or gospel message: "By his behavior, then, the false prophet and the true prophet shall be known."[11] This is a good example of moralism gone badly because it is set forth as the way of life to the detriment of the gospel or *gift living*. It is what we do or works living that is put forth as the defining way of grace.

An example from those that had great affinity with philosophy is worthy of mention, such as Justin the Martyr. We see in this class of men a moralism that is enlightened by philosophical truth or reason, which confirms and conforms a person in the way of virtue. Legalism as crass as the *Didache* type does not show here, rather a cleaner or elevated form of discourse that speaks of knowledge and virtue like a true philosopher. In other words, the Christian life and the virtues it enjoins upon people is advanced as the highest form of true philosophy, and Jesus as the incarnation of that truth, making it possible for his followers to live the life of the true philosopher. Socrates and the best that classical Greek philosophy has to offer are viewed as forerunners of Christ calling people to the logos or reason that can restore people to the right way of living. "Socrates attempted to make these things known and to deliver men from the demons, those very demons charged that he introduced unheard of gods, and brought it about through the agency of men who delight in evil that he was put to death as an atheist and impious person. Now they endeavor to do the very same thing to us."[12]

Justin attempts to vindicate Socrates by making a direct comparison between his reason and the reason, or the logos, Christ: "Not only did Socrates condemn these things among the Greeks by reason [logos], but even among the barbarians they were condemned by the Word [logos] Himself, who assumed a form and became a man, and was called Jesus Christ." Their philosophical approach is nonetheless a works paradigm that advances yet another formula for *work living* as evidenced in the following: "And if men, by their works, show themselves worthy of His design, they are deemed worthy, so we are told, to make their abode with Him and to reign with Him, being freed from all corruption and passion."[13] The emphasis lies on the illumination of truth on those who believe and then move on to exert themselves in order to follow in the way of truth and virtue in

---

11. Jurgens, *Faith of the Early Fathers*, 1:3–4.
12. Jurgens, *Faith of the Early Fathers*, 1:50–51.
13. Jurgens, *Faith of the Early Fathers*, 1:51.

the way of God's law so as to be accounted worthy of salvation. Here's an interesting and very telling summary of the Christian life for Justin:

> After we have thus washed the one who has believed and has assented, we lead him to where those who are called brethren are gathered, offering prayers in common and heartily for ourselves and for the one who has been illuminated, and for all others everywhere, so that we may be accounted worthy, now that we have learned the truth, to be found keepers of the commandments, so that we may be saved with an eternal salvation.[14]

We must recognize that these early men saw themselves embroiled in charges and accusations from society at large that they tried to fight off the best possible way. They set forth much that was good with what they had, considering their limitations, in terms of defending the divinity of Christ, the goodness of God's original creation, the identity of the Creator as the one true God and Father of Jesus Christ, the defense of the incarnation and the resurrection, as well as the unity of the church. However, they did so in ways that for the most part never clearly and unequivocally affirmed the free gift of forgiveness and reconciliation in Christ apart from works. And, in the best of cases, they saw this reconciliation and faith as a union or vivification that caused them to obey God's commands and thus attain to immortality. It is wholly an emphasis on what is given them: not first being fully forgiven and redeemed from guilt apart from works, but rather the power or grace to become obedient unto salvation, or as one of them would say, "The Word of God, our Lord Jesus Christ, who did, through His transcendent love, become what we are, that He might bring us to be even what He is Himself" (Iraeneus book 5, preface).

This emphasis sought after divinization or participation with God through the Spirit. Not that this is a wrong biblical sentiment insofar as we are being conformed to the image of Christ and eventually shall be glorified; but it is the centrality of such a focus on the work of the Spirit in us, rather than the work of Christ for us, that ultimately sets a very particular pace and strand of theological thought. The particular strand that we see here enunciated by Irenaeus of Lyons—in our estimation, one of the most articulate theologians of the early period—is one that is not necessarily unbiblical, but one that lends itself for confusion since it lacks the clarity of the work of God for us in Christ to deliver us from guilt and condemnation apart from our works. In other words, God's work of

14. Jurgens, *Faith of the Early Fathers*, 1:55.

redemption in Christ is subsumed in the category of vivification by the Spirit unto obedience, fruitfulness, or good works. There is no space for this vivification or fruitful obedience to be the result of faith alone unto salvation, no space for a vivification through faith alone unto salvation with the consequent result of the fruit of obedience. Thus, when Irenaeus talks about the fruit of the Spirit he refers to them as God's instrumentation unto salvation: ". . . he proceeds to tell us the spiritual actions which vivify a man, that is, the engrafting of the Spirit; thus saying, 'But the fruit of the Spirit is love, joy, peace, long suffering, goodness, benignity, faith, meekness, continence, chastity . . .' As, therefore, he who has gone forward to the better things, and has brought forth the fruit of the Spirit, is saved altogether because of the communion of the Spirit . . ."

We must notice that according to Irenaeus we are saved by the communion of the Spirit, not by the atoning death of Christ through faith alone. The clarity that we are saved apart from any works of love or obedience to God's law, through faith alone, is absent. It is the Spirit that is the controlling variable and all that it delivers to make us inherently righteous or participants in communion with God unto salvation. It can be said to be literally a case of salvation by faith and works, by faith and love, by faith and the fruit or obedience of the Spirit, definitely not by faith alone as Luther would later claim. It is a simple equation where those who do the works of the flesh manifest "through what things it is that man goes to destruction"; conversely, those who live in the fruit of the Spirit show "through what things he is saved." It is clear to see that faith alone is not the instrumentality through which undeserving, unworthy, unmerited sinners—who always remain thus—are saved. Rather, they must be saved through their renewal unto law or works obedience by the Spirit. Glaringly absent is the forensic righteousness of Christ alone as the basis for their acceptance before God through the instrument of faith alone, and for a grace that saves with the merits of Christ alone. Irenaeus goes on to assert, "In these members, therefore, in which we were going to destruction by working the works of corruption, in these very members are we made alive by working the works of the Spirit."

We contend that what we have just expounded in the foregoing example constitutes a train of theological thought that will be deeply embedded in the subsequent generations of Christian thinkers. It seems like the most articulate of theology of the time continues to reverberate and produce a strand of theological thought with tentacles even within a branch of the

Reformed tradition as will be discussed in later chapters. For now, we may consider this pattern of doctrinal thought in a few other Christian thinkers of subsequent ages as well as begin to delineate how such thinking leads to certain patterns of *works living*. It is thus that a free gift is no longer free; a free gift from the outset begins to be eroded by subtle and not-so-subtle attacks that undermine the outside-of-us nature of our righteousness and the life of faith or *gift living*. Right from the start, we see that the gift falls prey to the wrong packaging and shipping off down the subsequent generations, to keep using our gift and shipping metaphors.

CHAPTER 4

How Is a Free Gift Kept No Longer Free?

Lost in Transit, Ongoing Seeds of Corruption

We plan to continue our historical survey, now advancing into Early and High Middle Ages to continue to show the devastating legacy or influence that the "lost" free gift of the gospel had on whole new developments of Christian thought and practice. We shall focus not only on the doctrinal issues now, but also on the practices that began to shape a whole era that entrenched a way of living the Christian life by works, by fear, by ignorance, and, sadly, by abuse. Our historical samples must remain sketchy and selective at best of what we, arguably, consider good representatives of the shaping spirit of an age that would eventually become fertile grounds for the cries of reformation. While we present a strong critique of the early fathers and the Middle Ages period, we do not mean to negate many contributions made throughout in various other doctrinal areas. However, our scope is limited to an investigation of the gospel as the free gift apart from works that Paul announced. We could cite many good examples in the fathers and subsequently up to the Reformation, where the shimmering of grace is present; however, our focus is to highlight the theological pattern of an age that sadly did not stoke gospel fire and passions but rather obscured it. It is our contention that the fathers and the subsequent Middle Ages are not a good representation or continuation of the gospel taught by Paul, the gospel of the gratuitous free grace in Christ apart from works. While in defense of the fathers it is rightly argued that they focused on other issues than the one Luther or we have faced, we argue that they were not silent on soteriological matters, which clearly evidence a significant and consequential variation from the gospel of sola fide to offer a very "mixed" articulation at best, and downright legalistic at worst.

In efforts to claim historical legitimacy and pedigree for the gospel, reformers and their sympathizers have often sought to enlist the fathers and other predecessors for their doctrines; however, it is our contention that the fathers and much of what continued on into the Early Middle Ages was actually more in keeping, generally, with the Roman Catholic tradition and the tenets that they presented at Trent during the Counter-Reformation. While pro-gospel and pro-gift-living sentiments, as we have outlined here consistent with Paul, have existed, most of what has come to be known in print seems rather different at best, absolutely contrary at worst in many cases, with a few exceptions. For, rather different, we cite those who turn to the work of the Spirit to conform us to the image of Christ, our practical sanctification/holiness and good works, or our inherent righteousness as an intrical part of the condition or conditions to be saved, to be thus accepted by God. As absolutely contrary, we cite those that flat-out turn the gospel into the doing or working of the law by our obedience, those that simply view the gospel as a new law. Despite the usefulness this distinction may provide, we assert that in both cases the gospel is seriously compromised and gift living truncated.

It is interesting to see an emphasis on participating in Communion since very early that reveals a certain attitude about salvation that supports our thesis. The trend emerges early on where one is saved not by a simple childlike trust that unites the sinner to the person and work of Christ, which faith can be fed and strengthened at the Lord's Table, but one must look to the actual eating and drinking as if somehow we are intrinsically being saved by the actual doing of it. Without sorting out all the intricacies of the long-standing debates on the issue, suffice it to say that if participation in the sacrament is looked upon as the basis of getting life, of ingesting or being infused with something of worth I have to intrinsically possess or have by an obedient practice, this becomes the quintessential practice of *works living*. The eating and the drinking become the activity we perform to have something of worth in us whereby we may be saved, even if that something of worth is the body and blood of Christ. Immediately, the highlight is on me in a twofold manner: firstly, I must do or work some obedience to get right, and secondly, there must be something of worth intrinsically in me in order to be accepted by God. Such an attitude reveals the "in us" focus of the way to talk about salvation that rivals the "for us" focus of the gospel. Saint Basil the Great enjoins the following: "To communicate each day and to partake of the holy Body and Blood of Christ is good and beneficial . . . Who can doubt that to share continually in life is the same thing as having life abundantly? We ourselves communicate four times each week . . . and on other days if there is a commemoration of any saint."[1] This example of *works living*, which will color all of the Middle Ages, will serve to separate the good from the bad, the worthy from the unworthy, as the following example shows where a sinner who had fallen into a particular sin could be made to wait as long as ten years before being able to participate again in Communion: "And thus, when he has exhibited worthy fruits of repentance, let him be admitted in the tenth year to the prayer of the faithful without communion. And when he has assembled for two years in prayer with the faithful, then let him finally be deemed worthy of the Communion of the good."[2]

This great one among the Cappadocian Fathers, who so ably argued in issues that had to do with the person of Christ and the Trinity, is now seen to not speak as clearly on soteriological matters, or at least not as clearly as Paul speaks. While indeed these were men of their times addressing specific contemporary issues, one cannot say that they were silent on salvation and grace. What is obvious when they speak on the subject is the disconsonant note they strike with Paul's gospel of salvation apart from works, without being worthy or meritorious according to the law. Basil talks about the "exercise of piety" like a "ladder," making allusion to Jacob's ladder where, "What is necessary is that those who are being introduced to the virtuous life should put their feet on the first steps and from there mount ever to the next, until at last they have ascended by degrees to such heights as are attainable by human nature";[3] never mind that in Jacob's ladder Jacob never sets a foot to ascend on said latter. However, the trend continues to present a speech about salvation and grace that has mankind getting saved through their own sanctification, even if this is wrought by God's Spirit in grace. It is, nonetheless, their pious assent or obedience that saves them. The gospel becomes a model of virtue and love to imitate for such spiritual ascent: "This is the reason for Christ's sojourning in the flesh, for the models of His Gospel actions, the suffering, the cross, the tomb, the resurrection: that man who is being saved through his imitation of Christ, might receive that old adoption as son."[4]

1. Jurgens, *Faith of the Early Fathers*, 1:5.
2. Jurgens, *Faith of the Early Fathers*, 1:8.
3. Jurgens, *Faith of the Early Fathers*, 1:20–21.
4. Jurgens, *Faith of the Early Fathers*, 1:16.

Thus, adoption as sons is made conditional on *works living*. The following commentary further cuts the ground from *gift living* thus:

> I think that the noble athletes of God, who have wrestled all their lives with the invisible enemies, after they have escaped all of their persecutions and have come to the end of life, are examined by the prince of this world; and if they are found to have any wounds from their wrestling, any stains or effects of sin, they are detained. If, however, they are found unwounded and without stain, they are, as unconquered, brought by Christ into their rest.[5]

Basil's brother, Gregory of Nyssa, who would later enter into the monastery that his brother founded, follows in his footsteps. He makes an assertion that bespeaks much of what will plague the church even unto our modern times. It is basically the confusion that faith alone does not save, but that it must be conjoined to works for faith to save. He explains, "A soldier cannot be considered safely armored when either shield is disjoined from the other. For faith without works of justice is not sufficient for salvation; neither, however, is righteous living secure in itself of salvation, if it is disjoined from faith."[6] The mixing together of faith and works for salvation is the way that ultimately those that oppose sola fide will speak about salvation. Faith may be necessary but not sufficient on its own to secure justification before God; the righteousness of our own works and holiness is necessary. This seems to be the standard contemporary line that those who preach the unconditional, unmeritorious, and free grace of God in Christ find as the rallying cry of opposition. Their posture is well attested in the fathers, whom they can cite for support.

The themes of virtuous spiritual ascent, ascetic moral perfectionism, and a certain kind of mysticism were the theological atmosphere that began to take shape in the early fathers and into the Middle Ages. While many find a lot of good in these times and in such themes, we contend that the grace airs that Paul breaths becomes rarefied during such foundational times for many centuries to follow. The ascetic rigors of an age had begun to dawn in the initial monastic movement of the fourth century. It was rather logical after the gospel alterations of the first centuries to emphasize works, obedience, and virtue to somehow reason that separation from society for spiritual solitude and contemplation could be one way of bettering one's chances of communing with the divine unto holiness and salvation. The

5. Jurgens, *Faith of the Early Fathers*, 1:21.
6. Jurgens, *Faith of the Early Fathers*, 1:46.

story of John Chrysostom in the latter part of the fourth century exemplifies such a drive: "John sought solitude and the ascetic life outside Antioch. There he spent four years living with a hermit, after which he found his own cave, where he remained another two years. During this latter period he never lay down to sleep, night or day. As a consequence his gastro-intestinal system refused anymore to function properly and the cold and dampness caused malfunctioning of his kidneys."[7] While John would eventually reenter society and carry out a very popular preaching career, his instincts are those of a formative age where salvation lies deeply embedded in the virtue, holiness, or merit of our works as necessary conditions for the justification of his grace unto salvation.

We cannot abandon this transitional period without a look at one of the luminaries of such times, St. Augustine of Hippo. We proceed to cite Augustine knowing full well that the development of his thought and the copiousness of writings which embody such development call for more than some random interspersed citations. Such certainly does not do him justice, or any other writer of his width and scope for that matter. However, we will cite him in some lengthy quotes, keeping an eye out not necessarily for the right progression and evolution of his ideas, but rather for shades of theological meaning, practice, and content that would characterize the church for some time to come. So, we are looking for the paradigmatic in Augustine, of an age consumed by doing penance, obtaining ecclesiastical pardon, avoiding mortal sins, and achieving death in the sacramental graces of baptism and the Table. Such are the entrenched marks of an age that belie the loss of clarity on the gospel of the free grace of Christ from which many deviant innovations proceed. At peril of oversimplification, we offer the following quote as paradigmatic of the ensuing Middle Ages:

> Let no one say: "I did that; perhaps I will not be forgiven." Because you did it? How great is the sin you committed? Tell me what you have done, something serious, something horrible, something terrifying even to think about. Whatever you might have done, did you kill Christ? There is nothing worse than having done that, because there is nothing better than Christ. How great a wrong is it to kill Christ? But the Jews killed Him; and afterwards many of them believed in Him and drank His blood: and the sin which they had committed was forgiven them. When you shall have been baptized, keep to a good life in the commandments of God, so that you may preserve your Baptism to the very end. I do not tell you

---

7. Jurgens, *Faith of the Early Fathers*, 1:84.

that you will live here without sin, but they are venial sins which this life is never without (2). Baptism was instituted for all sins; for light sins, without which we cannot live, prayer was instituted. What does the prayer say? "Forgive us our debts as we too forgive our debtors (3)." We are cleansed only once by Baptism; by prayer we are cleansed daily. But do not commit those sins on account of which you would have to be separated from the Body of Christ; perish the thought! For those whom you see doing penance have committed crimes, either adultery or some other enormities: that is why they are doing penance. If their sins were light, daily prayer would suffice to blot them out. [8, 16] In the Church, therefore, there are three ways in which sins are forgiven: in Baptism, in prayer, and in the greater humility of penance; yet, God does not forgive sins except to the baptized.[8]

We see here a grace that is inextricably tied to works of penance, of prayers, of sacraments, and of church discipline. While there is much good that we may glean in some aspects from such traditions, there is also much obscurity of the gospel and *gift living*. There is a reason why the reformers appealed to St. Augustine, since he, while arguably being paradigmatic of an age, yet displays certain true dynamics of grace that can be appreciated: "In many passages [Paul] often bears witness to this, putting the grace of faith before works, not as if he wanted to put an end to works, but so as to show that works are the consequences rather than the precedents of grace. Thus, no man is to suppose that he has received grace because he has done good works but rather that he would not have been able to do those good works if he had not, through faith, received grace."[9] This is not to say that Augustine was the only writer or churchman of the period to evince grace dynamics in his teachings, certainly many more could be mentioned who display such good leanings, but Augustine can be said to be among the most prominent and forceful on the issue. Nonetheless, even the great one must be the object of our criticism insofar as we track a purer gospel trajectory. At the end of the day, Augustine embodies a grace that cannot be divorced from obedience for acceptation or justification before God. Again, on the issues of justification and sanctification, he is paradigmatic of an age that did not distinguish between both, and at the same time, the forerunner to an arguably better age that would indeed distinguish them, but separate them to the detriment of both.

8. Jurgens, *Faith of the Early Fathers*, 1:35.
9. Jurgens, *Faith of the Early Fathers*, 1:47.

While the language of by grace and by faith to refer to salvation may be present in this father's works, we must delve deeper for their meaning. Augustine provides a perfect case in point of one who circumscribes everything to grace and faith; yet, faith is more than just trusting and receiving Christ for us as sufficient for our forgiveness and righteousness before God without our works. For Augustine, emblematic of much of what the fathers taught and of much of what would follow, grace and faith are given with the Spirit in order to receive also love, good works, and merits whereby we are justified. We are saved by the way of the Spirit, which is the way of faith, namely, the way of being able to fulfill the law increasing in righteousness before God unto justification for salvation. Augustine explains the difference between the law of works, by which no one can be saved, and the law of faith, the only way to be saved. Both are the way of obedience to the law; the latter adds faith and grace by the Spirit to enable such obedience. This is another case of the lack of the proper distinction between law and gospel, which in the case of Augustine causes him to subsume the fruits of faith, good works, or our practical or progressive sanctification under justification:

> What the difference between them is, I will briefly explain. What the law of works enjoins by menace, that the law of faith secures by faith. The one says, "Thou shalt not covet"; the other says, "When I perceived that nobody could be continent, except God gave it to him; and that this was the very point of wisdom, to know whose gift she was; I approached unto the Lord, and I besought Him." This indeed is the very wisdom which is called piety, in which is worshipped "the Father of lights, from whom is every best giving and perfect gift." This worship, however, consists in the sacrifice of praise and giving of thanks, so that the worshipper of God boasts not in himself, but in Him. Accordingly, by the law of works, God says to us, Do what I command thee; but by the law of faith we say to God, Give me what Thou commandest. Now this is the reason why the law gives its command,—to admonish us what faith ought to do, that is, that he to whom the command is given, if he is as yet unable to perform it, may know what to ask for; but if he has at once the ability, and complies with the command, he ought also to be aware from whose gift the ability comes. "For we have received not the spirit of this world," says again that most constant preacher of grace, "but the Spirit which is of God, that we might know the things that are freely given to us of God." What, however, "is the spirit of this world," but the spirit of pride? By it their foolish heart is darkened, who, although knowing God, glorified Him not as

God, by giving Him thanks. Moreover, it is really by this same spirit that they too are deceived, who, while ignorant of the righteousness of God, and wishing to establish their own righteousness, have not submitted to God's righteousness. It appears to me, therefore, that he is much more "a child of faith" who has learned from what source to hope for what he has not yet, than he who attributes to himself whatever he has; although, no doubt, to both of these must be preferred the man who both has, and at the same time knows from whom he has it, if nevertheless he does not believe himself to be what he has not yet attained to. Let him not fall into the mistake of the Pharisee, who, while thanking God for what he possessed yet failed to ask for any further gift, just as if he stood in want of nothing for the increase or perfection of his righteousness. Now, having duly considered and weighed all these circumstances and testimonies, we conclude that a man is not justified by the precepts of a holy life, but by faith in Jesus Christ,—in a word, not by the law of works, but by the law of faith; not by the letter, but by the spirit; not by the merits of deeds, but by free grace.[10]

We do not wish to tire the reader by proliferating examples of such soteriological understandings of the period. We have provided some key notable examples and refer the reader to the source cited for a good and concise compendium on the fathers for further evidence. While we definitely do not advance this position on the fathers as any final word on the matter, we feel confident in making the case that such a position seems to be arguably the majority report among them, with variations, obviously, given their different emphases and contexts.[11] Hence, we must conclude of this transitional period into the Middle Ages that the seeds of gospel deviations and corruptions can be said to have been present from an early time. Even in the best of cases like the ones cited here, where much good is to be seen and commended, they become paradigmatic of a time where justification involves a more convoluted process where sinners are working hard to receive justifying grace and persevere under it, where sinners are to do their best to hope for grace, and where those in grace can never be sure of God's favor in any final way but struggle through their lives in penance, good works, sacraments and church discipline in order to hope for final

10. http://www.logoslibrary.org/augustine/spirit/13.html.
11. See Jurgens, *Faith of the Early Fathers*, vol. 2, for other important figures among the fathers, such as St. John Chrysostom (p. 108), St. Ambrose (160–61), and St. Jerome (192), to name a few, who speak in a similar manner including works, sacraments, and penance within the equation for justification.

justification in their sanctification journey. Ashley Null captures the legacy of such seeds by painting the following picture of a medieval inheritance under which a sinner made his spiritual journey:

> Nevertheless, even now his salvation from hell was not yet certain. In the normal course of events, upon emerging from the water, young Thomas would have been dressed with the chrisom, a white robe which symbolized his newly received purity, and instructed so to live his life as to be able to present his soul to God just as spotless on the day of judgment. For baptism remitted the guilt (reatus) of original sin inherited from Adam but did not remove its stirrings (actus), the former peccati. This "tinder box" remained within the pilgrim (viator) throughout his mortal life, always ready to spark the Christian's consent to the sins and offences which Satan and his demons ceaselessly suggested to him. Once the Christian had decided to commit a mortal sin, he would instantly lose both the supernatural goodness imparted by baptism and its concomitant promise of eternal salvation, until such time as he chose to restore himself to God's favor by penance. And so the robing and the warning represented the twin hope and threat under which the Christian viator made his earthly pilgrimage.[12]

---

12. Null, *Thomas Cranmer's Doctrine of Repentance*, 29.

CHAPTER 5

How Is a Free Gift Further Lost by High Middle Ages Handling?

WE HAVE SKETCHED IN the previous chapter what would be the marks of an age where we contend the free gift of the gospel and its concomitant gift living became deeply compromised and lost in transit, to use our packaging and shipping analogy, in the hands of those that were supposed to handle and deliver it faithfully to the people. Although the geographical, cultural, and theological contexts may have varied, some fundamental marks can be established along the lines of: sacramental infusion of grace, cooperation with grace unto further sanctification for final justification through works done in faith, works of penance to merit in some sense the reception or restoration of justifying or sanctifying grace, and ecclesiastical dependence for the inception, process, and progress of salvation. In short, faith alone does not justify, much less sanctify or advance one in works of holiness and obedience. Righteousness is, for sure, a matter of something I must do and manifest through my character and obedience for God to accept me as righteous—admittedly, still a matter of grace, but seemingly not a matter of faith alone, by his obedient sacrifice alone, unto the righteousness of Christ alone. Once again, Null sums it up for us well thus: "Although the aim of medieval piety was to die in a state of grace, no one could be certain that he would so live his life for that to happen. Remembering God's determination to punish sins encouraged people to do so themselves so that they would be prepared when called to account at their passing from this life. Godly hope, on the other hand, eliminated despair of inevitable damnation . . ." This was the combination of fear and hope through which medieval piety sought to attain salvation. The law was meant in the gospel to be kept with the help of the Spirit and the pardon available through Christ in order to not despair of God's acceptance. Null goes on to clinch it: "The letter of the law may have demanded eternal death for sinners, but its spirit promised forgiveness to all who turn to God in true penance."[1]

In the above quotes, we sense the tension between law and gospel, or even a fusion of them both. Interestingly, such a theological equivocation causes an existential and psychological fusion of fear and hope where, in most cases, fear wins over. When gospel and law are not properly distinguished and applied, law wins over as if swallowing the entire gospel in one gulp. The existential consequence is that similarly fear overcomes hope; hope is swallowed up by the clenching grip of fear. These two cannot coexist together as one; when an attempt is made to reconcile them through fusion, fear comes out on top—its power is such that it ends up squelching out hope. In order for them both to exist, they must be constantly ceding the place to the other, but never the twain shall meet, as the old adage says, or occupy the same place. Upon writing this, the memory of being in class with Dr. Null comes to mind when he made graphic allusion to what sentiments the imposing images of Christ inside the churches could evoke. Such overarching images and statues of Christ aimed at striking fear in people's hearts at the thought of judgment and retribution exacted by God's wrath through Christ. It was expected that such fear could pave the way through attrition unto contrition, that is, from the fear of condemnation unto the love of God through persistent pious effort aided by the ecclesiastical sacrament of penitentia, which included confession but was not limited to it. Sinners were supposed to struggle in their penitential pain and sorrow for fear of condemnation, and thus do whatever they could to hope for the gift of contrition—sorrow for sin out of love for God—which came with justifying grace. Once accomplished, the battle was on to remain in that state also spurred on by the two motivators of fear and love. Null offers magnificent characterizations that help illuminate:

> Like upper and lower millstones grinding the wheat kernels between them into flour for baking bread, hope and fear shattered hardened hearts, making the tears of contrition flow, and firing the heart with a love for God that made Christ welcome in the penitent's life. Fear of divine punishment caused grief, but because Christians had hope that this pain would bring about forgiveness, they also had joy. Pious Christians were always to live in reverent fear and godly hope. The first prevented presumption of assured salvation.[2]

1. Null, *Thomas Cranmer's Doctrine of Repentance*, 42.
2. Null, *Thomas Cranmer's Doctrine of Repentance*, 41. See chapter 1 for a whole perspective of the dynamics of contrition, where fear always plays a role even though the

HOW IS A FREE GIFT FURTHER LOST BY HIGH MIDDLE AGES HANDLING?

From relics, pilgrimages, images, statues, impressive buildings and elaborate adornments, vestments, altars, candles, incense, to the liturgies of the mass, prayers, and confessions—it was all designed as a very practical, sensorial, and hands-on approach to stimulate the penance and penitence work required and thus hope for justifying grace. Needless to say, it could be a very emotionally involved experience. We shall have more to say about fear as a motivator and the implications thereof; but for now suffice it to say that fear drove a system that nonetheless pursued love as an ultimate end, the love that was inextricably bound with the grace of justification. Thus, awakening and fueling the emotions for God were also seen as a necessity in this journey of salvation. A look at some of the different flavors from the spirituality of the times highlights the fact that there existed manifold ways to excite sinners unto the love of God. In the 1400s, the traditions and system of the Middle Ages would see the contributions of figures like Richard Rolle and Walter Hilton, who without abandoning what had preceded them made greater emphasis on the contemplative life to achieve union with Christ, and thus further move or motivate worshippers to obedience by tapping more deeply into their affections.

These people presented a stimulating and attractive road to God that both the plain uneducated as well as the learned Schoolmen and theologians could benefit from. Rolle extolls and recommends the gifts he has received in recompense for abandoning of all worldly vanity to pursue spiritual exercise in solitude and contemplation for the love of the name of Jesus, especially through the use of the name: "I think that no one would receive it unless he loved the name of Jesus especially, and also honored it, so much that never except in sleep, would he allow it to fade from his memory. I judge that the man to whom this has been given to do will reach that state."[3] Such meditation exercises and pursuits could deeply affect the worshipper by producing experiences of exquisite ecstasy-like states with all kinds of "fiery" physical and emotional manifestation. Rolle's account testifies to it thus: ". . . the heat of eternal love was felt in reality in my heart . . . suddenly I experienced within myself an unaccustomed and joyous burning ardor . . . delightful heat blazing in my senses to the infusion and

---

aim seems to be to leave behind servile fear and progress unto love for the sake of God. While love can expel or change fear into love, fear is an indispensable requisite for this transformation.

3. Rolle, *Fire of Love*, 148.

perception of the celestial or spiritual sound which belongs to the canticle of eternal praise and the smoothness of invisible melody . . ."[4]

Such an approach went beyond the traditional mere "purgation" of evil influences through external exercises, which had their place, to move beyond and higher into the realm of meditation and contemplation of the divine, and thus be moved inwardly or affectionately to love God, which was ultimately the end goal. Justifying grace here is framed in terms of fiery emotions and sweet experiences of song and delights of the soul in rhapsodious fellowship with God. The idea of the soul going beyond purification to achieve a certain illumination and communion with God was not new but established in the medieval notion of the "Three Ways," referring to purification, illumination, and perfection of the soul characteristic of Bonaventure's spirituality. While other notions or variations of the characterization of justifying grace existed, they could all be said to understand "justification as the establishment of rectitude within the higher nature of humans . . . The medieval statements concerning the nature of justification demonstrate that justification is universally understood to involve a real change in its object, so that regeneration is subsumed under justification."[5] In the case of our charismatic authors, this change and rectitude was full of mystical emotional experiences that could be described sensorially as melodious, sweet, and joyful. This soul's journey to God is another medieval way or expression of the path unto and through justifying grace, or as we would argue, away from gift living and unto works living. Indeed, works living can be masqueraded even in as sweet a framework as that of the spirituality that Rolle represents. Regardless of the flavor, we would argue works living seeks to fight off the fear it inhabits by enlisting hope to cohabitate in different ways. Rolle stimulates his comfort thus: "Many are the wonderful and great rewards, but there are none such among the gifts of life which so preciously confirm hope by a kind of invisible life in the loving soul, or which thus delightfully console the sitting man and snatch him up to the peak of contemplation, or to the harmony of angelic praise."[6]

We shall unpack this notion of fear and hope cohabitating together further in subsequent chapters, but for now we are simply saying that one cannot truly bear the fruit of love and good works in fellowship with God and neighbor if that arises out of a preoccupation with self unto salvation,

---

4. Rolle, *Fire of Love*, 147.
5. McGrath, *Iustitia Dei*, 67–68.
6. Rolle, *Fire of Love*, 149.

that is, of an underlying concern that the very love and delights of worship and service that I pursue are conditions to be able to stand before God justified. True love and service, while indeed a response of a contracted debt of love and gratitude to God, nonetheless, must be free, namely, free of fear. While both fear and love may be part of human emotions and attitudes we experience in light of God's revelation, they must each be accorded their rightful place where one must cede place to the other, but their cohabitation is antithetical to the spirit of Christianity and undermining of the gospel. The medieval worshipper may be said to have lived with an underlying anxiety about future torments, whether in hell or purgatory. Everything was designed to avoid both; the fear of future torment and the hopes of avoiding it drove the system. An apologist for the system provides great insight on this mindset: "Wherever one turns in the sources for the period one encounters the overwhelming preoccupation of clergy and laity alike, from peasant to prince and from parish clerk to pontiff, with the safe transition of their souls from this world to the next, above all with the shortening and easing of their stay in purgatory. It is a preoccupation which shows no slackening up to the very moment of Reformation . . ."[7]

Fears were stilled by work living, whereas in the gospel fears are stilled by gift living, namely, by Christ's promise through his death and resurrection. Hence, when it was all said and done, good works were of the essence for fear to join with hope, yet fearful uncertainty prevailed as confidence about avoiding future torment and the state of grace was viewed as presumptuous. The author goes on to explain, "It was the religious complex of these last things, death, judgment, Hell, and Heaven, that formed the essential focus of late medieval reflection on mortality, coupling anxiety over the brevity and uncertainty of life to the practical need for good works to ensure a blissful hereafter."[8] While a certain confidence was held out for extraordinary pious saints, the case of a woman who may have purported such assurances belies the anxieties of work living: "Margery Kempe, for all her mystical intimacy with Christ and repeated visionary assurances that she would never have to endure the pains of Purgatory, showed herself once again a woman of her time by taking the liveliest possible interest in clocking up the 'great pardon and plenary remission' of all the pilgrimage sites she visited . . . Margery's appetite for pardons was very widely

---

7. Duffy, *Stripping of the Altars*, 301.
8. Duffy, *Stripping of the Altars*, 308.

shared."⁹ Our criticism here is not with the fears of the people, not even with the aim of a system which in this regard can be considered pastoral insofar as it tries to provide answers to alleviate or comfort such fears. Rather, the point to be made is that fear itself was a necessary condition of the system unto and through the path for justifying grace. Once again, the apologist Duffy sums it up in a positive light that yet corroborates our point when he talks about visions of the future doomsday in Corpus Christi plays where Christ appears as judge of all:

> The whole machinery of late medieval piety as designed to shield the soul from Christ's doomsday anger . . . Such a vision must have seemed at times oppressive. But it was at this point that the relentless moralism of late medieval eschatology gave way to something else. It was fundamental to late medieval perception of human nature that, almost by definition, Everyman—every man and every woman—would be unprepared to meet the "Domesman," Christ, their good works inadequate, their sins overwhelming. Though the laity were endlessly exhorted to virtue, and to use their goods while they lived for the benefit of the poor and sick, and thereby of their own souls, preparedness for the moment of death could not be equated with a life of successful endeavor after charity, for in that pursuit almost no one was entirely, or even very successful. Everyman finds his good work too weak and feeble to help him when he calls on them to accompany him to the grave. His soul is saved not by them, but by the grace of repentance, mediated through the Church's sacramental system, confession, and penance, anointing and viaticum. Shrift, declares Everyman, is mother of salvation.¹⁰

Duffy has very succinctly captured for us the spirit of an age and the inner workings of a system that we argue promoted work living over gift living, the confusion of law and gospel, the comingling of fear and love, the irony of self-preservation and selfless service, the tension between the church as gatekeeper and Christ as the Door and Shepherd of his people. We have been taking a look from the bottom up to the spirituality of work living as practiced with and among the laity. But work living is not a respecter of class or intellect. Let us begin to shift our view unto another class

---

9. Duffy, *Stripping of the Altars*, 288–89. See all of chapter 8 for a whole intricate system and spirituality that belies the deeply held fears of an age that incentivized works living and the cohabitation of fear, hope, and love in a detrimental way.

10. Duffy, *Stripping of the Altars*, 309–10.

of work living as practiced by the Schoolmen and the theologians of the time, the intellectual and theological elite. Perhaps a good linkage there may be provided by looking at Walter Hilton and his approach. With him, a tradition that often borders if not outright sinks into magic, gross superstitions, ceremonialism, and mere sensory or sensual experience in many cases now reacts away from all that into a sharper focus on morals and the Bible. Notwithstanding the laudable emphasis on the Bible and the study of theology, it is no guarantee for the curbing of work living, but a mere variation of the same fallen inclination to deviate from Christ and his cross as our only chance at gift living, as we shall continue to unpack aided by Luther's theology of the cross. Hilton's goal is to pursue a reformation of morals and the curbing of sin in addition to feelings. His approach can be succinctly stated thus: "Those who fear God, reject the senses, and conduct their lives to please him will be reformed to his likeness in faith. The soul that avoids the senses and has no inclination to sin is reformed in feeling."[11] Hilton has replaced a mere physical sensation as the goal of contemplation for being reformed in morals.

His goal was to destroy sin through biblical meditation, to move the affections to obedience and thus bring about individual and societal moral reformation. Hilton has a greater appeal beyond the clergy since one does not have to abandon one's station in the world but rather the world becomes the stage for such transformation to take place. The incipient wind of humanistic reformation that shuns superstition and ignorance for an appeal to the Bible and morals begins to become very apparent. "The Pater Noster is probably best for the uneducated and the Psalter for the educated. The prayers of a contemplative is only for the soul, which will receive the gift of understanding Holy Scripture and see how God—concealed in the Bible—reveals himself to those who love him. His secret presence in the Scriptures is like his secret voice heard in the soul."[12] This author who appears very Christ centered at times yet enjoins a certain perfection of soul "through great spiritual labor . . . Only a person of great humility, charity, and faith, prepared to suffer much in body and soul, may reach Jerusalem, the city of Peace which is Contemplation . . . Grace and the desire for Jesus destroy all tendency to sin and become in the luminous darkness a beacon that marks the heavenly Jerusalem."[13] In some way, this is reminiscent to

---

11. Magill and McGreal, *Christian Spirituality*, 178–79.
12. Magill and McGreal, *Christian Spirituality*, 180.
13. Magill and McGreal, *Christian Spirituality*, 179.

us of revivalist and even puritanical-type spiritualties in a general sense, where extra efforts and zeal are conducive to further growth and nearness to God. It is emblematic of those visions that see beyond or in addition to faith, a way forward of progress and growth through the practice of virtues, namely, that some special good work and disciplines must be exercised in order to attain such lofty and noble goals beyond our justification and the gospel unto sanctification. We shall argue that the way forward is always the way of faith, of simply trusting, namely, gift living.

Let us end this brief survey of the work living spirituality of the High Middle Ages by now turning our attention to the Schoolmen theologians of the period that were part of the intellectual context in which the Reformation took place. Historians generally have seen the late eleventh and twelve centuries as a period where somewhat of a societal renaissance took place, especially in the realm of theological activity and education.[14] While it is not in the scope of our present study to analyze the different theological schools, some general thoughts can be offered in connection with the issues at hand. Perhaps the overall sentiment of the theological schools lies in the agreement that God has ordained that some kind of change in the individual informed by love or charitas is required for justifying grace. In keeping with the trajectory that we have been plotting, justifying grace is received or mediated through the change of the individual to turn away from sin and begin to love God. This can be summarized thus: "Although humanity has no claim to justification on the basis of divine justice, humans may look toward the divine generosity and kindness for some recognition of their attempts to amend their lives in accordance with the demands of the gospel."[15] All the schools seemed to concur on the fact that a change in disposition away from sin and unto the love of God was a movement required for justification. The details and particular characteristics of such a change vary from school to school, but the fact remains that such a change is of the essence of justification. McGrath offers the following summary on the medieval understanding of the nature of justification:

> Justification refers not merely to the beginning of the Christian life, but also to its continuation and ultimate perfection, in which Christians are made righteous in the sight of God and of humanity

---

14. See, McGrath, *Iustitia Dei*, 2.10, for a background in the reasons for the theological effervescence of the period and a study of the major theological schools with their positions on the issues of justification, grace, and related matters.

15. McGrath, *Iustitia Dei*, 141.

> through a fundamental change in their nature, and not merely in their status. In effect, the distinction between justification (understood as an external pronouncement of God) and sanctification (understood as the subsequent process of inner renewal), characteristic of the Reformation period, is excluded from the outset.[16]

This is nothing new but rather the actual general flow of continuity with the fathers that we have been tracking. The common understanding in justification appears to be one where God makes sinners righteous in order to justify them. Justification was about the process of transformation of a sinner from ungodly to righteous. There was no other way for God to accept sinners except through their moral transformation, their turning away from sin unto the love of God; hence, the love of God in the soul becomes the determinative factor. We see this in Augustine, whom we have characterized as emblematic of a period, notwithstanding his own peculiarities. McGrath agrees with our characterization of Augustine thus: "For Augustine, it is love, rather than faith, which is the power which brings about the conversion of people . . . The personal union of individuals with the Godhead, which forms the basis of their justification, is brought about by love, and not by faith . . ." We contend that this Augustinian implication and, by extension, paradigm of what follows lies at the root of much harm to the gospel and gift living. As we shall continue to unpack, any attempts at making our love of God the basis of our acceptance before him undermines the very love we pursue by the comingling of law and gospel, condemnation and acceptance, fear and love, God serving us in Christ and our serving him.

By referencing Augustine we are not saying that he initiates or creates such paradigm, only that he is paradigmatic of the sentiment of a whole age, notwithstanding their raging controversies and differences. Thus, it can be summed up that the ancients believed, generally—explicitly or implicitly—that love is part and parcel of the means for justification, that love is the ultimate ordained condition for justification. Whatever faith is for the period, there is no separation or distinction allowed between faith and love when it comes to justification. One can safely say, then, that if one is to be justified by faith, such justification unquestioningly includes obedience in love. Thus the fitting characterization: "it is unacceptable to summarize Augustine's doctrine of justification as sola fide iustificamur—if any such summary is acceptable, it is sola caritate iustificamur . . . There is no hint

---

16. McGrath, *Iustitia Dei*, 59–60.

in Augustine of any notion of justification purely in terms of 'reputing s righteous' or 'treating as righteous', as if this state of affairs could come into being without the moral or spiritual transformation of humanity through grace."[17] Interestingly, it is our contention that wherever the gospel of gift living is compromised, the same paradigm of change, love, and transformation emerges, as we have begun to note in some reputedly gospel orthodox authors. We shall argue that such paradigmatic view—for lack of a better term—goes into the Reformation and continues on to our present with the same, in our estimation, arguably maleficent influence.

The sacramentalism, penance, ecclesiastical discipline, ecstatic mysticism, ascetic rigorism, biblical moralism, and theological sophistication of an era can be summed up as a quest to love God, and in so doing be justified and find eternal life—in our view, simply put, work living. Let us take a look at some of the features that identified the theological schools of the High Middle Ages. At least eight theological schools have been identified in the late medieval period. [18] We will not proceed to mention them but simply to offer characterizations in terms of the commonalities among them that we would conceive as work living. We must evoke again the idea of an ontological change as a unifying common factor that the schools had as a necessity for justification prior to the challenge of the via moderna in the fourteenth century, which itself engendered a theological school. In general this change was conceived as a gift of God insofar as, one way or another, it was the operation or cooperation with the grace of God that produced such an ontological change.[19] In contradistinction from Pelagianism, the grace of justification was gratuitous yet required some preparation which, in general, also came to be considered due to the prior excitement or stimulation of God's grace. But the crux of the matter in terms of being justified hinged on the "intermediate" state within the person of an "ontological" change, which change, as we have already noted, involves the love of God. McGrath confers utmost significance to this theological piece as it unfolded at the time: ". . . one of the most significant theologoumena of High Scholasticism began to emerge—the idea that, as justification involves an ontological change in humanity, an

---

17. McGrath, *Iustitia Dei*, 46–47.

18. McGrath, *Intellectual Origins of the European Reformation*. See chapter 3 for the school identifications, and 2.10 in *Iustitia Dei* for distinctives.

19. See McGrath, *Iustitia Dei*, 2.5 for a discussion of how the dynamics of grace were viewed, and, 2.3 for the discussion on the subjective appropriation of justification.

ontological intermediate is required in the process of justification . . . to be identified with the created habit of grace or charity."[20]

All the schools advanced the necessity of such a change and posited that one had to do *quod in se est*, what is in one's power to do, what one can do. God would not deny grace to those who so prepared themselves for the reception of justifying grace. Aided by prevenient grace or not, depending on how the initial step was conceived, one had at their disposal the possibility of doing what one could do; helped by the church's sacraments and their system of penance, one could muster the necessary sorrow and separation from mortal sin through attrition, contrition, confession, and satisfaction so that justifying grace could be infused or restored after relapsed. The point to be highlighted here is that the abandonment of sin becomes a precondition for the forgiveness of sins and the eventual reception of justifying grace, as explained by McGrath: "Although only God is able to forgive sin, humans are able to set in motion a series of events that culminate in forgiveness of sins by the act of ceasing to perform acts of sin, which lies within their own power. Humans do what is asked of them, and God subsequently does the rest."[21]

At the point where one's *quod in se est* turned into the separation from sin unto the love of God for God's sake rather than a mere terror of condemnation, one could safely assume to be in the hope that a habit of grace had been received for the perfecting journey of love and obedience in justifying grace. In short: ". . . grace is given to those who dispose themselves to receive it by doing *quod in se est*—for example, by attrition. The subsequent gift of grace transforms this to contrition, which leads to the remission of sins."[22] Thus, remission of sins was contingent upon both prior preparation unto justifying grace by abandoning sin as well as the ensuing reception of a "habit of grace" that enabled one to further abandon sin in order to really love God for God's sake, walking in obedience with the sacramental help of the ecclesiastical system.[23] One could say, speaking "Reformed" and anticipating our intramural criticism, that the evidence of being on the path of salvation or justification lay on the abandonment of sin unto the love of God. This is the path of penance or repentance unto the beginning of jus-

---

20. McGrath, *Intellectual Origins of the European Reformation*, 76.
21. McGrath, *Iustitia Dei*, 109.
22. McGrath, *Iustitia Dei*, 110.
23. For the role of the sacramental system for justification, see McGrath, *Iustitia Dei*, 2.4, Justification and the Sacraments.

tification as well as the path forward, namely, the abandonment of sin, the holy evidence of a sanctified life, one that more and more abandons sin for the love of God. Such a disposition, which came to be accepted as aided by grace unto the change of created grace" or a habit of grace unto love, can be said to be the "transformative habitus upon which justification proceeded in the Middle Ages. This "habitus" is not only paradigmatic of an age but also continues to background every attempt that undermines the gospel in spite of the greatest and best of pious intentions.

Worthy of some further commentary is the via moderna and the challenge it posed to the "congruous" merit that most of the schools were willing to confer upon the dynamics of the change necessary for justifying grace. The via moderna severed the link of any correspondence of obligation by the nature of the entities involved in justification. Such a change as God would accept the via moderna viewed as simply grounded in the divine acceptation of God according to his ordained power. They rejected any notions that represented such transactions as indicative of any actual state of obligation or correspondence between God and the creature that imposed a necessity on God to accept such a disposition or change as worthy or fitting of acceptation by its own nature. The via moderna asserted a voluntarist view of God that posited justifying grace and the dynamics of any ontological change or habits of grace as conditions grounded in the concept of the pactum. Actually, this school would move away from asserting an ontological change as the ultimate necessity for justification to establish a voluntarist and personal approach. McGrath explains,

> The voluntarist position is particularly associated with the later Franciscan school and the via moderna. Its fundamental and characteristic feature is the recognition of a discontinuity between the moral and the meritorious realms, the latter being understood to rest entirely upon the divine will itself. For Scotus, every created offering is worth exactly what God accepts it for, and nothing more. The meritorious value of an act need therefor have no relation to its moral value, as it rests upon God's estimation alone.[24]

Interestingly, this position allowed the via moderna to agree with created habits and the meriting of justification de congruo because such merit was ultimately referred to the divine acceptation according to God's absolute power, without reference to anything in the nature of the entities involved in justification except what he has ordained to accept. Thus, the relation

24. McGrath, *Iustitia Dei*, 145.

between God and the justified inheres ultimately in a "covenantal causality" rather than in any direct correlation of any intrinsically moral and spiritual worth that God is obligated to recognize and reward. God is free to recognize and reward what he deems to be so purely out of the decision of his own will. It bears repeating then that in this framework "the moral abilities of humans are largely irrelevant, as the ultimate grounds of merit lie outside of humanity, in the extrinsic denomination of the divine acceptation."[25] The necessity of positing some kind of correspondence of righteousness between God and humanity for justification and the nature and dynamics thereof had undergirded many efforts during the period, which ranged from: the influence of Augustine's illumination and psychological approach, to the actual and created habits of grace that followed in the early schools, to the very influential Aristotelian notions of such grace via Thomas Aquinas, to the via moderna, which broke with the necessity of such a change as the ultimate moral and theological necessity for justification. Thus, the following can be highlighted as a fitting characterization for the state of affairs as they were evolving unto the eve of the Reformation and the theologically significant points of connection that begin to emerge:

> The ontological basis that the High Scholasticism of the thirteenth century established for the necessary involvement of created habits in justification was thus shown to be inadequate. Although it is not clear precisely what role the later theologians of the via moderna assigned to created habits, it is evident that there was a growing trend in the later medieval period, particularly within the schola Augustiniana moderna, to conceive primarily justification in personal or relational terms, and thus avoid the ontological conceptualization of the matter so characteristic of the earlier medieval period . . . the general trend among the Reformers to deny an ontological dimension to justification represents a continuation of this critique of the conceptual foundations of the habitus theology.[26]

One last point we wish to note upon the implications of the via moderna, as it will become significant in our later criticism of some trends among the Reformed, has to do with what McGrath calls a Christ "lacuna," or what we would label as deficient of a Christ-centered approach. In other words, if

25. McGrath, *Iustitia Dei*, 147.
26. McGrath, *Intellectual Origins of the European Reformation*, 77. Read all of chapter 3 for a detailed analysis of significant precursors and connections between late medieval theology and the Reformation.

justification ultimately only has a theocentric referent in God's will without any moral or theological reference to righteousness, justice, and rectitude, not only does such an approach preempt any claims from the human side, but it must be extended to also strike a preemptive attack on the necessity of the human Christ for atonement and righteousness. Thus, it is not just the necessity of a corresponding human righteousness that is negated, but also the necessity of Christ's sacrifice and righteousness on behalf of humans for the whole moral and spiritual rectification of the fallen created order. We shall unpack such a connection in detail soon; but for now let us ponder McGrath's "christological lacuna," which sets up our discussion to launch into the period of the Reformation and the dynamics of work living that continue to percolate through it in spite of its many triumphs:

> One aspect of the soteriology of the via moderna which is of particular interest is the Christological lacuna within their understanding of the economy of salvation. It is quite possible to discuss the justification of the viator . . . without reference to the incarnation and death of Christ . . . Both the Old and the New testaments hold out the promise of rewards to those who do good. While the new covenant abrogates the ceremonial aspects of the old, the moral law of the Old Testament remains valid. Christ is therefore more appropriately described as Legislator than as Salvator, in that he has fulfilled and perfected the law of Moses in order that he may be imitated by Christians. The justice which is required of humans in order that they may be justified is the same in the old and new dispensations.[27]

Notwithstanding their pactum theology in order to negate "habitus" the final cause in justification, the de facto reality even for the moderna way is one that amounts to work living for justification, even if such "habitus, transformation, or love" may be framed only as secondary causes rather than the ultimate reason or formal cause of justification. We shall adduce a very similar critique within Reformed theology where the necessity of good works, change unto holiness, and progressive sanctification is posited in such a way as to undermine or at least obscure the role of sola fide in justification as well as the power and motivation for transformation. If we may be allowed a rather cursi characterization, it sounds like the proverbial case of wanting to have the cake and eat it too! We propose that we have the cake and then eat it, that we have law and then gospel,

---

27. McGrath, *Iustitia Dei*, 200.

that we get fully accepted, pardoned, forgiven, accounted as righteous and then bear its fruits, that we fear and then hope, that we are killed and then made alive; in short, we receive gift and then gift ourselves to others! Let us see how the Reformation highlighted such a gift, especially with Luther's embrace of the gospel.

CHAPTER 6

How Can a Free Gift Be Recovered?

Lost and Found

THE FUNDAMENTAL INSIGHT THAT we want to highlight as the gift of the gospel being recovered has a twofold implication: one, that righteousness indeed is necessary to be accepted before God, and such righteousness as accords with what God has demanded in his law; and two, that such righteousness, as it is necessary to be accepted by God according to what the law demands, is all gifted unto sinners by faith alone on the basis of Christ's sacrifice and obedience alone. Thus, one can stand before God justified without any regard to our works but simply with regard to Christ's work. This will necessitate a forensic view of righteousness rather than the transformative or habitual grace paradigm of the Middle Ages that we have been tracking. This righteousness, then, can be said to be extrinsic to us insofar as it is not something we work or manifest in us in obedience to the law; rather, it is something we believe, and through faith receive as gift. This righteousness, more specifically, is Christ, namely, all of his person and work for us under the law—on behalf of sinners. Christ for us is the Christ in us that fully enables us to stand before God justified, and ready to live daily out of such justifying union. Thus, the internal process of sanctification as began at regeneration flows from a justifying grace or righteousness that is not conceived intrinsically but forensically and thus extrinsically. McGrath concedes this to be the unique distinctive feature from Catholicism thus: "The notional distinction, necessitated by a forensic understanding of justification, between the external act of God in pronouncing sentence, and the internal process of regeneration, along with the associated insistence upon the alien and external nature of justifying righteousness, must be considered to be the most reliable historical characterization of Protestant doctrines of justification."[1]

Thus, as one can see, a lot hinges on the concept and dynamics of righteousness and how it can be applied to humans before God. The Middle Ages generally conceived of it in the following fashion: either as on the basis of a personal relation to God in those changed by the uncreated grace of his Spirit that worked sanctifying/justifying righteousness in them (Augustine and early schools), or as the created habit of grace that provided an ontological intermediary of sanctifying/justifying grace (Thomistic and Dominican school), or simply as the ultimate acceptance of the divine will via pactum (via moderna) without a necessary correspondence of natures via righteous merit before God, while accepting some role for the latter as secondary cause at best. There are several implications that are worth noting in the above that somehow need to be addressed. First, does the biblical concept of righteousness involve a moral understanding or judgment of right and wrong? Can God be said to justify without regard to righteousness, namely, the moral rectitude that he demands? The via moderna answers that no such correspondence is necessary or exists, but rather a covenantal causality where God has simply ordained to consider a certain condition to justify; whereas the earlier schools do concede the necessity of some merit even if such merit is only fitting or congruous with God's righteousness, but still some kind of moral correspondence between God and the justified now exists in their natures. In the former, what God demands could have been different according to his power of ordination; in the latter, God could not demand otherwise than according to his nature, even if what humanity presents does not rise to the full and complete level of God's perfect righteousness or justice. Before we address the above questions, for which we shall provide a different answer as per the new solution that emerged out of the Protestant Reformation, let us briefly take a look at the concept of righteousness, and more specifically the righteousness of God.

It is with the concept of the righteousness of God as it appears in Romans that Luther had tremendous difficulty at first when battling against the Scholastic notions of the time. It appears that a view prevailed that posited that God would render unto each its own in an equitable and just way.[2] These were concepts that had percolated throughout Greco-Roman

---

1. McGrath, *Iustitia Dei*, 209–10.

2. See McGrath, *Iustitia Dei*, 2.2 for an analysis of the Ciceronian version of righteousness and other views that differed from it.

civilization through philosophical teachings of the time. The man who does what is within his sphere to do, what he can and ought to do, God will equitably or impartially treat him accordingly. They are thus poised to receive the congruous merit of justifying grace for the perfection of such a virtuous life, which God will ultimately reward once again with equity and justice according to his nature, or what he has established through the pactum. Luther soon came to reject the idea of created habits as the cause of justification in order to settle on the humility of faith as that which humans can provide according to the terms of the pactum. Luther then can be said to have been in continuity with the via moderna tradition, although a gospel trajectory is noticeable at this early stage. We say a gospel trajectory because what Luther conceives humans can do basically amounts to the recognition of their weakness and infirmity, thus, humility; whereas what preceded tended to emphasize one's hatred of sin and love for God, namely, the obedience of the law. While Luther's humility will need more development to arrive at his mature understanding of the righteousness of God, it definitely sets itself on a course toward faith and Christ. McGrath insightfully offers a characterization that may be seen to concur with the aforesaid analysis:

> Luther's early understanding of justification (1513–14) may be summarized as follows: humans must recognize their spiritual weakness and inadequacy, and turn in humility from their attempts at self-justification to ask God for his grace. God treats this humility of faith (*humilitas fidei*) as the precondition necessary for justification under the terms of the *pactum* (that is the *quod in se est* demanded of humans), and then fulfil God's obligations under the *pactum* by bestowing grace upon them. It is clear that Luther understands humans to be capable of making a response towards God without the assistance of special grace, and that this response of *iustitia fidei* is the necessary precondition (*quod in se est*) for the bestowal of justifying grace.[3]

Again, as noted by McGrath, while Luther remains within the parameters of the via moderna in conceiving of *iustitia fidei* as what humans need to do for *iustitia Dei* to reward them with justifying grace, we want to emphasize that this *quod in se est* can be said to be somehow emptied of one's achievement under the law. In other words, the acknowledgment of one's infirmity does not affirm positively an obedience of the law—it does not seem to fit well

---

3. McGrath, *Iustitia Dei*, 220.

with law category. In any case, it is the affirmation of a negative—I'm a sinner who is not worthy, or I bring nothing of worth but my unworthiness—that seems to fit better with the category of faith. Although, at the time, this humility of faith was what God was obligated to reward and looked for in justification according to the pactum theology of the via moderna. We must highlight this notion since it presents a contrast with other emphases prior that looked to faith as something intellectual, as in the case of Augustine, which does not rise to saving grace because it lacks love; it is not formed or infused by the love of the Holy Spirit. Not that Luther would have necessarily a pure notion of faith at this early stage, but a certain difference can be noticed. That Augustine does not seem to operate with this distinction or emphasis, which can be noted as paradigmatic of an age, is reflected in the following statement: "Faith can exist without love, on the basis of Augustine's strongly intellectualist concept of faith, but is of no value in the sight of God. God's other gifts, such as faith and hope, cannot bring us to God unless they are accompanied and preceded by love."[4]

We have been tracking how this blending or lack of distinction between faith and love actually compromises the gospel and gift living since love—law obedience, even if Spirit granted—is a necessary condition for justification before God, thus blurring the lines between law and gospel. While, indeed, we must maintain that he who does not love God has not been justified, we must also reject that faith alone is of no value in justification or even in practical sanctification. Thus, a distinction must be maintained between faith and love where each has a role in the Christian life and a certain dynamics between them as we shall elucidate in subsequent chapters. Faith needed to be formed by love to be saving or justifying grace, as we saw in Augustine. While Luther may have concurred with this at first, he does quite a switch on this notion at a later stage when he explains, "Afterwards, when Christ has thus been grasped by faith and I am dead to the Law, justified from sin, and delivered from death, the devil, and hell through Christ—then I do good works, love God, give thanks, and practice love toward my neighbor. But this love or the works that follow faith do not form or adorn my faith, but my faith forms and adorns love."[5] Faith is ascribed the forming or adorning quality as opposed to love, which rationale shall be further elucidated shortly. While in the former view one must be looking to love, its habitus, or transformation for the evidence of justifying

---

4. McGrath, *Iustitia Dei*, 45.
5. Luther, *Lectures on Galatians (1535), Chapters 1-4*, 161.

grace, in the latter view faith now becomes the focus, not at the exclusion of love, but certainly to validate love and everything that follows. Looking to love can only become a viable proposition insofar as such may be legitimized by faith. We shall contend that much of modern evangelicalism, including Reformed Protestantism, has suffered from altering this equation with damaging consequences for gospel or gift living.

Luther's next step would come to affirm the passivity of human agency. If the humility of faith is something humans can provide, then it is not so much a question of God's gift but of man's fitting response that determines any subsequent giving by God. Luther will take another decisive step toward gift living by affirming such humility of faith to be the gift of God. It is believed that sometime during Luther's Roman lectures of 1515–1516 another development takes place as Luther affirms that the beginning of justification lies with God. Luther affirms that God is active in giving righteousness for justification as a gift and not as a reward for humans doing *quod in se est*, which now Luther begins to attack as Pelagian.[6] At this time, Luther has moved away from the via moderna with its notions of humans beginning or setting in motion the course of justification, the idea of congruous merit for that to happen, and by extension a concept of *iustitia Dei* resting on equitable and human norms that God has established via the pactum. Thus, it can be said of Luther's framework that, in contradistinction from the via moderna and the Scholasticism of the time, he rejects that humans can do something of themselves to prepare for justification and thus merit justifying grace. He has affirmed that whatever they do consists in bringing their unworthiness and infirmities through faith to God in order to cry out for grace; and that such faith, which is the righteousness that God accepts for justification, is a gift from God, not their own doing. Luther set himself squarely against the *quod in se est* dictum thus: "The work of the law is everything that one does, or can do toward keeping the law of his own free will or by his own powers. But since under all these works and along with them there remains in the heart dislike for the law and the compulsion to keep it, these works are all wasted and have no value."[7] Augustinian influence can definitely be noticed here. Luther goes on: "Hence, you see that the wranglers and sophists are deceivers, when they teach men to prepare themselves for grace by means of works. How can a man prepare himself for good by means of works, if he does no good works without

---

6. See McGrath, *Iustitia Dei*, 220–21 for a discussion of such evolution in Luther.
7. Luther, *Commentary on Romans*, xv.

displeasure and unwillingness of heart?"⁸ Then he moves on to the final climax, which shows Luther's further evolution and separation from both the via moderna in a radical break, as well as Augustine in a more gradual way. The following deserves to be quoted in full length:

> To fulfil the law, however, is to do its works with pleasure and love, and to live a godly and good life of one's own accord, without the compulsion of the law. This pleasure and love for the law is put into the heart by the Holy Ghost, as he says in chapter 5. But the Holy Ghost is not given except in, with, and by faith in Jesus Christ, as he says in the introduction; and faith does not come, save only through God's Word or Gospel, which preaches Christ, that He is God's Son and a man, has dies and risen again for our sakes, as he says in chapters 3, 4, and 10.⁹

Thus, we begin to see in Luther a strongly anti-Pelagian and contra-Scholastic position, while at the same time a greater clarity and focus on the centrality of faith in Christ as the preeminent hub of the Christian life, and, consequently, of gift or gospel living. Indeed, "if it is God who bestows this quality upon humanity—rather than humanity that achieves it or acquires it—then the framework of *equitas* and *iustitia* essential to the *pactum* theology of the via moderna and the young Luther can no longer be sustained."¹⁰ While the above statement shows Luther moving in a different direction concerning righteousness and justification as the via moderna had conceived it, yet we continue to see the idea of a quality that, although bestowed by God, becomes the basis upon which God justifies. In other words, man must become righteous, and this righteousness, which for Luther now is faith, God bestows, namely, "righteousness is faith in Jesus Christ." And, thus, Luther begins to plot a course away from Augustine while still maintaining a participationist perspective on justification, one could say. McGrath bears this out pointing to the "Finish school,"¹¹ whose interpretation of Luther places particular emphasis upon the believer's actual participation in the divine life through union with Christ. "Christ is present with the believer in faith, and is through this presence identical with the righteousness of faith."¹² One can definitely see some merit in this

8. Luther, *Commentary on Romans*, xv.
9. Luther, *Commentary on Romans*, xv.
10. McGrath, *Iustitia Dei*, 221.
11. See McGrath, *Iustitia Dei*, 225 n. 43 for literature.
12. McGrath, *Iustitia Dei*, 225.

perspective upon hearing Luther expound such dynamics, which McGrath cites as corroborating evidence:

> Faith does not merely mean that the soul realizes that the divine word is full of all grace, free and holy; it also unites the soul with Christ . . . as a bride is united with her bridegroom. From such a marriage . . . it follows that Christ and the soul become one body, so that they hold all things in common . . . what Christ possesses belongs to the believing soul; and what the soul possesses belongs to Christ. Thus Christ possesses all good things and holiness; these now belong to the soul. The soul possesses lots of vices and sin; these now belong to Christ.[13]

Interestingly, as one begins to think in terms of such a union where there is a certain mutual commerce, or "happy exchange" as Luther would call it, participation in it can't seem to help but acquire a certain forensic or theological tone, rather than one strictly transformative or inherent in the natures of those involved. Something akin to the via moderna argument must be made insofar as the natures of the parties involved are concerned. And that is, to wit, that what Christ is in his own righteousness never really inheres within us by our own nature, except through the mediation or imputation of Christ's obedience for us under the law. And, conversely, the sin that really inheres within us never really inheres in Christ except through his standing in our stead under the condemnation of the law. Thus, any participation or transformation that seeks union with Christ as a reference will find in such personal reference a legal or moral reference that concerns righteousness—the doing of right and wrong—namely, conformity to God's moral standards as a necessary reference toward justifying righteousness. So, what could be posited as an anthropological ontology of transformation in terms of acquiring a new nature of sorts fails to adequately capture the "happy exchange" of such a union, and must enlist a theological lens to describe a union between the divine and the creaturely through Christ. Such a theological lens necessitates the forensic or legal framework to do justice to the biblical language of righteousness and justification. Stephen Westerholm reflects on the moral implications of righteousness, which in turn point to its legal reference according to the law thus:

> God has spelled out the good he expects of Jews and Gentiles alike in the law of Moses; informed by this law, Jews are in a

---

13. McGrath, *Iustitia Dei*, 225. Luther is cited from his work *The Freedom of the Christian*.

> position to teach Gentiles the moral responsibilities binding on them both (2:17–22) . . . Paul insists that what the law commands is (inherently) good (7:12; cf. 7:22; 13:8–10)—which is not the same as saying that only when the law commanded something did it become good, or right, to do. And as there is nothing arbitrary about the law's commands, so there is nothing arbitrary or negotiable about the claim that those who obey them will be righteous in God's sight . . .[14]

Such a view rejects the voluntarist view of the via moderna and affirms that God demands the righteousness that conforms to his nature and to the "wise ordering of creation," as Westerholm explains.[15] Thus, union with God necessitates a righteousness that justifies before God. This is a matter of right and wrong, namely, a matter of justice, God's justice or God's law; in short, it is a legal matter, a thing of law, which is tantamount to saying a moral thing. Thus, it is the doers of the law of Romans 2 that will be justified. In other words, justifying righteousness does not come except by way of doing what accords with his moral law, which, in turn, accords with his holy and good nature. However, there is not a human born of sinful parents that can match such moral demands, notwithstanding its claim over all humans. The author captures such a tension and its fitting conclusion:

> . . . that God finds righteous the doers of the law (2:13) is a simple statement of what makes the world go round, morally speaking. It is hardly an arbitrary Plan A that God, upon its failure, replaces with a Plan B for justification. On the other hand, it is not within the capacity of the law, however good its commands, to secure its obedience among human beings gifted with moral choice. As we have seen, the law can only condemn and curse transgressors, and hand them over as captives to sin. When a more positive role is sought for the law, it is said to make possible clear recognition of human sinfulness (Rom 3:20; 7:7–7–13). Those submissive to its demands can never be righteous on its terms (8:7–8). Since, as Paul sees things, that includes all human beings, it follows that 'a person is not justified by works of the law.'[16]

As Luther's thought continues to mature away from man's ability and merit, a forensic or legal element in his thinking about faith and righteousness begins to emerge. Thus, he asserts in the preface to his commentary on

---

14. Westerholm, *Justification Reconsidered*, 81–82.
15. See Westerholm, *Justification Reconsidered*, 81.
16. Westerholm, *Justification Reconsidered*, 82–83.

Romans, "For through faith a man becomes sinless and comes to take pleasure in God,"[17] which evinces both a forensic or legal view without abandoning a participatory framework. Sinners become sinless not in the reality of their daily practice but before God through faith, and such faith apprehends Christ in a transformative union where the sinner by faith is empowered to bear fruits unto obedience. Both elements in Luther—forensic and participatory—can be noticed to be in such a dynamic that they are hard to separate, but, as we have noted, their distinction begins to emerge very clearly. Certainly, such participation and transformation seem to have reference to faith as essential, rather than love, which explains why Luther wants to adorn or form love with faith rather than the other way around. Luther explains, ". . . if Abraham's circumcision was an external sign by which he showed the righteousness that was already his in faith, then all good works are only external signs which follow out of faith, and show, like good fruit, that man is already inwardly righteous before God."[18]

This righteousness Luther comes to see as the gift of God, as that righteousness with which we are justified by imputation, in distinction now even from Augustine. It was his meditation on the righteousness of God being revealed in the gospel in lecturing through the book of Romans, even though not fully developed at this particular point, that began to consolidate such insights and set the grounds for a more mature forensic or legal understanding in the years to come.[19] However, this did not happen in a vacuum since Luther had already been interacting with the concept of justifying righteousness through the course of his early lectures in the Psalms 1513–1515, during which period, McGrath contends, he sets himself at some point at odds against the via moderna. It may not be definitively clear at which point exactly Luther embraced a forensic view of justification. However, one can affirm that the journey led him through the Psalms (1513–1515) and Romans (1515–1516), as well as subsequent writings at the end of the decade and into the 1520s, in interactive reflection with the concept of the righteousness of God set in the larger context of what would consolidate as a theology of the cross. The following fragment McGrath cites testifies to his eventual mature conclusion:

---

17. Luther, *Commentary on Romans*, xvii.
18. Luther, *Commentary on Romans*, xx.
19. See McGrath, *Luther's Theology of the Cross*, ch. 4 for an analysis of the context for Luther's discovery.

> Afterwards, I read Augustine, On the Spirit and the Letter, where I found that he too, beyond my expectation, interpreted "the righteousness of God" in the same way—as that which God bestows upon us, when he justifies us. And although this is expressed somewhat imperfectly, and he does not explain everything about imputation clearly, it was nevertheless pleasing to find that he taught that the righteousness of God is that by which we are justified.[20]

By his later commentary on Galatians in 1535, the concepts of righteousness and justification are clearly and unequivocally framed in terms of imputation: ". . . this inestimable gift, excels all reason, that without any works God reckons and acknowledges as righteous the man who takes hold by faith of His Son, who was sent into the world, who was born, who suffered, and who was crucified for us . . . that righteousness is not in us in a formal sense, as Aristotle maintains, but is outside us, solely in the grace of God and in His imputation . . ."[21]

Interestingly, and in keeping with our language of gift living, the gospel and the cross are not mere intellectual or academic exercises, but very existential ones. They are a matter of life and death for all of life. It may not appear so at first, but we hope to bear witness as to how it is so throughout this project. Thus, everything that is theological can be said to be existential. We live *coram Deo*, before God, whether we like to acknowledge it or not. Our quest for living is a quest for or against God—but it cannot ignore him; it never proceeds without him, try though we may. Luther captures this very poignantly when he speaks of theologians rather than theology. Humans can be said to be theologians of sorts, which at the heart involves somehow or another wrestling with God, not just a mere subject matter.

This becomes evident in Luther's own struggle which can in varying degrees be emblematic of the human struggle before God. Before theology was a school subject matter for Luther, it was a matter that affected him at his existential core; he was more than simply a student of religion, but the affected object, the addressed subject, and compromised party of such an enterprise. Luther "drove [himself] mad, with a desperate disturbed conscience" because he felt accused and condemned by the righteousness of God even in the gospel. This existential/theological crisis Luther revealed as one that robbed him of the love of God. He couldn't seem to love the God

20. McGrath, *Luther's Theology of the Cross*, 97.
21. Luther, *Lectures on Galatians (1535), Chapters 1–4*, 234.

who condemned him with unrelenting righteousness, an active righteousness that called him to be righteous by obeying the law, which he kept on failing to obey no matter how good and obedient a monk he proved to be. He speaks of his terrors: "I was angry with God, saying 'As if it were not enough that miserable sinners should be eternally damned through original sin, with all kinds of misfortunes laid upon them by the Old Testament law, and yet God adds sorrow upon sorrow through the gospel, and even brings his wrath and righteousness to bear through it!'" After God apprehends him with the good news of God's mercy in Christ through the righteousness in the gospel for him, he then speaks of heavenly consolations:

> I began to understand that righteousness of God as that by which the righteous lives by the gift of God, namely by faith, and this sentence, "the righteousness of God is revealed," to refer to a passive righteousness, by which the merciful God justifies us by faith . . . This immediately made me feel as though I had entered through open gates into paradise itself . . . And now, where I had once hated the phrase "the righteousness of God," so much I began to love and extoll it as the sweetest of words . . .[22]

Thus, righteousness is a very practical and necessary thing for our existence. It will provide comfort for the soul that suffers what could be said to be at the heart of every human, namely, the need to be justified. Justification can be said to function almost as the permission moral fallen creatures need to live. Let us say it is the moral and spiritual occupational license sinners need to live in God's world. They must apply to God for such a license. Consequently, it is a God problem that requires a God solution. The creature's sinful rebellion against God's word of judgement upon sin has brought untold suffering, death, and condemnation, which only God can alleviate and ultimately eradicate. Sinners separated from God live under the futility and burden of death according to God's word of judgment; the knowledge of evil was forewarned as death. Such a death involves an enmity against God's word of judgment where the sin, guilt, shame, death, and fear experienced under such a word sinners resist, struggle against, and seek to rid themselves of. God forewarned a verdict of death, but after such a death promised a verdict of life. One must receive the death word in order to receive the life word. God gives both words. God executes both verdicts, namely, God kills and he makes alive! Luther captures this reality in a loaded theological statement: "Through the Law, therefore, we are condemned

---

22. Luther, *Lectures on Galatians (1535), Chapters 1–4*, 98–97.

and killed; but through Christ we are justified and made alive."[23] The way to God's comfort word necessitates a word of suffering and death before such a comfort can be obtained through the word of peace and life. Such is the nature of righteousness—what is not righteous must die and, conversely, what is righteous must live. The gospel contains what appears to be a great riddle or paradox that can be stated thus: "Out of death life, yet never really doing either but receiving them—who am I?" The Christian! At the heart of the Christian faith lies death and resurrection; it is not first and foremost about changing, reforming, improving, or transforming, but always first and foremost about dying and rising! But even this we must receive from God through Christ and by his Spirit. It is the Lord's doing!

Only Christ is the truly righteous Lamb of God destined to die for unrighteousness, the one who, in the service and for the sake of justifying righteousness for sinners, will die and rise. Sinners can only receive this at his hand through faith, hence the need for a forensic view that nonetheless affirms participation and transformation. Luther begins to move in this direction as we hear him say, "We are righteous 'outside ourselves' when our righteousness does not flow from our works; but is our alone by divine imputation." Luther rightly realizes that man needs a covering, and as his thought matures he sees in this covering the twofold blessing of forgiveness and imputed righteousness: ". . . Blessed are they who by grace are freed from the burden of iniquity, namely, of the actual sins which they have committed. That, however, is not sufficient, unless also their 'sins are covered,' that is unless the radical evil which is in them, (original sin), is not charged to them as sin. That is covered when, though still existing, it is not regarded, considered and imputed by God . . ."[24] While one must say that still here in Romans by the year 1516 his thought on these issues has not fully developed, yet the ideas are in the oven, so to speak. He is cooking the imputation of righteousness beyond what Augustine taught. But he's still quoting Augustine thus: "Grace was given, in order that we might fulfill the law. It was not the fault of the Law that it was not fulfilled, but the fault was man's carnal mind. This guilt the law must make manifest, in order that we may be healed by divine grace."[25] But if that radical evil holds and cannot ever be changed now no matter how much transformation, it follows then that not transformation, but the double-sided forgiveness/righteous-

---

23. Luther, *Lectures on Galatians (1535), Chapters 1–4*, 151.
24. Luther, *Commentary on Romans*, 83.
25. Luther, *Commentary on Romans*, 77.

ness covering of God's declaration becomes crucial. Zahl has captured this poignant reality in a very simple but profound statement: "Sin is a disease that is never healed. It is forgiven."[26] In a time when much effort is spent in transformation and change, the truth of the power of forgiveness and forensic righteousness may be elusive.

Going back to Luther, it seems, at least, that at this time Luther is still ambivalent about the righteousness whereby we are justified. Let us just say that the underbelly of his doctrine is still medium cooked and deeply marinated in Augustinian dressing. Its flavors smacks of one that is justified by faith but not without a certain spiritual observance of the law, that is, a faith through whom one is indeed pardoned and received but, nonetheless, a faith that fulfills the law as it ought to be fulfilled "willingly and truly." Luther can be said to have a via media of sorts at this time between Augustine and the well-done Luther, no pun intended. To follow the cooking analogy, his doctrine of justification is medium cooked between a righteousness or grace of the Holy Spirit, which he calls the work of faith and grace, and the well-done fully forensic imputation of righteousness without any observance or works of the law by grace. In this medium position, the faith that justifies is not without certain "works" of faith and grace as averred by his clarification, "When the Apostle says that we are justified 'without the deeds of the law' he does not speak of the works of faith and grace; for he who does such works, does not believe that he is justified by doing these works. (While doing such works of faith), the believer seeks to be justified (by faith)."[27]

What then does the apostle refer to by "without the 'deeds' of the law"? Luther goes on to explain the works that are excluded from saving faith, or the ones without which we are justified: "What the Apostle means by 'deeds of the law' are works in which the self-righteous trust as if, by doing them, they were justified and so were righteous on account of their works. In other words, while doing good, they do not seek after righteousness, but they merely wish to boast that they have already obtained righteousness through their works."[28] Thus, works in which one would somehow boast as meritorious and as accomplished unto the attainment of righteousness, that is, in the doing of them lies righteousness accomplished, cannot justify; such works must be excluded from the way of justification. Notwithstanding the exclusion of such works, others are not so excluded and one

---

26. Zahl, *Grace in Practice*, 97.
27. Zahl, *Grace in Practice*, 80.
28. Zahl, *Grace in Practice*, 80.

is not justified without them; certainly not because of them, but through a faith that operates with them. Luther establishes the need for such works thus: "When James and Paul say that a man is justified by works, they argue against the false opinion of those who think that (for justification) a faith suffices that is without works. Paul does not say that true faith exists without its proper works . . . Justification therefore does not presuppose the works of the law, but rather a living faith, which performs its proper works."[29] What are these "proper" works with which a man together with faith is justified? Luther makes a subtle but poignant distinction: ". . . the Law is established and confirmed when its demands or injunctions are heeded . . . We say that it is obeyed and fulfilled through faith. But you teach that the works of the law justify without faith, make the law void; for you do not obey it; indeed, you teach us that its fulfillment is not necessary: The law is established in us when we fulfill it willingly and truly. But this no one can do without faith."[30] Thus, fulfillment of the law is necessary, but it can never happen except through faith. God grants justification by faith indeed, but not by a faith that does not fulfill the law, since only faith truly works a "spiritual" fulfillment of the law.

We see then how Luther has been tracking a journey where faith is on the ascendancy as the explanatory defining factor of everything else in the Christian life unto justification and sanctification. While Augustine and the Middle Ages seek to form faith with love, the bond of union with the Spirit, with some grace of the Spirit or some habitual virtue built in for justifying sanctification, Luther is on a trajectory of singling out faith and forming, adorning, or building everything else through it. It should be noted that there is much more that Luther draws from Augustine in rejecting some of the Scholastic and Aristotelian notions of the High Middle Ages, but it is not in the scope of this work to address it.[31] This process, to keep using our metaphor of cooking, undergoes the roasting fires of the theology of the cross. His evolving thought on righteousness, faith, justification, and the Christian life takes him in the direction of a more focused and wider theological cogitation throughout those very formative years of 1515–1519, issuing in what came to be known as his theology of the cross,

---

29. Zahl, *Grace in Practice*, 75.

30. Zahl, *Grace in Practice*, 80.

31. See McGrath, *Luther's Theology of the Cross*, ch. 3 for a detailed discussion of Luther as a late medieval theologian and the various streams of influence upon his thought, including Augustine. Luther embraces Augustine's "bond of love" union notions over the "habitus" intermediary Aristotelian notions.

or his distinction between theologians of glory and theologians of the cross. McGrath sheds light on these dynamics:

> Luther's discovery of the righteousness of God is but one step in the process leading to the theology of the cross—but it is nevertheless the decisive catalytic step, which forced Luther to reconsider the theological matrix within which this concept was set. The old wineskins of the theology of the *via moderna* were simply incapable of containing the new wine which Luther thereby introduced. Luther's passing reference to his rethinking of the meaning of the terms such as *potentia Dei, sapientia Dei, fortitudo Dei,* and *gloria Dei* is practically a programmatic description of the development of the theologia crucis.[32]

One could say that it is out of the cross "oven" that Luther's thought matures, which is tantamount to saying that theological maturity and growth for life must traverse the simple but deep waters of the scriptural gospel. His lectures in the Psalms, Romans, Galatians, Hebrews, as well as other writings,[33] led him to the concept of the righteousness of God vis-à-vis the cross or the gospel. The scriptural fires were stoked by the fuel and heat of the gospel therein, which would eventually set ablaze a heart gripped by the struggle with the crucified and risen Christ. The concept of the righteousness of God revealed in the gospel, as a catalyst in the process, came to be known as that righteousness with which God justifies us, and so forth with other attributes of God; it involved a shift from a posture of doers to now one of being recipients, from giving to receiving, from being driven by performance and works to being shaped by gospel grace, or from work living to gift living. And such is not just an intellectual or academic endeavor but a very existential or practical one where we go from being in control to being graciously surprised by the One in control. We do not mean to say by this that the intellect, will, and affections are not engaged in the process, but that Christ crucified and risen crucifies and raises sinners through the gospel; sinners are brought from death and through death unto life through the gospel. Only the crucified and risen can bear witness because they have seen or rather they have been seen, they have known or rather have been known, they have apprehended or rather have been apprehended. We shall

---

32. McGrath, *Luther's Theology of the Cross*, 99–100.

33. For a good compendium of other writings beyond the initial commentaries into the end of the 1510s and early 1520s, a crucial maturing time for Luther, see Lull, ed., *Martin Luther's Basic Theological Writings*.

have more to say on these practical dynamics, but let us keep sketching what it meant for Luther and how he explained it.

Luther has gradually come upon the realization that God's righteousness whereby he justifies sinners is in opposition to the conceptualizations of righteousness and justification espoused by the theologians and philosophers of the time. He believes God justifies the ungodly in such a way as it does not appear rational or even equitable and just by human standards, or by the standards of the theological philosophy of the times. Luther critiques the wisdom of his age with the assertion that God justified those worthy of death. It was not so among an age stepped in Aristotelian-Ciceronian notions of law, equity, virtue, and merit; within these parameters, the via moderna, as we have mentioned, allowed for human beings to do what they could, what lay within their natural powers, in order to attain some God-ordained status of congruous merit that God would reward with justifying grace. The philosophy of the day dovetailed perfectly with such notions, which Luther comes to reject outright:

> Luther's attacks on the "enemies of the gospel" frequently involve the linking together of ratio, lex, Aristotle and the Jurists . . . Aristotle's equation of *ho dikaios* and *ho nominos* inevitably means that the righteous man is understood to be the man who keeps the law—an opinion which Luther later attributes to reason . . . Similarly, the Aristotelian dictum that a man becomes righteous by performing righteous deeds is rejected by Luther: it is only when a man is justified (*iustus coram Deo*) that he is capable of performing good deeds. Underlying this criticism of Aristotle is Luther's basic conviction that man is naturally incapable of performing anything which is good *Coram Deo*, and which could be regarded as effecting his justification.[34]

Thus, Luther has landed on imputation terrain fertile for more fruitful development. His reflections on the righteousness of God through his lectures vis-à-vis man's sinfulness and the justifying dynamics of the God who acts in righteousness for sinful man rather than against him, as well as the formulation of the humility of faith and its righteousness as the gift of God, would eventually set him apart as a unique theological phenomenon of his time. Indeed, his theology becomes alien to his times because it literally entails an "alien righteousness," one that cannot be discerned by the naked eye or the common wisdom of the age. Luther advances the language of

---

34. McGrath, *Luther's Theology of the Cross*, 138–39.

imputation because God in order to justify must cover the sinner, whose sin always remains his except God removes it from his sight. In other words, it is not sufficient that God pardons sins committed, but sinners must be helped with their sinfulness or that sinful corruption that remains with them for all of their lives. In Luther's own words in his commentary on Romans of 1515, where, although still far from is mature position, he begins to speak a language of imputation: "Blessed are they who by grace are freed from the burden of iniquity, namely, of the actual sins which they have committed. That, however, is not sufficient, unless also their 'sins are covered,' that is, unless the radical evil which is in them, (original sin), is not charged to them as sin. That is covered when, though still existing, it is not regarded, considered and imputed by God; as we read: 'Blessed is the man to whom the Lord will not impute sin.'"[35]

The problem resides with a man who cannot just be partially righteous *coram Deo*; some righteous quality or portion of man as such will not suffice if he still remains a sinner, which in Luther's understanding was always the case even after justification. "Luther did not divide up man in higher and lower faculties a la Augustinian in a Neoplatonist fashion, but rather understood that 'flesh' (*caro*) and 'spirit' (*spiritus*) are not to be regarded as man's lower and higher faculties, respectively, but rather as descriptions of the whole person considered under different aspects. Thus *caro* is not man's lower nature, but the entire man (*totus homo*), considered as turned in upon itself . . . in its irrepressible egoism and its radical alienation from God."[36] If that is the case, no portion of mankind remains unsullied by sinful contamination at any time, which means righteousness cannot advance through certain spaces, portions, or dimensions of the human being as if to gradually reclaim the whole house. A different conceptualization must be formulated that Luther presents as a man who is simultaneously *iustus et peccator* in justification. McGrath explains, "For Luther, justification relates to the entire person, both flesh and spirit: although the individual comes to put his trust in the promises of God, he nevertheless remains a sinner. Thus the *totus homo* is *iustus et peccator simul*—a sinner inwardly, and yet righteous in the sight of God."[37] In contradistinction from Augustine and his mentor Staupitz, for both of whom justifying righteousness is "inherent to man, *iustitia in nobis*, which, although originating from God, may be

---

35. Luther, *Commentary on Romans*, 83.
36. McGrath, *Luther's Theology of the Cross*, 133.
37. McGrath, *Luther's Theology of the Cross*, 133.

regarded as part of the person of the believer"; for Luther, "justifying righteousness is a righteousness which is alien to man, *iustitia extra nos*, which can never be said to belong to the person of the believer,"[38] except through the "covering" of imputation.

This alien righteousness that the believing sinner has by imputation is not one visibly discernable as Luther would indicate in his Heidelberg Disputation of 1518, where he presented what has been known as his theology of the cross. What concerns us from this disputation for our tracking of the gospel is his emphasis on the "hiddenness" of God. This theme is related to the theme of righteousness and has great implications for justification and the practice of our Christian life. Luther in this disputation, in keeping with his emphasis on faith, says in thesis 25, "He is not righteous who works much, but he who, without work, believes much in Christ."[39] As has been noted, this phrase stands in sharp distinction from the spirit of an age that seeks righteousness on the visible, tangible, and comprehensible things such as good works, reason, creation, law, virtue, etc. For Luther, the believer's righteousness and the knowledge of God are hidden in the cross, or we would say in the gospel. Rather than speculative theology, plumbing the depths of philosophical and doctrinal mysteries, the ecstatic uplifting escapades of mystical fancies, the rigorist conquests of strict ascetics, or the moral and social advancement of the socially and ethically engaged, true knowledge of God and his righteousness can only be apprehended via the cross, and such is a "matter of faith." McGrath explains, "This revelation is to be recognized in the sufferings and the cross of Christ, rather than in human moral activity or the created order. Both the moralist and the rationalist expect to find God through intelligent reflection upon the nature of man's moral sense or the pattern of the created order: For Luther, 'true theology and knowledge of God are found in Christ crucified.'"[40] Forde eloquently captures the same dynamics in his words, "The righteousness that avails before God is a being claimed by the crucified and resurrected Christ. It is not like accomplishing something but like dying and coming to life. It is not like earning something but more like falling in love. It is not the attainment of a long-sought goal, the arrival at the end of the process, but the beginning of something absolutely new, something never before heard of or entertained."[41]

---

38. McGrath, *Luther's Theology of the Cross*, 134.
39. Forde, *On Being a Theologian of the Cross*, 103.
40. McGrath, *Luther's Theology of the Cross*, 150.
41. Forde, *On Being a Theologian of the Cross*, 105–6.

It is in the cross as the gospel is proclaimed that everything visible, reasonable, and valuable that resides in human beings is consigned to death vis-à-vis God's judgment. No one can stand *coram Deo* on the basis of anything they have, do, see, or reason by human standards. The cross demands the death of all we bring; its balance must all be accursed and consigned to vanity and death, thus, righteousness is hidden because we do not possess it, bring it, produce it, or even cooperate to initiate, grow, or improve it. Forde calls such attempts to establish one's righteousness "a glory road" to which Luther consigns all theologians of glory. This is he "who looks upon the invisible things of God as though they were clearly perceptible in those things that have actually happened (or have been made, created)."[42] Luther advances in thesis 23 the crusher of human glory thus: "The law works the wrath of God, kills, curses, accuses, judges, and damns everything that is not in Christ." As if to say, God will not have any of our own glory before him but only the glory of his Son, and the holy and righteous law of God is there to ensure that. Whenever we look to ourselves to establish anything or worth or value before God, God crushes it with the holy weight of the law, which denounces and exposes our utter failure in righteousness. Only perfect righteousness can be presented *coram Deo*, namely, Christ righteousness; and this righteousness is alien and invisible to the world! Forde explains the ministry of the law with very plain words: "The law does not work the love of God, it works wrath; it does not give life . . . it kills; it does not bless, it curses; it does not comfort, it accuses; it does not grant mercy, it judges. In sum, it condemns everything not in Christ."[43] Or, as Paul would say in Romans 4:15, "For the law brings wrath," and in 7:10, "The very commandment which promised life proved to be the death of me."

Righteousness is all of Christ, who died and rose for us as our righteousness before God. This is what Paul affirms throughout chapter 3 in his letter to the Philippians, when he says that he wants to "be found in him, not having a righteousness of my own that comes from the law, but that which comes through faith in Christ, the righteousness from God that depends on faith" (3:9). Before such affirmation Paul has emptied himself of what was visible according to his works under the law, his birth, his nationality, his education, etc. In other words, he flushes what belongs to him literally down the toilet to affirm the righteousness of another for him as

---

42. Forde, *On Being a Theologian of the Cross*, 72. See theses 19–22 (pp. 71–95) in Forde for a contrast between a theologian of glory and a theologian of the cross.

43. Forde, *On Being a Theologian of the Cross*, 95.

not only his hope for the future but also the way of knowing God: "I have suffered the loss of all things and count them as rubbish that I may gain Christ . . . that I may know him and the power of his resurrection, and may share his sufferings, becoming like him in his death, that by any means possible I may attain the resurrection from the dead" (3:10). Luther offers in his mature commentary of Galatians (1535) an insightful explanation on the phrase "yet not I" (2:20) that corroborates the Christian's righteousness; though lengthy, it warrants fully quoting:

> That is, "not in my own person or substance." Here Paul clearly shows how he is alive; and he states what Christian righteousness is, namely, that righteousness by which Christ lives in us, not the righteousness that is in our own person. Therefore when it is necessary to discuss Christian righteousness, the person must be completely rejected. For if I pay attention to the person or speak of the person, then, whether intentionally or unintentionally on my part, the person becomes a doer of works who is subject to the law. But here Christ and my conscience must become one body, so that nothing remains in my sight but Christ crucified and risen. But if Christ is put aside and I look only at myself, then I am done for. For then this thought immediately comes to my mind: "Christ is in heaven, and you are on earth. How are you now going to reach Him?" "I will live a holy life and do what the Law requires; and in this way I shall enter life." By paying attention to myself and considering what my condition is or should be, and what I am supposed to be doing, I lose sight of Christ, who alone is my Righteousness and Life. Once He is lost, there is no aid or counsel; but certain despair and perdition must follow.[44]

It may seem paradoxical that one must abandon one's person in order to gain it, but that is precisely the biblical teaching, for "whoever would save his life will lose it, but whoever loses his life for my sake will find it" (Matthew 16:25). This is the denying of self Jesus enjoins upon those who would follow him. In other words, one must deny and lose one's own righteousness to gain the righteousness of another; one must give up their own person to the person and the work of Christ. It is much harder to rescue a drowning person amid their self-preserving efforts and struggle for survival than one who has already drowned, passed out, or collapsed. Similarly, we must accept God's damning judgement over all our own self-preserving, self-affirming, and self-establishing, that is, our self-justifying efforts, in order

---

44. Luther, *Lectures on Galatians (1535), Chapters 1–4*, 166.

to receive life out of death through the death and resurrection of the Son for us. Paul indeed had acted out of concern for his own righteousness before God when he pursued righteousness by the law, but such visible, reasonable, and glorious way does not lead to righteousness. Such concern and works act contrary to the way of faith God has established through the cross. It is only in Christ that we can be considered righteous by faith in his own person and work for us. Forde points out some important implications of this truth in explaining thesis 25 in Luther's Heidelberg Disputation:

> . . . God simply is not interested in works issuing out of the self's concern for its own righteousness. "Whatever is not of faith is sin." Only those who believe much in Christ are righteous before God, period. It always seems incredible to us, but getting used to that fact is what it means to die and be raised to newness of life in Christ, to be born anew. Only then will works that can be called "good" begin to be done. Good works, works done for the neighbor without calculation or claim, can begin when the Old Adam is put to death and the new appears.[45]

To go the way of our works, the visible and glorious way of our performance and achieved righteousness is tantamount to challenging God's way through Christ, and thus we are left without both Christ and true righteousness. We are left with a lot of visible, attractive, and seemingly powerful and reputable things in the eyes of man, but actually ruined and rejected in the eyes of God. To go the way of the cross is to go an invisible route, not discernable to the naked eye, but apprehended, reputed, and elevated in God's eye, for Christ sits at the right hand of God and we are seated with him through faith alone. Consequently, Luther enjoins upon believers to make a clear distinction between the law and the gospel, between the way of the law and the way of grace:

> But we who, by the grace of God, accept the doctrine of justification know for certain that we are justified solely by faith in Christ. Therefore we do not confuse the Law and grace, or faith and works; but we separate them as far as possible. Let everyone who is concerned for godliness observe this distinction of Law and grace diligently . . . Consciences should be carefully taught to understand the doctrine of the distinction between the righteousness of the Law and that of grace.[46]

---

45. Forde, *On Being a Theologian of the Cross*, 104.
46. Luther, *Lectures on Galatians (1535), Chapters 1–4*, 152–58.

To err here is to forfeit death and resurrection, that is, to forfeit Christ for us as our only righteousness *coram Deo*. One could gain much personal change, healing, and transformation of life but if all of it is not first dammed, killed, aborted, flushed down the toilet, if one does not first curse all of our own self-justifying efforts, we are left challenging God's righteousness as revealed in the gospel. We are left not submitting ourselves to God's killing word of law in order to be crucified and buried with Christ; and it must be so in order that the good news of the gospel may freely declare us forgiven, holy, and righteous apart from any of our own works, apart from our own personal efforts, and only through the holy, righteous, and satisfying efforts, obedience, and sacrifice of Christ for us. We affirm that much transformation, change, and healing is available to the Christian, as we shall see when we deal more closely with practical or progressive sanctification, but a point that must *not* be lost is that any true and spiritual change—or as the Bible calls it, fruit of the Spirit—is but the consequence of a liberated conscience, of a glad heart, of a spirit made free by the good news of the gospel, thus made alive for gift living![47] One paragraph from Luther may suffice at this point to illustrate such dynamics:

> Who, then, is living? "The Christian." Paul living in himself, is utterly dead through the Law but living in Christ, or rather with Christ living in him, he lives an alien life. Christ is speaking, acting, and performing all actions in him; these belong not to the Paul-life, but to the Christ-life. "You malicious person, do not slander me for saying that I am dead. And you weak person, do not be offended, but make the proper distinction. There is a double life, my life and an alien life. By my own life I am not living; for if I were, the Law would have dominion over me and would hold me captive. To keep it from holding me, I am dead to it by another Law. And this death acquires an alien life for me, namely, the life of Christ, which is not inborn in me but is granted to me in faith through Christ."[48]

---

47. See Luther, *Lectures on Galatians (1535), Chapters 1–4*, ch. 2 for analysis of how this liberated conscience comes into being and operates vis-à-vis the distinction between law and gospel, works and faith, Moses and Christ.

48. Luther, *Lectures on Galatians (1535), Chapters 1–4*, 170.

CHAPTER 7

How Is a Free Gift "Mixed Up" in Reception?

Sorting Out Reformed Abuse and Confusion

WHAT WE ARE ABOUT to do, which has already been hinted at, may not be popular, but remains the necessity of a gospel-minded reforming spirit, namely, criticize our own. Let it be said from the start that the present writer claims to maintain affiliation by heart and practice within a Reformed perspective. Many of the authors cited here, if not all, are people whom the writer of this paper highly respects and has learned much from. However, in the interest and for the sake of the gospel and its centrality in the life of the church, we only hope that this exercise can be taken as a clarion call for further discernment and critical engagement about the central tenets and practice of our faith. This we believe to be the gospel in its proper relationship and distinction from the law.

Having said that, let us set the grounds for this intramural criticism that we want to offer by presenting the following quote and asking how the Reformed church or even the evangelical church at large would respond to it: "I believe it is not sound and orthodox to teach that we must forsake sin in order to our coming to Christ, and instating us in Covenant to God."[1] The proposition above was required of candidates to licensure for ordination in the presbytery of Auchterarder in Scotland in the year 1716. To such a proposition one candidate by the name of William Craig took exception and was rejected by the said presbytery. But that was not to be the end of the matter, as said applicant appealed to the General Assembly, which ruled in his favor opining that it was "'unsound and most

---

1. *From the Register of the Acts and Proceedings of the General Assembly of the Church of Scotland . . . 1717,* 839–40, as cited in Vandoodewaard, *Marrow Controversy and Seceder Tradition,* 24.

detestable,' arguing that it would lead to spiritual sloth and unholiness." Without saying more at this time about the controversy that ensued,[2] let us use it as a good point of departure for our contention on the lack of distinction between law and gospel.

It is our contention that the proper distinction between law and gospel keeps the categories of faith and works, or faith and love as the obedience of the law, in their proper place and relationship dynamics. Let us explain further using an analogy: there is faith on the one hand as a receiving grace whereby the sinner hears, trusts, and rests in the work of another, that is Christ; and, there is the obedience or works of love as a giving grace whereby the justified sinner offers himself in service to God and neighbor. Thus, the believer receives two hands—a receiving hand named faith and a giving hand named love. By the former, we always go out of ourselves to God and his forgiveness and righteousness for us in Christ; this hand is always grabbing or apprehending this alien righteousness on our behalf without bringing anything to offer in said hand but the lack and need for such a hand to be filled—"Blessed are the poor in spirit, for theirs is the kingdom of heaven . . . blessed are those who hunger and thirst for righteousness, for they shall be filled" (Matthew 5:3, 6). These are they who acknowledge their lack, their emptiness in themselves, not their fullness. Such are filled always with the perfect righteousness and forgiveness of Christ, which is God's grant and gift to the receiving utterly empty believing hand. In other words, such a hand apprehends Christ in all the splendor and glories of his propitiating life, death, and resurrection on our behalf. This is why Paul says in Romans 3 and 4 that it is all "by his grace as a gift" and "to the one who does not work," and further, "apart from works" that God counts or imputes righteousness.

On the other hand—pun indeed intended—the justified sinner becomes a channel through which they give themselves in loving gratitude to God and neighbor in a variety of good works of adoration, praise, and service. This is love in action and love "does not seek its own" but connection, intimacy, service, and the well-being of others. This hand, which in order to give must be full, can't help but open itself, surrender, give, serve, and bless. It is full of good works and, as Luther would say, it is always "busy" carrying out its good designs. It is not the design of the "receiving" hand of faith to give; it must be busy receiving instead. And, vice versa, it is not the design

---

2. See Vandoodewaard, *Marrow Controversy and Seceder Tradition*, ch. 1 for historical background and chronology.

of the "giving" hand to receive; it must be busy giving. Every time we mix up the hands they get confused and their specific roles each are affected; we become defective in both receiving and giving, or in believing or trusting and loving or working. Notwithstanding this distinction, an intricate and close dynamics exists between both hands where the giving or loving hand is always being filled and exercised by the receiving believing hand. In other words, what the giving hand gives, the receiving hand receives first. The former depends on the latter so that one must be filled by faith with gospel treasure before one can deliver the goods in loving service, or as Paul would say it is "faith working through love" or the Spirit being supplied in mighty works and perfecting by the "hearing of faith" (Galatians 5:6; 3:3–5). Luther illustrates this for us thus: ". . . Christ as a gift nourishes your faith and makes you a Christian. But Christ as an example exercises your works. These do not make you a Christian. Actually they come forth from you because you have already been made a Christian. As widely as a gift differs from an example, so widely does faith differ from works, for faith possesses nothing of its own, only the deeds and life of Christ."[3]

These simple interdependent and consequent dynamics of love and works issuing from faith as a result or fruit must always be carefully preserved and communicated in all Christian endeavors lest the gospel of Christ be subverted. The whole fallen cosmos militates against this truth, being that it seeks the ground of being in itself and not in another. This is the essence of Christianity as opposed to the mindset of the flesh, the world, and Satan. Ever since the fall, humankind has been on a quest to hide, deny, resist, and subvert God's verdict of death and condemnation on their self-driven and resourced pursuits. A guilty condemned sinner who cannot see the way of forgiveness and life through grace will only further entrench themselves in their own self-justifying, self-affirming ways in rebellious opposition to God's word. When all they see is judgment without the kindness of his mercy and grace, they remain stubbornly and willingly enslaved in their own ways running away from God's judgment. That is why the Bible reasons that "the power of sin is the law" (1 Corinthians 15:56b) and that deliverance is needed for "those who through fear of death were subject to lifelong slavery" (Hebrews 2:15). We must conclude that sinful humans cannot extricate themselves from God's guilty verdict passed by the law; and, furthermore, the fear of death and condemnation aroused by such a verdict hammers the nails tight of their alienation and slavery to sin

---

3. Lull, *Martin Luther's Basic Theological Writings*, 107.

in rebellion against God's holiness and righteous indignation. Not that God causes such a terrifying rejecting disposition, but that it is the natural reflex and impulse of those shut under judgment. Fallen humanity lives under the sinful reflex or impulse to resist their death sentence, to hide their shame, to deny their guilt. The law of God, however, pursues them relentlessly, whether it be the written law or the law written in their hearts; they cannot avoid moral judgments and the corresponding accusing or excusing that goes along with it through their conscience.

Such a burden can only be relieved in the natural by the searing of conscience to avoid its nagging voice, the numbing and dark surrender of despair, or the deceptive and hardening voice of hypocritical pharisaicalness. The Spirit, however, provides a different response because the Spirit is the revealer of grace and the kindness of God, which is the only way leading to repentance unto life. "Or do you presume on the riches of his kindness and forbearance and patience, not knowing that God's kindness is meant to lead you to repentance?" (Romans 2:4). And then in Titus 2:11 and 3:4, "For the grace of God has appeared, bringing salvation for all people, training us to renounce ungodliness and worldly passions . . . But when the goodness and loving kindness of God our Savior appeared, he saved us, not because of works done by us in righteousness, but according to his own mercy . . ." Thus, all work of redemption and the fruits thereof have reference to the kindness, mercy, forgiveness and loving grace of our God. The fear of torment, punishment, and condemnation does not work or produce love but rather more alienation and enslavement.

The very dynamic of love calls for a free, unhindered, unconcerned, unafraid disposition as it relates to one's well-being, safety, and provision. Any time the self is threatened without an attaching anchor of security and comfort elsewhere, it will inevitably panic, fight, flight, or despair. Loving is the attitude and actions of those securely attached and provided for, as can be clearly seen in children, to take a case from the natural world. Children whose parental attachment is ambivalent and insecure may manifest unhealthy coping behaviors. Likewise, when the love of God is made conditional and contingent upon our performance with the threat of wrath and torment hanging over our heads, love of God does not stand a chance, no matter how much outward conformity may be had. 1 John 4:16–19 testifies to such a powerful truth: "So we have come to know and to believe the love that God has for us. God is love and whoever abides in love abides in God, and God abides in him. By this is love perfected with us, so that we may have confidence for the day of judgment, because as he is so also are we in this world. There is no fear in love, but perfect love casts out fear. For fear has to do with punishment, and whoever fears has not been perfected in love. We love because he first loved us." But what would happen, though, if in order for God to deliver us from punishment and condemnation we were required to satisfy his demands that we love him? In other words, if God made his love conditional upon our love, our freedom from torment and judgment only through our compliance with his law, what would happen to the very love God demands? What would happen if, rather than being justified through faith alone in order to be able to love, we were justified, accepted, and delivered from his wrath conditional upon our obedience? Would this fear of torment and punishment to wrath drive us unto the true transformation of love? It is our contention the Bible answers no. Any attempt to cause obedience on such a framework may indeed exact outward conformity but not the true fruit of righteousness. It is our contention that any attempts to achieve obedience conditional upon obedience-or-else-wrath-and-torment subvert true evangelical and spiritual obedience, which also reveals the fundamental error of the proper distinction between the law and the gospel.

One could say that gospel battles are ever current as the ground we must always fight on. In other words, while other issues have been important historically, we neglect the centrality of the gospel at its own peril. Actually, when the gospel is assumed or taken for granted to move on to other issues, one can almost affirm that the gospel battle has receded, defeats have been inflicted, although not visible at the time due to the distractions of other important issues, and festering wounds loom ominously large on the horizon. Such can arguably be said to be the case with the early fathers that we have cited here. Readers of this work could get the impression that a biased or negatively slanted view of the fathers is proposed that does not consider their circumstances of the issues and battles they had to fight. We have already conceded such truth and the contributions they made. However, we must maintain and propose the thesis that the main highway to God's arsenal, namely, the gospel, seems to have been neglected while fighting these other battles, thus receiving gospel setbacks and defeats that would haunt the church for centuries to come.

The craftiness of the enemy is such and his fear of the gospel so great that very important battles will be presented as ploys to stop, delay, or muddle the powerful canon attack of gospel proclamation for sinners freely through Christ's sacrifice and righteousness. That is the main defense that actually turns into offense, and the enemy knows it. With that hopefully useful word of clarification and warning, let us return to our historical survey and sample some examples we would consider right in line with fighting the gospel battles even within the Reformed camp. The beginning of the Marrow controversy cited above with the statement the Assembly condemned highlights the issue. The Auchterarder presbytery seemed actuated by the desire to safeguard the offer of salvation to sinners from being made conditional upon their obedience to the law, thus their proposal that abandoning sin is not required to be able to stand saved within the covenant of grace; rather, God calls sinners to be saved from sin with the unconditional forgiveness and grace of Christ. It is one thing to be called to abandon sin to be saved and another to be called to salvation because of and in spite of our sin. No amount of trying to connect faith to the call to abandon sin for salvation will save either the sinner or the faith required with it unto such a result.

The Marrow controversy illustrates the gospel issues at play. Insightfully, it starts at the very practical level of proclamation. The Marrow men defended a gospel call that did not condition the gospel to the obedience of abandoning sin. And we believe the rationale for doing so lies in yet another issue that may be said to undergird such practice. It is the issue of assurance as it relates to saving faith. The Marrow men believed that assurance was of the essence of faith. Vandoodeward has carefully selected the following quote by the Assembly in response to the Marrow because it clearly delineates the contrasting positions:

> The Assembly of 1720 selected quotes from The Marrow that were argued in its 5th Act to state that "saving faith commanded in the Gospel a man's persuasion that Christ is his, and died for him; and that whoever hath not this persuasion or assurance hath not answered the Gospel call, nor is a true believer." Against this perceived error of the Marrow theology, the Assembly stated that both the Westminster Confession and Catechisms 'show that assurance is not of the essence of faith.[4]

Let us explain the Marrow position by offering the following quote from the book in the prior century from which Marrow men drew their ammunition.[5] When the character Evangelist is questioned about how a person

---

4. Vandoodeward, *Marrow Controversy and Seceder Tradition*, 33.
5. See the reproduction of an original work by Fisher, *Marrow of Modern Divinity:*

may be sure of being in the faith, they begin to respond with what we would call the direct or primary witness to assurance as it hinges first in the very gospel promise proclaimed: "... I would have you to close with Christ in the promise, without making any question whether you are in the faith or no; for there is an assurance which rises from the exercise of faith by a direct act, and that is, when a man, by faith, directly lays hold upon Christ, and concludes assurance from thence."

One of the assaults on the gospel that we seek to correct is the direct recourse not to Christ but to works and obedience for assurance. The author, we believe, wisely counsels to always run first to Christ as he is offered in the gospel, wherein we have a promise that all who hear may recur to without any conditions but faith—but coming, but turning to him from whatever conditions we may find ourselves in. Nothing is required from those who hear the gospel but to recognize their need of the Savior therein freely offered and turn to him who will by no means reject the coming one, namely, the believing one (Isaiah 55:1; John 6:35–40; Romans 10:13). Thus, assurance is of the nature of faith because the grounds for such a faith repose with the free promise to be had by all who come. Simply put, if I am coming, I am believing, and thus received, justified, saved; because the promise is a Savior for sinners, for every such to come! Faith cannot be discussed, or assurance for that matter, without the objective grounds for it, namely, the person and work of Christ offered for sinners. The Marrow men would affirm that he is offered as a "Deed of Gift and Grant unto all Mankind," which was heavily contested by the Assembly because it seemed to threaten the particularity of election and a limited sense of the atonement as well as the conditionality of the covenant—the latter being another point of significant contrast that we must further elaborate on. But let us hear the Marrow men on the free gospel offer, which was deeply disliked by the Assembly but in our opinion boldly lifted up the gospel call:

> that the following passage is condemned, viz. The Father hath made a Deed of Gift and Grant unto all Mankind, That whosoever of them shall believe His Son, shall not perish, is surprising to us: When in the condemned passage itself, extracted forth of the sacred records, we read that Deed of Gift and Grant, by which we understand no more, but the Revelation of the Divine Will in the Word, affording a Warrant unto all to receive him. This Treatment of the said Passage, seems to incroach upon the Warrants

In Two Parts, annotated by Thomas Boston. It is believed to have first appeared in print during the summer of 1645 in London.

> aforesaid, and also upon Sovereign Grace, which hath made this Grant, not to Devils, but unto Men, in terms than which none can be imagined more extensive.⁶

The Assembly's fear about such language, as Vandoodeward explains, was grounded in the suspicion "that the brethren were propounding a gospel offer rooted in a theology that lay somewhere between universalism and Amyraldianism."⁷ The Marrow men's response clarifies such fears while maintaining the clarity of what the gospel offers universally to every sinner unconditionally through faith:

> . . . although we believe the purchase and application of redemption to be peculiar to the elect, who were given by the Father to Christ in the counsel of peace, yet the warrant to receive him is common to all: ministers, by virtue of the commission they have received from their great Lord and Master, are authorized and instructed to go to preach the gospel to every creature, i.e. To make a full, free, and unhampered offer of him, his grace, righteousness, and salvation, to every rational soul, to whom they may in providence have access to speak.⁸

Their view on gospel offer, we contend, is linked to gospel assurance because if men are called to only believe in order to be saved, they must of necessity have recourse to faith and the promise for assurance before anything else. However, if the gospel calls people not just to believe the promise that inherently speaks assurance but to a promise that must not only be believed but also demands some other obedience, said obedience must share equal grounds to establish assurance. The Marrow book provides an excellent case in point to illustrate our argument as it deals with a new young Christian seeking assurance, which quote deserves full citation:

> Wherefore, my dear Neophitus, to turn my speech particularly to you, (because I see you are in heaviness,) I beseech you to be persuaded that here you are to work nothing, here you are to do nothing, here you are to render nothing unto God, but only to receive the treasure, which is Jesus Christ, and apprehend him by faith, although you be never so great a sinner; and so shall you obtain forgiveness of sins, righteousness, and eternal happiness: not as an agent, but as a patient, not by doing, but by receiving. Nothing here

---

6. Vandoodeward, *Marrow Controversy and Seceder Tradition*, 66–67.
7. Ibid., 67.
8. Ibid., 67.

comes betwixt but faith only, apprehending Christ in the promise. This, then, is perfect righteousness, to hear nothing, to know nothing, to do nothing of the law of works; but only to know and believe that Jesus Christ is now gone to the Father, and sitteth at his right hand, not as a judge but is made unto you of God, wisdom, righteousness, sanctification, and redemption. Wherefore, as Paul and Silas said to the jailer, so say I unto you, "Believe on the Lord Jesus Christ, and thou shalt be saved"; that is, be verily persuaded in your heart that Jesus Christ is yours, and that you shall have life and salvation by him; that whatsoever Christ did for the redemption of mankind, he did it for you.[9]

Anywhere you find clarity on what the gospel offers in terms of the centrality of a promise that itself offers assurance because it offers Christ as the propitiation for sinners through faith, you are likely to find that assurance is made of the essence of faith. In other words, the primary grounds for assurance lie with faith or with the object of that faith which assures what it promises upon simply resting in it or believing it. The object of faith is Christ for sinners as their: forgiveness, propitiation, righteousness, sanctification, and everything necessary to stand reconciled before God. What do we need to do to receive it? Just take it; it is for you! We can see in John Calvin another witness to such a truth, which may surprise some as he also believed that assurance was of the essence of faith. Let us hear his definition of faith: "We shall now have a full definition of faith if we say that it is a firm and sure knowledge of the divine favor toward us, founded on the truth of a free promise in Christ, and revealed to our minds, and sealed on our hearts, by the Holy Spirit." And then, "The true knowledge of Christ consists in receiving him as he is offered by the Father, namely, as invested with His Gospel . . . knowledge of the divine favor toward us, and a full persuasion of its truth."[10] Calvin employs the language of "full persuasion" and "knowledge" grounded in how he is offered in the gospel of God's "divine favor." How is Christ offered in the gospel? To be taken freely as the pardon and favor of God for sinners. Furthermore, Calvin explains that the object of this faith speaks or beckons one to believe not just with any word of God but such as specifically testifies of mercy and grace in Christ. Let us quote at length again:

---

9. Fisher, *Marrow of Modern Divinity*, 97–98.
10. Calvin, *Institutes of the Christian Religion*, 358–62.

> ... we are only inquiring what faith can find in the word of God to lean and rest upon. When conscience sees only wrath and indignation, how can it but tremble and be afraid? And how can it avoid shunning the God whom it thus dreads? But faith ought to seek God, not shun him. It is evident, therefore, that we have not yet obtained a full definition of faith, it being impossible to give the name to every kind of knowledge of the divine will. Shall we, then, for "will," which is often the messenger of bad news and the herald of terror, substitute the benevolence or mercy of God? ... Hence, there is need of the gracious promise in which he testifies that he is a propitious Father; since there is no other way in which we can approach him, the promise being the only thing on which the heart of man can recline.[11]

Now, the reality of a direct and primary assurance that sinners who come to Christ can have by virtue of the promise itself as Christ is offered in the gospel freely does not negate that such persuasion inherent with faith can be assailed by much doubting and anxiety, or that God has also provided for other evidences of faith and the grace of God at work in our lives. That Christ is offered freely in the gospel promise means, "There is forgiveness for you here, sinner: take it, receive it, believe it. You can be assured that it is here for you." "At what cost?" someone could ask. "None to you, but priceless to God because it cost him his Son's life; there is infinitely sufficient worth and virtue in his sacrifice to save you upon simply coming to receive by believing, by trusting his promise to do so for anyone who comes—yes, indeed, for you!" Now, it is important to understand that insofar as the sinner comes, in the act of doing so they are assuredly and persuadedly exercising saving faith. They cannot come unless they are assuredly persuaded of the promise; if they are not, they simply do not come, namely, they do not believe, they are still in unbelief.

It does not matter how small one's faith may be, just an ounce of such a persuasion or trust will be enough to believe unto salvation. Just a little trust enough to reach out for him will find Christ. The disciples were scolded, "O you of little faith" (Matthew 14:31), while others were commended for their great faith; but any size faith gets persuaded enough to touch Jesus and be saved, for the power lies in the object of faith and not faith itself. Thus, faith can be great or small, even assaulted and shaken by doubting, fears, and anxieties; however, true persuasion and assurance in Christ as it is the nature of true faith will never fade away in those who truly believe. Those

---

11. Calvin, *Institutes*, 359.

who never find such a persuasion of assurance in Christ's promise simply do not believe, have not trusted Christ, no matter how much profession or obedience they have shown. It is on their lips and outward conduct but not on their hearts. Such were the Pharisees, but yet they were unbelievers. Calvin affirms that ". . . the elect alone have that full assurance which is extolled by Paul, and by which they are enabled to cry, Abba, Father." Notwithstanding such assurance, believers, Calvin also maintains, "have a perpetual struggle with their own distrust, and are thus far from thinking that their consciences possess a placid quiet, uninterrupted by perturbation. On the other hand, whatever be the mode in which they are assailed, we deny that they fall off and abandon that sure confidence which they have formed in the mercy of God."[12] Thus, the apostle Peter reminds us that we "by God's power are being guarded through faith for a salvation ready to be revealed in the last time" (1 Peter 1:5); although now that faith will have to undergo many trials, testing, and temptation.

Not only is the trial of faith not denied by such a primary direct assurance, but neither are the need for self-examination as well as the reality of other evidences of grace for further strengthening assurance. We will call this a secondary or indirect line of evidence that can never be sought or engaged apart from the primary or direct line of evidence, namely, the gospel promise. Now, we contend that such an examination for other evidences must issue from the window of seeing the promise through faith. In other words, self-examination is not to be made disconnected from the direct evidence of faith in the promise; rather, upon seeking and seeing the promise in Christ, and only then, do we recommend looking for secondary evidences of grace issuing from faith. This is the biblical testimony for assurance as we hear in 1 John 3:23–24: "And this is his commandment that we believe in the name of his Son Jesus Christ and love one another, just as he has commanded us. Whoever keeps his commandments abides in God, and God in him. And by this we know that he abides in us, by the Spirit whom he has given us." Notice the order, namely, faith and love; this is how John sums up the commandments. John begins his letter pointing our attention to the need of walking in the light of God's fellowship through our confession of sin and trusting in Jesus as our propitiation (1:7–10, 2:1–2); then he calls us to love one another because he has first loved us, and we ought and can do so, having been set free from the fear of punishment and condemnation (4:13–19).

---

12. Calvin, *Institutes*, 362, 366.

Also in his gospel, John evinces the same order as we hear an inquiry made of Jesus followed by his insightful response: "'What must we do, to be doing the works of God?' Jesus answered them, 'This is the work of God, that you believe in him whom he has sent.'" And then later on, "A new commandment I give to you, that you love one another: 'just as I have loved you, you also are to love one another'" (John 6:28–29; 13:34). Thus, we see two lines of evidence, one having to do with faith in the promise, and the other with love. But the dynamics of how these two are related cannot be ignored. One can only look to affections of love and display of good works as we are looking to the Son, who assures us of his propitiating love to freely produce our loving response. A sinner assured by the promise in Christ as they look to him will never fail to thank and praise him in loving adoration, from which neighborly and brotherly love and service also arise. Calvin affirms the reality of a faith that can and ought to be examined as well as the presence of other evidences that help assurance. Calvin says, ". . . believers are taught to examine themselves carefully and humbly, lest carnal security creep in and take the place of assurance of faith . . . because the Spirit properly seals the forgiveness of sins in the elect only, applying it by special faith to their use," and in another place, "faith cannot possibly be disjoined from pious affection."[13] Calvin's instinct is to seek the promise in Christ first and from there the pious affections of the sanctifying Spirit for the whole assurance dynamics. One could only wish that Calvin's Christ-centeredness were followed by much of today's contemporary church.

The Marrow affirms the same with arguably even more explicitly Christ-centeredness than Calvin himself. And by Christ-centeredness in assurance we mean the clarity of seeking assurance first directly in the free promise of the gospel, and only derivatively or reflectively from and through faith in loving affections and other works. Thomas Boston in his annotations on the Marrow calls this secondary evidence "assurance by a reflex act."[14] Evangelist proceeds to explain assurance to the young Christian with the following points and order:

> Consider, then, I pray you, that you have been convinced in your spirit that you are a sinful man and thereupon have feared the Lord's wrath and eternal damnation . . . and you have been convinced that there is no help for you at all in yourself, by any thing that you can do [and] that Jesus Christ alone is an all-sufficient

---

13. Calvin, *Institutes*, 362, 358.
14. See Boston's notes in Fisher, *Marrow of Modern Divinity*, 215.

help; and the free and full promise of God in Christ has been made so plain and clear to you, that you had nothing to object why Christ did not belong to you in particular, and you have perceived a willingness in Christ to receive you . . . and you have thereupon consented and resolved to take Christ and give yourself to him . . .

Up to here, we can call this the objective self-authenticating and assuring promise the sinner receives, and from there, as a reflex, the following:

> . . . and I am persuaded you have thereupon felt a secret persuasion in your heart, that God in Christ doth bear a love to you; and answerably [reflexively] your heart hath been inflamed towards him in love again, manifesting itself in an unfeigned desire to be obedient and subject to his will in all things, and never to displease him in anything.[15]

Upon hearing such an enlighteningly refreshing explanation, the young Christian is relieved of his fearful burdens and confirms what Evangelist has explained with joy, which, upon the hearing of it, Evangelist proceeds to speak the following words of comforting absolution: "And to you yourself, Neophytus, I say, as Christ said unto the woman, 'Thy sins are forgiven thee, thy faith hath saved thee, go in peace.'"[16] Such is the comfort gospel shepherds ought to provide their flock upon their confession of sin and trust in Christ for the promise, which gives rise to much holy affection. Sadly, such comfort is denied when assurance does not proceed first to Christ directly in the promise and only reflexively to love and other fruits of faith. The comforting absolution shall be the reflective grounds for the reflex of faith to issue in renewed obedience and devotion to God and one another. The practice of making assurance dependent on obedience, not as a faith reflex but as a faith requirement where obedience is of the essence of faith, turns the seeking of assurance into a works project that undermines, nay, destroys any hope for true evangelical assurance and the true free loving obedience that flows from it.

The last issue that we want to delve into using the Marrow as our case in point is the issue of the conditionality of the covenant, which is the logical assumption underneath what we have discussed so far. We shall speak more at length on this topic as it regards the covenant of grace and whether or not it is a conditional covenant. But let us begin tackling the issue from the very practical standpoint of the doctrine of repentance. One of the chief

---

15. Fisher, *Marrow of Modern Divinity*, 216.
16. Fisher, 217.

Marrow opponents objected to its "Antinomianism" by alluding to the necessity of repentance as a condition of forgiveness. Vandoodewaard highlights how James Haddow conditions faith unto forgiveness on repentance with the following quote, which we provide in its entirety:

> ... that the evangelical grace and duty of repentance goeth before pardon of sin, in God's method of bestowing them; and remission of sin is a consequent blessing annexed unto repentance by divine promise; and that therefore ministers in preaching the gospel, may, and ought to call sinners to repent, and forsake their sins, in order unto their obtaining the pardon of them, as well as to believe in Christ for their justification . . . Repentance is placed before pardon, in the proper order, wherein Christ bestows his purchased benefits . . . Repentance, or forsaking of sin, hath the promise of pardon annexed unto it, and the duty is enforced from the encouraging promise of this gracious benefit following thereon.

We can see in this assertion, firstly, the very clear identification of repentance with the forsaking of sin, and secondly, that such forsaking of sin precedes pardon and justification. It's important to understand that such a position has confused law and gospel and turned the doing of the law into a condition for forgiveness and justification, which Paul says happens without the works of the law in Romans 3 and 4.

Let us try to explain further. The category of law explains what Jesus sums up as loving God with all our strength, heart, mind, and soul, and our neighbor as ourselves. This is the summation of all of God's commands in his law. Simply put, it means love—the love of God and neighbor perfectly without failure: "Cursed be everyone who does not abide by all things written in the Book of the Law, and do them"; "For whoever keeps the whole law but fails in one point has become accountable for all of it" (Galatians 3:10; James 2:10). Another way of saying the same thing is that the law forbids any lack of conformity to God's moral will, and that the Bible calls sin: "for we have all sinned and fall short of the glory of God" (Romans 3:23). When we talk of the law of God proper, we are referring to that which forbids all sin; it commands us to forsake sin, namely, to live righteously or to love, since "love is the fulfilling of the law" (Romans 13:10). Here, as a side note, we agree with Westerholm that the "moral commandments God gave to Israel spell out unmistakably the kind of wise behavior that is in harmony with all the ordered goodness of the cosmos and therefore expected of all human beings."[17] Consequently, if we take the definition of repentance to mean forsaking sin, or somehow involve the forsaking of sin in it, we have encumbered repentance with the freight of the law. Thus, calling people to salvation and forgiveness in Christ conditioned upon repentance would sound like, "Stop sinning; quit your sins and believe in Christ to be forgiven and justified."

It is clear to see that such an appeal conditions forgiveness and acceptance in Christ to the actual obedience of the law, at least in some sense, even if not granted that the law demands perfect obedience, namely, perfect and total forsaking, quitting, abandoning of all sin. On a grander scheme, to use Westerholm's language, if repentance understood this way is the condition for forgiveness and justification, then we can only be justified when we exhibit the right and wise behavior demanded of the ordered goodness of the cosmos. Or at least, as some would put it, we must have a beginning of such ordering or submission to God's law in order to be justified. Thus, Christ can only be applied to us in his forgiving and justifying virtue as we demonstrate some virtue, some sense of ordering, of wisdom, of law obedience ourselves. To evoke the justification language of the Middle Ages and Roman Catholicism, we must be made righteous to be justified, and this is a process of getting more and more ordered, just, sanctified, and conformed to God's commands. In this vision, obedience to law and some conformity to it is of the essence of being justified, thus repentance and faith are both mingled with such obedience. Null in his work that deals with repentance sums up one theologian of the time thus: "Fisher outlined three steps necessary for reconciliation with the Creator. A sinner needed to amend his life, to call to God for help, and to have a full trust in His merciful Lord."[18] It is interesting to note a similar inclination, although differently nuanced, in the Reformed objection to the Marrow. Here, we must forsake sin to be justified once for all, but the implication for acceptance unto such justification is both repentance, or the obedient forsaking of sin as the law demands, and faith unto pardon and justification. The clear implication is that the latter cannot be effective and valid without the former.

This may be why John Calvin with his accustomed Christ centrality chooses to assign repentance a place after faith. He may agree that repentance involves the forsaking of sin, but he distinguishes repentance from faith as if to signal that the sole reason why we are accepted before God

---

17. Westerholm, *Justification Reconsidered*, 81–82.
18. Null, *Cranmer's Doctrine of Repentance*, 60–61.

has nothing to do with our obedience and merit and everything to do with Christ's obedience and merit. Because, we must emphasize, to condition acceptance with God upon our forsaking of sin in repentance confuses law and gospel and destroys the grace by which we are accepted and empowered to live in his love. While we have some disagreement with Calvin on this issue, let us highlight Calvin's fundamental thoughts on the issue before we begin to disagree. Calvin's arguments on the topic of repentance after he has dealt with the topic of faith thoroughly undermine the Marrow opponents. Citing Psalm 130:4, "There is forgiveness with thee, that though mayest be feared," Calvin explains that "no man will ever reverence God who does not trust that God is propitious to him, no man will ever willingly set himself to observe the Law who is not persuaded that his services are pleasing to God."[19] We strongly concur with the aforesaid. Calvin also affirms that "repentance not only follows faith, but is produced by it . . . those who think that repentance precedes faith instead of flowing from, or being produced by it, as the fruit by the tree have never understood its nature . . ."[20] We disagree with Calvin's placement of repentance after faith for reasons we shall soon elucidate, but agree that if repentance is taken to mean some obedience to God's commands, some real holiness and righteousness in man, it must be referenced to always as fruit, consequence of, the result of the free favor of God being embraced by faith alone.

Indeed, for Calvin repentance means a man "betaking himself from the errors of his former life into the right path, and making it his whole study to practice repentance," which involves "that holiness of life, real holiness [which] is inseparable from the free imputation of righteousness,"[21] but, as we have noted, always as a consequence and fruit of a faith that alone embraces the free promise of pardon and righteousness offered as a "deed of grant and gift," as the Marrow speaks, for those who hear. Then, if we apply Marrow language going back to Boston and his nomenclature for loving obedience as a "reflex act," repentance construed as obedience is nothing but the "reflex act" of faith, of a faith that has assuredly and gratuitously received free pardon and righteousness in Christ. While Calvin advances that repentance is "a real conversion of our life unto God, proceeding from sincere and serious fear of God; and consisting in the mortification of our flesh and the old man, and the quickening of the Spirit," he sees "faith and

19. Calvin, *Institutes*, 387.
20. Calvin, *Institutes*, 386.
21. Calvin, *Institutes*, 386.

repentance as two different things," and insists that "although they cannot be separated, they ought to be distinguished . . . though constantly linked together, are only to be united not confounded."[22]

This good practice of rightly dividing, discerning, and distinguishing what ought to be so in light of a proper understanding of the knowledge of Christ and the centrality of the gospel is necessary for every argument and analysis that involves the gospel and the fruits thereof. Nay, we would contend that such protection or republication of gospel truth is a necessity when treating with any doctrinal issue. The distinction between the law and the gospel, we advance, is always the unspoken battle and casualty of any doctrinal warfare that fails to address it. To use an analogy, it is the hub from which all other spokes proceed, receive, and transmit spiritual energy. Thus, Calvin shows his judicious skill in the much-nuanced arguments that he offers on repentance for the purpose of not undermining the free gospel of Christ; he begins to conclude:

> Forgiveness of sins is preached when men are taught that Christ "is made unto us wisdom, and righteousness, and sanctification, and redemption" (1 Cor 1:30), that on his account they are freely deemed righteous and innocent in the sight of God. Though both graces are obtained by faith (as has been shown elsewhere), yet as the goodness of God, by which sins are forgiven, is the proper object of faith, it was proper carefully to distinguish it from repentance.[23]

It is our contention that emphasis on the distinction between law and gospel stands behind every clear attempt at safeguarding the free nature of God's grace as offered in the gospel. Every time the lines between them are blurred these categories become so bunched up almost to the point of merging or assimilation. Such is the case when good works are said to be of the essence of faith as in its defining element, or faith is said to consist in holy affections or in obedient surrender, the forsaking of sin, the necessity of works for salvation, final justification according to works, and the like. This bunching up abounds and the confusion entrenches itself so that gospel battles must be constantly reengaged and refought for the heart capital of Christianity. Now, we want to highlight a difference with Calvin that we consider to be a better way of speaking about repentance that more aptly

---

22. Calvin, *Institutes*, 388.
23. Calvin, *Institutes*, 388.

safeguards law/gospel distinction. For that we offer the Augsburg Confession section on the issue in its entirety:

> Concerning repentance it is taught that those who have sinned after baptism obtain forgiveness of sins whenever they come to repentance and that absolution should not be denied them by the church. Now properly speaking, true repentance is nothing else than to have contrition and sorrow, or terror about sin, and yet at the same time to believe in the Gospel and absolution that sin is forgiven and grace is obtained through Christ. Such faith, in turn, comforts the heart and puts it at peace. Then improvement should also follow, and a person should refrain from sins. For these should be the fruits of repentance, as John says in Matthew 3 [:8]: "Bear fruit worthy of repentance."
>
> Rejected here are those who teach that whoever has once become righteous cannot fall again.[24]

A couple of things must be noted: firstly, repentance and faith are distinguished as in Calvin, yet, secondly, repentance is not assigned a value of obedience or righteousness according to the law, or equaled with the obedience of the progressive/practical/real sanctification that ensues after being justified or converted unto Christ. In other words, repentance is placed as an indivisible and constitutive part of the instrument to justification together with faith, but never are the two viewed in the sense of any obedience to the law that commands righteousness. For it they, either repentance or faith, were assigned law value in the sense of being obedient acts of righteousness according to the law, then the gospel is compromised to be made a gospel that calls for both faith and works unto salvation. This is somehow what the Lutherans protested against the Roman Catholics, but, sadly, what continues to be the ever-present danger in gospel battles. In order to further clarify what is at stake and the importance of the contrast with Calvin, we must nuance the argument a bit more, and we shall continue to enlist the Lutheran confessional view to help us in the matter.

Going back to Calvin in book 2 on faith, he labors to show that reprobates are not in possession of true or genuine faith. It behooves us to understand how Calvin explains this, and while much of it, if not most, we find agreeable, there is however a slight problem to be noted. Calvin proceeds to refute those who claim that there can be such a thing as a bare faith that needs the supplementation of love to be true by affirming that faith cannot

---

24. Kolb and Wengert, eds., *Book of Concord*, 44.

be spoken of in those who have no "fear of God, and no sense of piety."[25] The legacy of the Schoolmen provided for a distinction between formed and unformed faith. In other words, some could have faith, a bare assent to all that is necessary to know unto salvation, but if this faith was not formed by love, namely, the fear and love of God, such was not true faith but could be spoken of as faith in some sense. Calvin refutes that distinction, negating that such "bare" faith can be spoken of as faith in any sense at all. He wants to reject the Scholastics, who maintain that faith, which is bare assent, needs to be formed by love; it needs the additional quality of love, infused by God when infusing justifying grace into the hearts of sinners, for it to be true faith. Calvin may be said to succeed in refuting the Scholastic distinction, but in doing so arguably muddles the waters just a bit—but enough for later generations to wallow deep in the mud seeds that he has created.

What Calvin says next, we contend, is a seed that will be used by many later in the Reformed tradition in many harmful ways not intended by Calvin himself.[26] Thus, we should hasten to add that Calvin's gospel centrality almost redeems him from such a misstep, but nonetheless the seeds are already planted. Let us delve into the muddy seed. Calvin refutes the distinction between unformed faith and formed faith not, like Luther, by flipping the terms as noted much earlier. Let us remember, the Scholastic distinction allows for a love-lacking faith that needs to become a love-present faith, namely, unformed or not saving faith into a formed saving faith. When a person believed what the church taught, he also did everything in his power to receive from God justifying grace—*quod in se est*; this was the infusion of love from and for God. Once such a love for God or justifying grace was received, the person is on his way through cooperation with said infused/received grace of loving God to his sanctifying justification goal. Love of God was the virtue, the habit, the grace that they were supposed to long for, work for, wait for, receive, and cooperate with in order to remain on that sanctifying path of grace. To affirm such a framework implies that faith is what it is, or rather, of any worth or value for acceptance before God because of its love-unto-God or affections-for-God component, to wit, its yield in terms of righteous obedience unto God/law.

---

25. Kolb and Wengert, eds., *Book of Concord*, 360.

26. See Kendall, *Calvin and English Calvinism to 1649* for a very lucid and persuasive case for how Calvin is either misinterpreted or ignored on his views on the nature of faith, the atonement, the gospel offer, etc.

Luther turns the above framework on its head, which ends up like this: God demands love, i.e., the obedience of his law, namely, perfect righteousness; but no one, no matter how much they do *quod in se est*, how much *dolor* in their contrition and confession, how much obedience in their satisfaction, how much devotion and love they might claim before God for acceptance, it is never enough, not true unless formed by faith; it is actually all damnable works unless formed by faith. Thus, we could say, there was a "bare" love that was not sufficient, nay, actually accursed because God demands perfect love, perfect obedience or righteousness. Only Christ's perfect righteousness and sacrifice will do, and Christ is attained only by faith. Consequently, sinners could only be accepted before God by the faith that apprehends the only grounds for acceptance before God, namely, Christ's sacrifice and righteousness, or to put it in other words, the Son's perfect love in his life and work for us. Luther, again, explains: "By faith alone, not by faith formed by love, are we justified. We must not attribute the power of justification to a 'form' that makes a man pleasing to God; we must attribute it to faith, which takes hold of Christ the Savior Himself and possesses Him in the heart. This faith justifies *without* love and *before* love."[27]

Hence, we have a sinner whose love cannot save him, but the love of Christ can; and that love can only be received by faith, so that now a sinner loves God with a love formed by the faith that apprehends Christ. When asked about their love, such people will say, "Look to my faith because it is looking to love, to perfect love for me, to Christ!" Indeed, it is a faith that works in love, but its essence, confidence, and assurance lies in receiving all freely from the Son's love; that is the essence of faith, its object for us. True love, saving love, resides with Christ, whose perfections and glories for us in the gospel we receive by faith, a Christ-apprehending, -resting, and -trusting faith that forms, sustains, adorns, and perfects our love, namely, a faith/Christ-formed love. Our salvation, then, is not a path of cooperating with an internal grace that enables us to love and thereby be saved, but a path of delighting, rejoicing, and serving a God whose love, demonstrated in Christ as proclaimed in the gospel, saves, feeds, sustains, and transforms us through faith for his own glory. Luther further corrects the opponents illuminating the issue at hand:

> The pope and his scholastic theologians say clearly that the Law and grace are distinct things, but in his practice he teaches the very opposite. "Faith in Christ," he says, "whether it is acquired by man's

---

27. Luther, *Lectures on Galatians (1535), Chapters 1–4*, 137 (italics added).

natural powers, actions, and qualities or whether it is infused by God, is still dead if love does not follow." What has happened to the distinction between the Law and grace? He distinguishes them in name, but in practice he calls grace love. Thus the sectarians demand works in addition to faith.

We see here the need to not simply rely on familiar terms because for others they may carry a different connotation and meaning. We must proceed to theological precision in gospel matters. Luther concludes about their error:

> So far as the words are concerned, they admit that the two are distinct things; but in fact, as I have said, they confuse them, because they do not concede that faith justifies without works. If this is true, then Christ is of no use to me. For though I may have as true a faith as possible, yet, according to their opinion, I am not justified if this faith of mine is without love; and however much of this love I may have, it is never enough.[28]

Calvin in his reply to the Scholastics refutes them in their distinction but, we contend, does not clearly disavow the obedience of love, or affections unto God for that matter, as the defining essence of faith. Although he clearly defines faith, on the one hand, as the apprehension of Christ in the gracious promise of the gospel, on the other hand, he argues in such a way for something more in faith as will pave the way for the undermining of the effectiveness of faith alone for salvation, for acceptance before God. What is that something else, that "muddy" seed? Let us quote Calvin for the answer as he is offering his answer to the Scholastic distinction: ". . . that they talk absurdly when they maintain that faith is formed by the addition of pious affection as an accessory to assent, since assent itself, such at least as the Scriptures describe, consists in pious affection."[29] Thus, Calvin rejects part of their opponents' argument but could be said to tacitly agree with their main premise, namely, that true faith is only faith insofar as it loves God, has pious affections for God, or obeys the law. To repeat Calvin, "it [faith] consists in pious affection." He considers his opponents roundly routed because he has shown that what they view as an addition—the supplementation of love, of righteousness, of obedience to the law, of pious affection—is what faith consists in, instead of, as we have argued, the fruit thereof.

While Calvin now speaks of faith as receiving the promise, he then speaks of faith as the affections of love, the pious obedience to the law. Does

---

28. Luther, *Lectures on Galatians (1535), Chapters 1–4*, 144.
29. Calvin', *Institutes*, 360.

that mean that one is to believe that faith can exist without love? No, we must reply; but we must quickly make absolutely clear that what Calvin describes as of the essence of faith and later assigns more properly to repentance should properly be assigned to their fruits, or more strictly and properly speaking, as the resulting consequence of both. We must affirm that God accepts us through the instrument of repentance and faith without works of the law, which, to be redundant, in no way can be meant to include any law obedience or mixing thereof with the instrument, but the sole apprehension and imputation of such forgiveness and righteousness in Christ; and from there, then, affirm that such faith and repentance shall be demonstrated in much fruit of law obedience, of pious affection, of righteous living. There is a theological cause-and-effect rationale that the Bible provides for repentance/faith, on the one hand, and the fruit of obedience, of holy affections, on the other, which inheres in the distinction of law and gospel as we have explained. Augsburg speaks more properly here, where no law, love, or works are conceived under the category of repentance but simply as another aspect of the faith instrumentation unto justification, and then any obedience arising thereof as its fruits, namely, the fruits of repentance and faith. This we contend is the testimony of Scripture that guarantees no confusion between law and gospel between faith/repentance and the new work of obedience that results.

Someone might ask whether this is not the splitting of theological hairs and argue that it does not matter how repentance is construed in the grand scheme of things as long as we repent. But we must reply that given the nature of how many are wont to condition salvation upon repentance, it becomes necessary to have a right view of repentance and faith and their proper relationship with the new obedience of the believer. Indeed, the Bible records that the calling to salvation proceeds with now calling sinners to believe, and another time calling them to repent, and yet other times to do both. In Acts 3:19–20, we hear the apostolic injunction, "Repent therefore, and turn again, that your sins may be blotted out, that times of refreshing may come from the presence of the Lord," and thus the calling to salvation proceeds often. We must affirm with the biblical record that we are saved through faith and repentance, that is, with faith and repentance. They are both instruments in God's way of reconciling sinners unto himself. Because this is so, it is crucial that neither element gets charged the freight of the law, works, or love obedience, because to do so presents a conditional covenant of grace that adds the demand of the law in order to be saved. In other words, if repentance is the giving up of sin, the pious affection of love, the commitment and desire to obey, the total surrender of sanctification, then forgiveness can only be tendered upon our rendering such obedience, which unquestionably goes under the category of law obedience. If so, we must affirm that we are saved with or through both faith and love, grace and merit, trust and works; in other words, we are not saved by faith or repentance alone, meaning, without *any* works of the law as a condition.

Undoubtedly, there are many who so construe salvation, and this is why they have no problem making such claims. Yet, there may be others who do not share such notions but in practice communicate such a perspective. We believe Calvin does not share such a perspective, and this is why he reserves for repentance a place after faith in order to avoid such notions. However, we contend, we can remain more faithful to the biblical record by keeping repentance on the side of faith, namely, distinguishable from faith, but together with faith on the side of instrumentation rather than on the side of fruits, result, and consequence within sanctification. This is the better way of assuring that sinners hear the unconditionally of the covenant of grace whereby they are called to receive all things freely, meaning without works or any law obedience. As we have noted, Augsburg keeps these lines clear and even Calvin seems aware that such a proposal exists when he concedes, "The other they term evangelical ; or that by which the sinner, through grievously downcast in himself, yet looks up and sees in Christ the cure of his wound, the solace of his terror, the haven of rest from his misery . . . Examples of evangelical repentance we see in all those who, first stung with a sense of sin, but afterward raised and revived by confidence in the divine mercy, turned unto the Lord."[30] Bingo, we would say to Calvin, however, he is not content and goes on express, "Though all this is true, yet the term repentance (insofar as I can ascertain from Scripture) must be differently taken."[31] And thus he proceeds to define repentance by its fruits, loading the concept with the full weight of the sanctifying fruits of regeneration as he sums it up, "In one word, then, by repentance I understand regeneration . . ."[32]

Again, one could live with Calvin's view were it not for the fact that a whole tradition after him seemed to have ignored what he said on faith, the nature of faith, the centrality of Christ as the object of faith, the gratuitous

---

30. Calvin, *Institutes*, 388.
31. Calvin, *Institutes*, 388.
32. Calvin, *Institutes*, 390.

pardon, the free universal offer of the gospel, the direct assurance, choosing instead to emphasize repentance as the law-abiding obedience that the sinner must begin as the condition and evidence of grace for salvation. While for both Luther and Calvin a true and genuine faith does not fail to produce good works, these are never affirmed as conditions for salvation but rather as consequences and results thereof. However, there is a strand of entrenched Reformed theology that affirmed such a necessity in such a way that colored the covenant of grace as conditional upon such obedience. The scope of this chapter and book does not suffice to provide a detailed tracking of such outcome, but a sampling of such attitudes is in order. The Marrow debate provides our main case sample, but the evidence is wider and more comprehensive. Beeke and Jones note such attitudes among the Reformed approvingly thus:

> Protestants did not all agree on whether good works were necessary for salvation. In article 4 of the Epitome, the Lutheran Book of Concord addresses this issue at the beginning of the Negative Theses: "1. Accordingly, we reject and condemn the following manner of speaking: when it is taught and written that good works are necessary for salvation; or that no one has ever been saved without good works; or that it is impossible to be saved without good works." The writings of Reformed theologians paint a very different picture, however. In fact, they affirmed the very opposite, namely, that good works are necessary for salvation. But they would defend this truth with a great deal of care to include the requisite distinctions that kept them from denying justification by faith alone, by situating this doctrine in the context of their doctrine of the covenant.[33]

If we take a look at the Affirmative Theses of the Epitome in said article, Thesis 5, we hear the following enunciation, which does not deny the "necessity" of good works but rather establishes them on a basis that clarifies the separation of such works from their justification and their proper place in grace in distinction from the law covenant: "Of course, the word ... ('necessity' and 'necessary') are not to be understood as a compulsion when they are applied to the reborn, but only as the required obedience, which they perform out of a spontaneous spirit—not because of the compulsion or coercion of the law—because they are 'no longer under the law, but under grace' (Rom. 6:14)." By citing Lutheran sources we do not aim at

---

33. Beeke and Jones, *Puritan Theology*, 312.

endorsing all of their theology since much in them can also be subjected to critical scrutiny; we are simply highlighting in some parts a better way of handling a particular issue or way of speaking about it. Theses 7–9 go on to explain that this is said:

> 7 . . . regarding the liberated spirit, which acts not out of fear of punishment, like a slave, but out of the love of righteousness, as children (Rom.8 [:15]). 8. However, in the elect children of God this spontaneity is not perfect but is encumbered with great weakness, as St. Paul complains about himself in Romans 7 [:14–25] and Galatians 5 [:17]. 9. Of course, because of Christ, the Lord does not reckon this weakness against his elect, as it is written, "There is therefore now no condemnation for those who are in Christ Jesus" (Romans 8[:1]).

The Lutheran difference lies in attempting to keep the proper distinction between the law and the gospel so that each may have its place and not be comingled in their proclamation, usage, and functions. The preaching of repentance as the preaching of obedience to God's commands in the regenerate does have a place but it is not the gospel proper. Neither can the gospel unto life ever be conditioned upon such law preaching as useful as the latter may be in the Christian's life. In regards to the preaching of the gospel in distinction from the law, the Book of Concord in section V, affirmative thesis 6 clarifies ". . . that the gospel is not a proclamation of repentance or retribution, but is, strictly speaking, nothing else than a proclamation of comfort and a joyous message which does not rebuke nor terrify but comforts consciences against the terror of the law, directs them solely to Christ's merit, and lifts them up again through the delightful proclamation of the grace and favor of God, won through Christ's merit."[34]

In other words, sinners are not called to salvation conditioned upon their obedience to the law, partial or not, but on the basis of their freedom from condemnation incurred justly under the law but delivered thereof graciously or freely under the gospel. Neither are saints spurred forward along the path of sanctification by the terrors of the law, but by the sweet comforts of the Spirit through the gospel, which again speaks deliverance and freedom from condemnation as sanctioned under the law for transgressors. This does not negate the use of the law as in article VI, thesis 4: "in order that people do not resolve to perform service to God on the basis of their pious imagination in an arbitrary way of their own choosing, it is

---

34. Kolb and Wengert, eds., *Book of Concord,* 501.

necessary for the law of God to light their way"; yet a crucial difference is maintained in thesis 4: "Concerning the difference between the works of the law and the fruits of the Spirit . . . that the works performed according to the law remain works of the law and should be so called, as long as they are coerced out of people only through the pressure of punishment and the threat of God's wrath."[35] Such is the case when the preaching of the obedience of regeneration or repentance is preached or emphasized in such a way that characterizes salvation as conditioned upon such obedience. That would be the preaching of the law and would lead to nothing but works of the law, which are not gospel or Spirit fruits of obedience.

Beeke and Jones rightly point out the careful and nuanced arguments among the Reformed on the issue of the necessity of works. And, while good examples exist, we want to highlight the examples that run roughshod over the covenant of grace, turning it into a conditional covenant in the worst of cases, and in the best into a conditional search for assurance on the basis of works. Both assault the free grace of the gospel to save and sanctify, not on the basis of terror and fear of judgment, but as the free grateful adoring response of grace. One such example is the attempt at a unifying confession of faith for Presbyterians and Congregationalists, where renowned names were involved and included such articles as: "14. That whoever do not prize and love Jesus Christ above himself, and all other things cannot be saved. 15. Whosoever allows himself to live in any known sin, upon any pretense or principle whatsoever, is in a state of damnation."[36] It is clear here to see in article 14 the statement of the law that Jesus summed up in loving God above all things as a condition of salvation, as well as the rigidity of outright condemnation of those living in sin. Missing is the distinction between law and gospel and the grace foundation to lead fallen saints out of sin through grace rather than the fear of judgment and wrath. It is one thing to call saints to love Jesus supremely, above all things, forsaking sins on the basis of the free grace and deliverance received, and another to cajole them to abandon sin out of fear of damnation and thus assure their state before God. Consequently, nothing but works of the law is assured as a result, which is not truly the new spiritual obedience of the Christian but the old legal mold.

However, this theology dovetails nicely with a conditional view on the covenant of grace. Beeke and Jones advance such conditionality as

---

35. Kolb and Wengert, eds., *Book of Concord*, 502–02.
36. Beeke and Jones, *Puritan Theology*, 311.

emblematic of the Reformed when they showcase Francis Turretin in support of the necessity of works thus: "They do not contribute to the meriting of salvation, but they are necessary for possessing salvation. Moreover, Turretin's understanding of the covenant as two-sided, which accords perfectly with the British understanding of the covenant of grace, necessitates that the promises of God are met with obedience from those in covenant with him."[37] We could tacitly agree on the basis that the redeemed are called into a new life where good works are the way of manifesting the life they have freely received, namely, the necessity of new life, new light, and new precepts to live by. But we could never agree if such good works were enjoined upon the believer in any way as a condition for God's acceptance, for God's deliverance, for God's Spirit to be given. On the contrary, the testimony of Scripture is that the Spirit is freely given by the hearing of faith, and that obedience and good works flow from the Spirit in those who trust and believe the free promise announced in Christ. Is this what is being advanced? Let the reader judge on their own as the authors continue, "Believers are 'bound to new obedience by an indissoluble and indispensable bond . . . not only by the necessity of precept, but also by the necessity of the means. Turretin adds that the gospel demands not only profession of the truth, but also (principally) the practice of piety . . . [these] are related to glorification antecedently and ordinatively because they are related to it as the means to the end."[38]

The key phrase to note is "means to the end," the end being salvation in its final manifestation or state, namely, glorification; and works are necessary not just because they are the precepts and ways of the new life but because they are the "conditional" instruments to receive such ultimate state. So, one could say that faith alone is the instrument to receive justification; we are justified by faith alone, but we are glorified by adding to faith another instrument necessary, namely, good works. We are glorified through our piety and good works. Again, to say that they will be present in all of God's children as a consequent of faith or regeneration and enjoin them upon believers as such we warrant, but to cast them, in any way, as conditional means required to our final glorification, we must reject. Thus, the authors believe the doctrine of justification by faith alone is safeguarded while strongly advancing the need for sanctification as part of what the gospel in the covenant of grace demands for ultimate salvation.

37. Beeke and Jones, *Puritan Theology*, 312.
38. Beeke and Jones, *Puritan Theology*, 313.

Thus, they run to the English Davenant, who affirms that the gospel requires good works from the justified from "infused grace." The authors reach the happy conclusion supported by Davenant, who "argues for his position by noting that the gospel demands faith alone as the condition for justification; 'yet in the subject and doctrine of sanctification, [the gospel] demands the fruits of faith.' That is to say with Turretin, the gospel commands not only faith, but also obedience."[39] Notice the turn of events: the gospel, to wit, the proclamation of God's free promise in Christ to save sinners, demands that we call sinners unto salvation, unto their acceptance by God not only by faith, but also by the obedience of the law, by their sanctification. God will accept sinners who believe and through faith produce good works in sanctification for them to be ultimately received into God's heaven. And thus the gospel is turned into law keeping as enabled by the Spirit. This is the "principal" demand of the gospel and its defining essence according to those who view the covenant of grace as conditional. This is what Calvin wanted to avoid by separating faith from repentance; this is what the Marrow men sought to avoid by supporting the Auchterarder proposal; this is what Luther pursued in the distinction of law and gospel; and this is what we fight for in this paper.

We contend that all in the Christian life is given freely and unconditionally. Although many things are received by believers on their way to glory, such as good works, new obedience, and the fruit of the Spirit in their sanctification, these are all theirs freely, not conditionally. Their final glorification is not conditioned upon their obedience; rather, their obedience is conditioned upon the One who was glorified for them. Their being accepted in Christ even unto glory without works, without their obedience, without their sanctification [practical obedience to the law], their receiving the Spirit of Christ unconditionally (without their obedience unto the law) by the hearing of faith, guarantees their glorification and everything they receive along the way. They are not accepted or admitted unto glory or, as some espouse, justified on Judgment Day because of their sanctification, piety, holiness, or good works. In other words, God is not filling them with good works to use them as the rationale for his acceptance of them; rather, they receive all manner of good in their sanctification because the issue of their acceptance, their standing before God, their merit before him was definitively settled by the only merit, sanctification, obedience, piety, and righteousness that counts, namely, Jesus'! It is a love formed by faith, not

---

39. Beeke and Jones, *Puritan Theology*, , 313.

the other way around, namely, a love that rests on perfect holy love received and covered therein, Christ's love!

The situation of the lack of distinction between law and gospel, a conditional covenant, and the preaching of repentance as the obedience of the law remains ever present today, especially among some very influential preachers. One of them, as has been previously mentioned, is John Piper. Let us see the same kind of a "turn" of events with Piper, where statements about faith and the gospel turn into statements that are properly speaking law. Piper quotes Jonathan Edwards as saying ". . . that love is the main thing in saving faith, the life and power of it, by which it produces great effects," and goes on to explain, "Another way to say it is that faith in Christ is not just assenting to what God is for us, but also embracing all that he is for us in Christ." One has to wonder what the term "embracing" means. If he means trusting, believing, being persuaded of all that he is for us, no problem there, because that is exactly what faith is. But that is not where Piper is going with the term. Let us see what he loads it with in the following quote: "True faith embraces Christ in whatever ways the Scriptures hold Him out to poor sinners. This 'embracing' is one kind of love to Christ—that kind that treasures him above all things."[40] And thus the unfortunate "turn" converts faith into the keeping of the law, namely, loving Christ/God above all things. Because we fail to treasure God and Christ in all things, God gave Christ that treasured the Father above all things for us; this is gospel truth that faith embraces in all of its rich splendor and sufficiency for sinners. We embrace, trust, receive, and rely on God's embrace of us in Christ. We are inflamed and burned with the passion and the love with which we have been loved and thus reciprocate in love. Faith trusts, or to put it another way, it abandons, commits, and forgets all lack, misery, and failure to his embrace. And the result translates into an embrace back to him that cherishes him and loves him, though still not supremely or perfectly, much less as the condition for our acceptance before God. Those who love God in Christ are those who are also always confessing their failure to love him above all things as the law demands, but are nonetheless affected to love him back the more we see God's love and faithfulness for us in spite of our unbelieving, hateful, and sinful attitudes toward him.

The other author in the same vein although with different peculiarities is John MacArthur. Piper takes his framework on future grace and posits a future final justification, which he calls "the future grace of eternal

---

40. Piper, *Future Grace*, 159.

life,"⁴¹ on the basis of working, sanctifying faith, following many in the Reformed tradition of the conditional covenant. One must keep in mind when reading Piper that faith for him includes the works, the sanctifying affections of obedience that love God/Jesus supremely above all things. This is the faith that justifies us in the grand scheme of things. MacArthur advocates a view of lordship salvation that they would advance as the unarguable notion that whoever receives Jesus as Savior receives him as Lord too. No arguing there for us; the problem emerges with the implications of how this is presented, which clearly confuses again law and gospel, conditioning our salvation to our obedience to the law. It is our contention that MacArthur in a somewhat different theological presentation or nuance suffers from the same problem.

MacArthur warns of "separating faith from faithfulness"; he equates the obedience of faith unto salvation with the demands, duties, and obedience of discipleship. To simply believe Christ in his atoning work for salvation amounts in his view to "easy believism" because being saved is conditional on one's total surrender and commitment to follow Jesus in obedience to God's commands. Thus, MacArthur asserts, "The call to Calvary must be recognized for what it is: a call to discipleship under the lordship of Jesus Christ. To respond to that call is to become a believer. Anything less is simply unbelief."⁴² Now, who can be opposed to clarifying that although God accepts sinners without works or obedience of any kind on our part, once we believe his atoning love there will be much to work, sacrifice, and obedience as his blood-bought disciples in a life that increasingly seeks to conform to the image of the Savior? Who could be opposed to affirming that whoever is called to believe should also be made aware who God is as sovereign Lord, and the kind of life he will work to bring about in us as a result of our reconciliation? Not us for sure. But this is *not* what MacArthur is seeking to advance. He is not simply trying to make sure that sinners understand that although God receives them freely, without anything they offer, bring, or obey, they will then be transformed in a life of sacrificial discipleship. He rejects critics thus: "[faith] is inseparable from repentance, surrender, and a supernatural longing to obey . . . They assume that because Scripture contrasts faith and works, faith must be incompatible with works. They set faith in opposition to

---

41. Piper, *Future Grace*, 228. See all of chapter 18, especially discussion of conditional graces and how to believe conditional promises.

42. MacArthur, *Gospel According to Jesus*, 46.

submission, yieldedness, or turning from sin, and they categorize all the practical elements of salvation as human works. They stumble over the twin truths that salvation is a gift, yet it costs everything."[43]

Responding directly to his quote above, we again agree that true faith is inseparable from many things such as he mentions, because through faith all these things are received, caused, and produced by God in our lives. But to say that is a far cry from making faith equal with those things that flow, derive from, and are received through it. The practical elements of our salvation such as our obedience and works are *not* what faith is, because if they are we are indeed saved by works, or at least faith and works. In other words, we would be called to salvation by the call to the practical obedience of our sanctification and discipleship or by loving in conformity to the law as empowered by the Spirit. To ask for conformity to the law, namely, the abandoning or turning from sin, the total surrender of obedience, the full forsaking everything in repentance, as conditions for salvation, for deliverance from judgment, is to be saved by the works of the law. It is to make Jesus not the fulfiller of the law for us, to simply trust him in the sweet persuasion that in him, through childlike faith, all our sins are wiped out and his righteousness imputed to us freely; but to dispense through him the obedience of the law by the help of the Spirit so that we may be accepted through such supernaturally "infused" obedience. This is flat out another gospel, not the gospel according to Jesus, as much as Jesus may be cited and advanced as a Lawgiver that saves disciples who must obey the law he came to fulfill, the righteousness he came to freely give. Indeed, we agree that salvation is costly; it cost the Son his precious life to ransom enslaved sinners freely and without cost to them, as the prophet exclaims joyfully, "Come, everyone who thirsts, come to the waters; and he who has no money, come, buy and eat! Come, buy wine and milk without money and without price" (Isaiah 55:1).

Law and gospel clarity and the preaching of both in their proper roles and functions are of the essence in our Christian endeavors and proclamation. We want to close this chapter by citing a clear enunciation of both and hope that what we have contributed so far provides food for thought into rightly dividing the Word of God thus. The chapters that follow shall try to make some application of such principles and distinctions as well as providing exegetical and hermeneutical ammunition for doing

---

43. MacArthur, *Gospel According to Jesus*, 46–47.

so. The Book of Concord in article V, sections 2–4, set forth the following, and we quote at length:

> 2. We believe, teach, and confess that the law is, strictly speaking, a divine teaching which gives instruction regarding what is right and God-pleasing and condemns everything that is sin and contrary to God's will. 3. Therefore, everything that condemns sin is and belongs to the proclamation of the law. 4. However, the gospel is, strictly speaking, the kind of teaching that reveals what the human being, who has not kept the law and has been condemned by it, should believe: that Christ has atoned and paid for all sins and apart from any human merit has obtained and won for people the forgiveness of sins, "the righteousness which avails before God," and eternal life.

CHAPTER 8

A Redemptive Cognitive-Relational Narrative Framework to Pastoral Counseling

In Search of Christ-Centered Applications to Counseling Psychology in Christian Practice

It has been said that all truth is God's truth. It is not in the scope of this paper to track a history of the relationship between theology and psychology, but suffice it to say that such a dictum has been used by Christian integrationists both in the theological and psychological side to borrow "truth" from each other. While in the best of cases practitioners of both spheres in the Christian camp would recognize that truth originates from God mediated to us through creation partially and the Bible especially, integrationists would seek knowledge in other camps or disciplines where God has seen fit to reveal other "kinds" of truth of great significance and importance for human functioning. Eric L. Johnson summarizes well this attitude of the modern integrationist movement: "The movement has sought to take legitimate research and theory from contemporary psychology and cultivate a psychological and clinical sophistication in their understanding of people, in order to help promote the well-being of Christ's people."[1]

We are grateful for the efforts of integrationists in seeking God's truth everywhere and their attempts to draw important connections of interdisciplinary significance, which benefit the lives of God's people and even of all people in God's common grace. Integrationists have provided different approaches in their perspective of bringing God's truth to bear on humans wherever it is found. Johnson helps us better grasp the issue of the wide diversity of integration efforts by dividing them between those

1. Johnson, *Foundations for Soul Care*, 88.

who seek to integrate conceptually and others who emphasize doing so ethically. The author identifies strong conceptual integration "by evidence of a substantial impact of Christian belief on the discourse"; also, within the conceptual camp, "there are two different formulations of integration: interdisciplinary integration (II) and worldview integration (WI)."[2] So, whether we may be seeking to draw psychological insights from the modern discipline today to bear upon the functioning of humans in our communities, or drawing from theological and biblical knowledge to illumine or enhance our psychological practice and approaches, we are attempting to establish connections between two disciplines and seeking a wide-enough lens to integrate the ideas, assumptions, theories, and practices that arise from each camp. Reflecting on ethical integration, the author explains, ". . . integration involves fundamentally, the bringing of one's Christian's values, beliefs, and relationship with God into one's personal and professional life such that Christian counselors act with integrity and coherence throughout their faith and life."[3]

In light of such efforts, we cannot but praise such attempts in their good motivations and purposes. We ought to be open to what God reveals through other disciplines in his general revelation that helps us better understand and improve our human functioning, even as we realize that ultimate final truth and certitude can only be found through his special revelation in Christ. Having said this, we want to join our voice to the author in calling for a wise measure of caution and warning. These must be in effect constantly because of three main factors: 1) the fact that modern psychology arose at a time of questioning and rejection of Christian discourse in the scientific arena, 2) the opposing foundational theoretical assumptions to Christianity present as a result, and 3) the ongoing effects of such an antithesis not only outside from a hostile world but from inside through our own sinfulness. Thus, let us register with the author the following criticism worthy of note for the alertness and discernment needed:

> Modern soul care deals with the core religious issues of life-human meaning, fulfillment, abnormality and recovery—but it is secular and grounded in evolutionary and naturalism or humanism, and it assumes the Self as the source of morality and recovery and its well-being as the ultimate value. In various ways, modern soul care is based in, perpetuates and fosters a fundamentally

---

2. Johnson, *Foundations for Soul Care*, 89.
3. Johnson, *Foundations for Soul Care*, 95.

> human-centered orientation . . . some integrationists are naïve about the intellectual conflict that has been waged over the past few centuries and have underestimated, on the one hand, how profoundly non-Christian worldview assumptions distort the research choices, data interpretations and conclusions, and theoretical formulations of modern psychology, and on the other hand, the tremendous soul-care resources organic to Christianity . . .

With this in mind, it is important to seek beyond a mere integrationist stance a reflection framework or grid that may help us think theologically and biblically without shying away from the common grace that God affords through other disciplines in their discoveries, knowledge, and application. All truth is God's truth not because creation and scientific research produce truth on equal footing or just as the Bible reveals it, but because the God of all truth revealed in the Bible has given us a world where much of the true workings of the ultimate truth of creation and his nature can be discovered. Let us propose the following analogy for clarification of this point. When we were first exposed to learning the use of a watch, it was fascinating to become acquainted with what it does and how to keep it working. We learned to use the crown or button(s) to set dates, times, and even chronometer as well as other features. We can say that everything we learned was true; however, it is not ultimate truth. To know ultimate truth in this case would be to go beyond its exterior and penetrate to the inner mechanisms and systems that make it work and discover exhaustively why it works the way it does in all the intricacies and interconnectedness of all its parts, to the minutest of them. It would be to know comprehensively and exhaustively. The scientific method cannot provide such comprehension, but indeed, by God's common grace, it allows us to see, understand, and apply some of the outward, visible, tangible, and experiential true working knowledge of reality.

However, since all that we discover in nature or creation scientifically can only apply to a limited number of cases (N), while true statistically, it always needs to press on to further discoveries that often deepen the realities that once were thought final. God has given us such a world to discover and some basic but important knowledge of himself and mankind to grasp also at this level. So, the physics of yesterday are not the physics of today; much more has been discovered that does not necessarily negate any true workings discovered prior but deepens, enhances, and further develops what one knew to be true yesterday, while also correcting any false prior conclusions.

What we knew about the brain yesterday does not come near to what has been discovered today, and so forth with physical or, let us say, earthly realities. What about spiritually or heavenly ones? When it comes to God, while what we know of him may be progressively grasped, his character and works unto us are unchanging although dynamic and live. In other words, what God seeks to reveal spiritually, while channeled differently throughout cultures, times, and settings, remains the same; namely, God wants us to trust and love. He wants to restore us to an image bearing person or community in and through Christ. While a certain basic understanding of God's loving gifts could be grasped from creation in such a way that mankind should thank and adore him, it falls short of the comprehensive redemptive narrative that gets to the inner workings and intricacies of God's purposes for creation in his ultimate gift, namely, Christ.

Consequently, we need to go beyond a mere integrationist view to a framework that may listen to creation's voice and output as we interact with it, but in such a way that such a dialogue may always be channeled through a larger very specific metanarrative, namely, the gospel redemptive narrative. I would liken this movement to a centrifugal/centripetal force where the weight of research and earthly experience leads us centrifugally/outwardly in a certain direction and to certain findings but always suspended, guided, and shaped by the centripetal/inwardly core of our redemptive narrative framework in the gospel. Without such constant gospel force, we shall succumb, if only by inertia, to the multiplicity of narratives that equally compete or seek to coexist when it comes to the existential and psychological life and purposes of mankind vis-à-vis the transcendental. Thus, "integrationist authors in the future will have to do a better job convincing their readers that they are reading secular psychology critically as Christians."[4] Our innate rebellion and blindness to God's goodness especially demonstrated in Christ usually causes any reflection along these lines to be deeply challenged, resisted, and distorted, which is why we need to intentionally fight gospel battles in all spheres, beginning with ourselves—a fight that does not have to be nasty, intrusive, rude, and unsophisticated, but a fight nonetheless. Johnson concurs with this assessment by showing the nature of the challenges in the following representative statements:

> . . . given human finitude and the antithesis principle, Christians ought to expect that human scientific activity will yield some distortions in human understanding, particularly when dealing

---

4. Johnson, *Foundations for Soul Care*, 100.

> with issues of ultimate significance . . . not all the assertions of modern psychology are true . . . the integration label is being used by some to rationalize a false dichotomy between one's faith and one's professional life . . . [and] secular counseling in Christian garb is especially tragic, because it would seem to imply to its Christian counselees that the Christian faith is irrelevant to the healing of their souls.[5]

A proper centripetal gospel force shall ground our understanding in the Bible's redemptive gospel narrative. This necessitates a doctrine of creation, of sin and the fall, of promise and covenants, of law and gospel, of Spirit and flesh, of faith and works, of redemptive suffering in hope, faith, and transformative love. It is the narrative of pain, suffering, disorder, mess, chaos, shame, and death in light of God's eternal communicative and transformative word of grace in and through Christ; or, the language of hope and faithful transformative waiting and confessing in the midst of anxiety, depression, addictions, compulsions, societal and behavioral disorder complicated with divorce, abuse, murder, suicide, grieving, betrayals, lust and pornography, and the whole array of our sinfulness on display; or, better yet, a redemptive gospel framework for those whose life narrative does not seem particularly complicated or challenged but actually well put together, religiously, orderly, composed, ethically and morally excellent, as well as financially and professionally solid or established. We need a framework that allows our centrifugal weight of living in the world to be centripetally guided and interpreted by the weight of gospel redemptive narrative.

Johnson seeks something better than poor and weak integration because such cannot bring the full weight of our hope to bear on our lives. And this requires a challenge of human views that cannot account more comprehensively, like in the case of the watch, for the inner workings of reality in the face of God. To do otherwise is to deny reality, to bury our face in the sand and be content with superficial and vain approaches to healing. By the same token, the author supports going beyond a mere reactionary and rejecting stance on anything coming from the discipline of psychology. While the author mentions many positives of Jay Adams's nouthetic approach, he also sees it as having the potential to produce an unhealthy relationship with the integration movement and anything in the modern discipline of psychology. He highlights Adams's approach as one that "tended to focus on behavioral dynamics like personal discipline, dehabituation

---

5. Johnson, *Foundations for Soul Care*, 100–105.

and rehabituation, and practical homework (Adams, 1973)." The dangers of moralism and legalism are never too far behind when such an emphasis prevails. However, it should be noted that "The most important theme sounded by Adams and the movement he founded is the belief that God must be recognized as the center of the counseling enterprise . . . Consequently, sin is the greatest soul care problem there is . . . and God's deliverance through Christ is the supreme solution to that problem."[6]

Notwithstanding the good contributions of Jay Adams and what came to be known as Traditional Biblical Counseling (TBC), we agree with Jones that a more comprehensive and cooperative view with modern psychology can be established. An utterly hostile relationship with modern psychology will, at one level, deprive Christian counselors of a place at the discourse table, or counseling room, with the redeeming gracious voice of Christ, and, at another level, fail in its discerning stance of examining and interacting, within God's common grace, with whatever is "true" in other disciplines as we have defined it. With that in mind, we view counselors who go beyond John Adams and his most reticent followers with approval, who maintain an uncompromising and strong biblical and theological stance. Such has been the case among successors of Adams in whom there has been a wiser course, in our opinion, which the author calls Progressive Biblical Counseling, and could be said to be characterized by very positive efforts at addressing things like:

> the dynamics of the heart, particularly the problem of idolatry (Powlison, 1986, 1995a; Tripp, 2001; Welch, 1997b, 2001b) . . . a more complex model that combines a primary focus on sin with a theology of suffering and examines the biological and social contextual factors that are interwoven with sin in the human heart . . . so that some allow for a discerning use of psychotropic medication . . . [also], the Progressives typically place greater positive value on the role of the counseling relationship . . . [and] a greater willingness to interact with others.[7]

What we are saying is that our healing efforts in the world, even when we act within the centrifugal force (outward) of common-grace "true" knowledge from other disciplines—including psychology—must issue, be guided, sustained, and filtered through the centripetal force (inward pull) of a redemptive metanarrative, namely, the gospel. This will have tremendous

---

6. Johnson, *Foundations for Soul Care*, 107.
7. Johnson, *Foundations for Soul Care*, 110.

ongoing implications for counselors as well as counselees since it provides a whole Christian outlook or worldview based on God's redemptive story. Mark R. McMinn insightfully sums it up like this: "A theological worldview has been supplanted by a therapeutic paradigm . . . In the process we may have lost our understanding of what it means to be fallen humans in God's world."[8] Without the reflection of sin and grace, healing is at best an outward "massaging" or management of outward symptoms that can never penetrate to the deeper issues and realities of the heart vis-à-vis the transcendent, namely, God. Learning how to control anger, staying away from addictive and destructive substances, improving relationships, and better coping with pain and loss can never touch the deeper underlying issues of meaning, identity, purpose, worth, suffering, death, and the eternal. More specifically, without God's story of redemption in Christ, man is at a loss at truly knowing himself, the world, reality, and the only ultimate hope for these. We propose to add our voice to the many voices that have made contributions and offered solutions to the problem.[9] Our voice remains indebted to many who have done excellent more in-depth work on the issues. Our contribution on the shoulders of others lies in providing a very concise framework that is laser-focused on the gospel as its interpretive and practical core. It will incorporate some practical insights from psychology within the framework of gospel redemptive narrative truth. The former will justify or manifest the truth of the latter, and the latter will prove itself to be the illuminating power and fountainhead of the former.

We want to call our approach the Redemptive Cognitive-Relational Narrative (RCRN). Let us begin to unpack what we are after as contained in this title. Firstly, we aim to advance a redemptive framework, namely, one that provides deliverance, liberation, or healing by the actions, works, or sacrifice of another. Christian healing is not a self-funded and -resourced process, but involves the person, presence, payment/sacrifice, and work of another for the one in need. This does not negate that the counselee has a responsibility in the matter; by the redemptive term and its explanation we seek to highlight the redeeming person's role in liberating/helping the one in need. Secondly, such redemption, deliverance, help, or healing happens in the context of "relationshipping" or relating to God

---

8. McMinn, *Sin and Grace in Christian Counseling*, 19.

9. See McMinn and Campbell, *Integrative Psychotherapy* and chapter 5 in McMinn's *Sin and Grace* for an example of such a contribution. See also parts 3 and 4 in Johnson's *Foundations for Soul Care* for another worthwhile massive contribution.

and neighbor, and occurs by the cognitive affectation that results from the redemptive encounter with both. Here, we are not dismissing the affective or emotional component, but conveying the instrumentally crucial role of the cognitive or the understanding. Thirdly, such healing or liberation by the sacrificial work of another through "relationshipping" or relating to God and neighbor provides a specific metanarrative wherein all our life stories can be reframed and restoried. We are reoriented, redefined, redirected, and reframed to the meaning, purpose, goals, identity, and ultimate hope of such grand metanarrative with its grand actor, grand act, and grand finale, namely, the gospel story of death and resurrection in Christ. This relational aspect goes hand in hand with the cognitive since the cognitive is employed in the exercise of the relational and the relational assumes and necessitates the cognitive.

The Redemptive aspect of the framework consists in the healing grace, transformation, hope, comfort, patience, love, and other fruit of the Spirit that opposes our sinfulness and sinful patterns in our lives as a result of another's kind and merciful gift. It involves, on the one hand, an orientation to the love, hope, and comfort found in the person and work of Christ, as well as the redeeming influence that counselors can have on their counselees by virtue of their gracious presence, time, effort, and sincere helping efforts. Redemption speaks to the reality of sinful slavery, boundedness, oppression, even impotence and death. It is not cheap positive talk or motivation, or even a quick path to change and healing. It does not deny, hide, or distort the reality of darkness, sin, and suffering but rather begins to face it with a slow but steady and firm exposure to the truth of law and gospel dynamics. Biblical and theological concepts such as sin, guilt, shame, and death are explored in order to chart a path toward grace, forgiveness, adoption, justification, sanctification, and the hope of glory through Christ. The counselee is faced with the reality of their slavery and corruption as well as directed to the source and hope of life in and through another. The direction goes from self out to Christ, from our failures and our efforts or lack thereof to the finished, completed, rich and abounding life in the Son's person and work. Redemption through the gift of another involves forging an identity in union with Christ wherein self begins increasingly to find the rest of living in the asking, waiting, receiving, delighting, sharing, and thanksgiving for God's gifts, namely, intimate and experiential knowledge of God's assuring love and care of us through Christ even in the face of great affliction, suffering, and trials. The counselor becomes a model of one who is also traveling this journey and through a gracious empathic presence almost "joins" the counselee on the path. The counselor gives the counselee the gift of his unconditional presence and care through a compassionate, interested, supportive, and sharing stance.

Cognitive-Relational has to do with the fact that we were created as image bearers in fellowship with God and one another. An image bearer is one that lives reflecting the life of another, namely, the life of God. Adam and Eve participated in fellowship with God and one another, receiving and sharing God's bountiful love and care. Now, this relatedness among them involved the rational and moral communication of their being one to another. It was not just an emotive or affective relationship of the senses but one that entailed rational moral thought, discourse, and discernment. Persons, language, commandment, naming, good, bad, power, temptation; these are all concepts that demand the exercise of moral and rational attributes. These attributes are primarily cognitively exercised, meaning that they involve mental processes of judgment, reasoning, discriminating, perceiving, memory, analysis, etc., in distinction from the emotional and volitional. The emotional and volitional are operating in combination and inextricably tied with the cognitive, but the cognitive ultimately supplies the meaning, the direction, the outlook, the goals, the purpose and conclusions of a matter in human life. We cannot relate to God, one another, and creation without the cognitive attaching some kind of moral/spiritual normative value or directional judgment to our experience. We are not attempting here an epistemological philosophy but simply noting the eminent domain of the cognitive in our lives. Through such cognitive filter with its accompanying affective and volitional resources, we relate to God and one another.

Furthermore, it seems like human experience is best and even primarily interpreted in the framework of a story. Everyone has a story to tell and it seems like sharing it is not only part and parcel of living it, but also an ongoing shaping, framing, and reinterpreting of said story. God also has a story to tell and our stories can be subsumed or interpreted in light of God's redemptive story. The gospel is a narrative of God's suffering holy love demonstrated in the atoning sacrifice of the Son to save sinners, which is God's ultimate gift and demonstration of his goodness. This is the story of death and resurrection, of old and new creation, and the pilgrimage or journey that goes on in between. Interestingly, God's story is also man's story in an archetypal way. The story of the incarnate, holy, sacrificial, and atoning God is the ultimate cognitive-relational bridge between the earthly and temporal and the heavenly and transcendentally eternal. A disconnect from the transcendental and eternal has vacuumed the soul of humanity from their archetypal defining and interpretive story. Granted, humans have spared no effort at trying to fill such a vacuum with manifold ultimate narratives or the lack thereof, with no end in sight. We submit the gospel narrative has the interpretive and redeeming power of truth to re-story anew the minds and hearts of stories lost in the wide dark chasm of self-made interpretations to fight the ever-recurring experience of fear, guilt, shame, and death. This Narrative aspect is ever seeking to frame any story in God's redemptive story; it is ever gently nudging, showing, illuminating, convincing, and advancing that there is indeed *the* story, the grand story of God gifting his precious and enriching Trinitarian life to man through his story with man, namely, the gospel of Christ!

Before we delve into some practical examples of the RCRN framework at work, we want to delineate some elements or principles from counselling psychology that we believe are compatible with the framework. Actually, these could be said to be "true" elements that modern psychology has derived from studying human interactions in their attempt to come up with therapeutic interventions and practices that work. We submit these are discernable from a common-grace platform but deeply illuminated and resourced by the gospel narrative. We will draw primarily from group psychotherapy insights and hold these principles to be at work as signs of the psychologically "healthy" maturing church. Irvin D. Yalom's work in the area of group psychotherapy shall be our main source of valuable insights, and whence our principles will be eminently drawn.[10] The principles we want to enumerate are by no means exhaustive but they represent a good embodiment of the best truth that God in his common grace and also, we believe, the influence of Judeo-Christian values through the Scriptures have translated into modern psychology. They are the following: 1) Instillation of Hope (H), 2) Universality (U), 3) Imparting Information (I), 4) Altruism (A), 5) Imitative Behavior (IB), and 6) Corrective Interpersonal Relationships (CI). While these are drawn from group counseling dynamics, individual principles will also emerge inextricably tied to group and family or systems dynamics. An individual is never seen or counseled isolated from their network of relationships. Their individuality must be maintained at the same time that it is placed in the symbiotic life context of

---

10. Yalom, *Theory and Practice of Group Psychotherapy*.

relationship dynamics. Likewise, the church provides another such group or family dynamics that call for a new socializing approach that necessitates the rethinking and reframing of old family/group dynamics around the new gospel redemptive narrative.

A brief word or explanation of the foregoing principles is necessary before we see them in their application.[11] Installation of Hope (H) has to do with an expectation of a positive therapy outcome. A redemptive approach to counseling is constantly providing hope to sinners no matter the condition they find themselves in. Granted, it is not the hope of denial or "positive" thinking; many positive people will ultimately find their lives shipwrecked on the rocks of sin, death, and condemnation without Christ. But no matter how dire circumstances may be in the world for a counselee or church group, they have a hope through faith that transcends and overcomes the world. This hope is instilled by the metanarrative of the gospel, which reframes our suffering into a grander eternal story through Christ. Hence, our tears, pain, loneliness, and even death can be borne in hope. Such hope begins to pay transformative/sanative dividends in people even now.

Universality (U) involves suffusing the counselee in the reality that although different—contextually and experientially—we are all "messed up"; we all need help because we all have issues, namely, we are all in need. Yalom writes, "Many individuals enter therapy with the disquieting thought that they are unique in their wretchedness, that they alone have certain frightening or unacceptable problems, thoughts, impulses, and fantasies." This does not negate each person's unique experience and individuality; rather, it affirms that we all suffer, that we all do not have it put together, that we all lack, falter, and stumble in different ways. The author powerfully describes the therapeutic implications of such realization: ". . . the disconfirmation of a client's feelings of uniqueness is a powerful source of relief. After hearing other members disclose concerns similar to their own, clients report feeling more in touch with the world and describe the process as a 'welcome to the human race' experience."[12] We contend this is a common-grace factor in the help that many sufferers find in groups like Alcoholic Anonymous, where they all unite under the common confession, "Hello,

---

11. Check chapters 1 and 2 in Yalom's *Theory and Practice of Group Psychotherapy* for detailed full psychological counseling perspective; our perspective on them is colored by the lens of a biblical redemptive approach.

12. Yalom, *Theory and Practice of Group Psychotherapy*, 6.

I'm an alcoholic." The church could benefit from equally confessing as we come together, "Hello, I'm the first of sinners." This realization ought to be present even in the counselor-counselee relationship of a Christian context as well as the pastor/elders–church members' relationship.

Imparting Information (I) in an anti-intellectual age may be not immediately welcomed as society "feels" better attuned to the language of instincts, emotions, sensations, images, pictures, and experiences in general. We are by no means discounting these elements; however, we cannot overemphasize the importance of the cognitive, the rational, the understanding, or the mind. The author describes this element under the rubric of didactic instruction, where formal instruction or psychoeducation becomes an important part of the program. And, while this is an explicit component in some therapy groups, the author recognizes the following: "Most participants, at the conclusion of successful interactional group therapy, have learned a great deal about psychic functioning, the meaning of symptoms, interpersonal and group dynamics, and the process of psychotherapy. Generally, the educational process is implicit; most group therapists do not offer explicit didactic instruction in interactional group therapy."[13] Our counseling efforts are also teaching opportunities and, whether the teaching is explicit or not, one thing cannot be avoided, namely, the cognitive-relational aspect of the encounter with God and one another. What this means is that the imparting of information ultimately becomes a quest for meaning—for understanding—for a moral and spiritual reason or justification to our lives. This is how we relate both to God and one another; we seek meaning, reason, justification, purpose, direction to and in the relational story. We simply do not relate without attaching some value judgment to our stories, some significance, some meaning and worth to what we do. This is best expressed in the proverbial "Without a reason for living, life is not worth living," or in the theological truism that "Doctrine is for devotion." Affections or emotions, the sensorial and experiential, do not happen in a vacuum but in the moral-spiritual meaning-making endeavor that defines humanity. While Yalom in this element simply signifies didactic endeavor, we are addressing the deeper cognitive-relational need for an examined life vis-à-vis others in light of the gospel story.

Altruism (A) or simply loving others in mercy and grace is an intricate part of the journey we want to embark on with counselees and the church at large. Only one joy tops the joy of receiving or enjoying something

---

13. Yalom, *Theory and Practice of Group Psychotherapy*, 9.

valuable: the joy of sharing it with someone else. From the simple ministry of presence or connecting yourself with others, to the sharing and contributions such relationships will produce in terms of their mutual help, comfort, and growth, these dynamics altogether provide the topping off or the coming around full circle of gift living. The full redemptive orbit of the cognitive-relational narrative of the gospel liberates us to know God, ourselves, and others while sharing and participating with God, ourselves, and others in mutually enriching, benevolent, and beneficial relationships. The author insightfully explains,

> Many psychiatric patients beginning therapy are demoralized and possess a deep sense of having nothing of value to offer others. They have long considered themselves as burdens, and the experience of finding that they can be of importance to others is refreshing and boosts self-esteem. Group therapy is unique in being the only therapy that offers clients the opportunity to be of benefit to others. It also encourages role versatility, requiring clients to shift between roles of help receivers and help providers.[14]

We must hasten to add that the concept of self-esteem should be replaced by the concept of Christ-esteem. In other words, the reason we can find worth to acknowledge in ourselves and others in order to share is found with God in Christ. We were not created to validate ourselves but to be validated in our relationship with God and through him unto others. Hence, any attempt at self-esteeming, -validating, or -justifying that does not look to God's gifts in creation, especially the gift of Christ in redemption, provides a sure recipe for further moral, spiritual, and relational alienation and disaster. Our ultimate health does not reside with independence but with utter self-dependence in God through Christ and the inevitable life-giving and sharing fellowship that results. Such altruistic giving is actually grace or gift giving that delights in the freedom of creaturely living through God's daily gifting, favor, mercy, or grace in Christ. We are free to live in the God-exalting freedom of our creaturely dependence and fellowship. The creature, then, was designed to live in the joy of receiving and giving, of having a dependence-based joy, yet a reflective giving, sharing joy.

Imitative Behavior (IB) speaks to the power of inspiring and compelling others by modeling the example we want them to follow. The power of a life on display for others to see and follow has to do with the dictum that our actions speak louder than words and the necessity of a

---

14. Yalom, *Theory and Practice of Group Psychotherapy*, 9.

good testimony to back up the redemptive truths we proclaim. How we relate to others in church, family, and community becomes a wonderful stage for our counselees to grasp the practicalities of faith. Also, since pastors, counselors, and mentors are themselves on the same journey, those coming for help benefit from seeing our actions and behaviors through challenging circumstances and may be prone to imitate what we have done or seek after the same set of spiritual/moral resources through grace to tackle their own challenges. Interestingly, it has been said that churches may begin to look like their pastors. Regardless of how much truth there may be to this, the shaping and formative influence of leaders cannot be overemphasized. A grace-filled leader in word and deed will be a powerful force for healing and change through the dynamics of imitative behavior alone. The author's experience corroborates this:

> Clients during individual psychotherapy may, in time, sit, walk, talk, and even think like their therapists. There is considerable evidence that group therapists influence the communicational patterns in their groups by modeling certain behaviors, for example, self-disclosure or support . . . In group therapy it is not uncommon for a member to benefit by observing the therapy of another member with a similar problem constellation—a phenomenon generally referred to as vicarious or spectator therapy.[15]

Corrective Interpersonal Relationships (CI) speaks to the truth that we are relational beings. Interestingly, this is also the nature of our Creator, who lives in an eternal relationship within the Godhead among the three divine Persons. It is almost as if God created a world to resemble such part of his nature and invited us to participate together with him in such relational dynamics. While God is also rational, spiritual, and moral, he is also a relational communicative being. Truth, reason, logic, speech, beauty, excellence, perfection, delight, and power embrace his creation in a union or bond where his communicable attributes and life enriches everything and everyone related to his being. God does this to a certain extent by the relational dynamics of creation, and in an ultimate and special way through the dynamics of redemption in Christ. With such theological underpinnings established, one can safely warrant what psychology has also discovered, namely, that humans can only properly develop and thrive in a relational matrix. The author cites some seminal works that support such an assertion thus: "The person is comprehensible

---

15. Yalom, *Theory and Practice of Group Psychotherapy*, 17–18.

only within this tapestry of relationships, past, and present . . . personality is almost entirely the product of interaction with other significant human beings. The need to be closely related to others is as basic as any biological need . . ."[16] On this aspect, let us be quick to add that some assumptions of secular modern psychology regarding relationships are evolutionary and atheistic although cognizant of an important aspect of human life. The piece we need to add or perhaps correct lies in God being the ultimate relationship all humans need. So, we would say that the person cannot fully and truly develop—in a spiritual moral and rational sense—without relating to God. Relationship with God is part, nay, even more, provides the ultimate relational grid through which persons can know themselves, make themselves known unto others, and know others.

Thus, we place relationship with God as a fundamental part of this web or matrix of relationships necessary for human thriving, psychologically speaking. This does not negate the absolute necessity of interpersonal relations among humans, nor do we imply that humans are totally incapacitated functionally without God, although radically depraved or enslaved to their sinful nature. What it does mean is that their optimal functioning and healing lies in the context of a reconciled relationship with God and neighbor as best explained, we contend, through the framework of Redemptive Cognitive-Relational Narrative. Within this framework, the story of God's favor and approval of sinners in Christ gives birth, in a new therapeutic and salvific way, to a self that can adjust, correct, and heal through the reflection of God's love and favor upon their lives. God's appraisal of them in Christ becomes the sanative force that restories their lives and reframes every other relationship as well. The author cites another interesting "truth" that psychology seems to have discovered: "The self may be said to be made up of reflected appraisals . . . This process of constructing our self-regard on the basis of reflected appraisals that we read in the eyes of important others continues, of course, through the developmental cycle."[17] Amen, we say, as the truth of God shining down his face upon us with the approval and favor of Christ has forever changed our lives and the way we relate to others, through grace, for the better!

We should not fail to mention, at least in passing, other more specific factors that are essential in a therapeutic counseling relationship. They all could be said to be part of that grace-filled stance or posture by which our

---

16. Yalom, *Theory and Practice of Group Psychotherapy*, 20–21.
17. Yalom, *Theory and Practice of Group Psychotherapy*, 21.

presence carries redemptive fragrance to our counselees. They are a non-judgmental attitude, active listening, and empathic understanding. When we season the above principles with a good healthy intervening dose of these factors, the outcomes can be very gratifyingly transformative. By a non-judgmental attitude we do not mean a lack of confrontation when needed, but a disposition to form such an alliance with the counselee where they may feel they can share anything without eliciting a shocking, negative, or rejecting response on our part. Helping others requires a willingness to stay connected with the person even when what they have to share may reflect very badly on their morality, spirituality, capacity, or judgment. This non-judgmental attitude comes close to God's unconditional love in Christ shown at the cross, and his relentless pursuit and commitment to rescue unworthy sinners.

Out of this attitude flows a genuine desire to gain knowledge and understanding about the counselee's plight. Active listening describes listening with the intent to fully comprehend and build rapport with the speaker. It allows the listener to get a full grasp of understanding about the speaker and the situation from facts, emotions, and other nuances. It conveys to the speaker that he has connected with someone genuinely involved, fostering the further building of trust in the therapeutic relationship as well as allowing the listener to acquire a deep perception of the person and the whole situation. An empathic understanding is the underlying motivation or goal in the dynamics of interconnectedness among these factors. It addresses the proverbial walking in or wearing somebody else's shoes. I think this speaks to the Spirit-fruit biblical attitude of being moved to compassion as we see the plight of others, especially more so as we are framing our helping endeavor as fellow travelers in the same journey. We propose to integrate these principles, factors, and framework (RCRN) into a cohesive approach to provide pastoral counseling in individual as well as small group settings. But we want to further enhance our counseling proposal by a biblically informed theological or doctrinal confession on the gospel. The next chapter will provide a biblical catechism on chapters 1–8 of Romans to help us bathe our counseling proposal in a Christ- or gospel-centered doctrinally sound approach. This catechism shall be mostly a biblical one, meaning not a *loci communes* structure, but following the biblical exposition of the Romans text.

CHAPTER 9

A Romans Catechism with Counseling Vignettes and Implications within the RCRN Framework

Romans 1

1. What was Paul set apart for? V. 1: The gospel of God.

2. What does the gospel consist of? Vv. 2–5: The person and work of Christ in his incarnate life, death, and resurrection for sinners everywhere according to the Scriptures.

3. How does Paul view his role when present with fellow believers as in Rome? Vv. 10–12: The mutual encouragement and edification of each other in faith.

4. What is the power of God unto salvation? V. 16: The gospel, the good news proclamation of Christ's person and work to save sinners.

5. Where is the righteousness of God revealed unto salvation? V. 17a: In the gospel.

6. How is the righteousness of God unto salvation revealed? V. 17: By faith.

7. Can the righteousness of God in the gospel be discovered outside of the person and the work of Christ? V. 17: No; it can only be discerned by revelation according to the Scriptures through faith.

8. How is a believer, the righteous person, supposed to live the Christian life? V. 17b: By faith; believers live the Christian life by faith, just in the same way they began the Christian life by faith.

9. Is the righteousness of God as revealed by faith in the gospel of Christ a saving righteousness? V. 17: Yes, this is a saving righteousness in Christ.

10. What is the condition of mankind outside of the righteousness of God through the gospel? V. 18: They live in ungodliness and unrighteousness in rebellion against God's truth.

11. How does God respond to mankind's rebellion in ungodliness and unrighteousness? V. 18: With wrath; God is against them because of their rebellion.

12. Does mankind have enough knowledge of God to be without excuse before him even without knowing the gospel? Vv. 19–21: Yes; they know his existence, power, and goodness and should have honored and thanked him accordingly.

13. How does mankind have this knowledge of God that renders them inexcusable? Vv. 19–21: They can perceive this knowledge from creation, namely, the divinity, power, and goodness of God in the realm of creation.

14. What is the essence of mankind's rebellion? Vv. 21–23: Not trusting God and honoring him as such but rather trusting and honoring themselves in their own wisdom and pursuits.

15. How does mankind's rebellion manifest itself? Vv. 22–32: The hardening of sin in idolatry and unbelief manifested in the works of the flesh.

16. Does sin consist in the corrupt outward acts or works of the flesh only? No; the outward works of the flesh are the issue of an evil heart of self-centered and -directed idolatry in unbelief.

Romans 2

1. Can anyone excuse themselves by judging another? Vv. 1–2: No; not if one is also guilty of practicing the same things.

2. What is the sin of the one who judges another while practicing the same things? Vv. 1–3: The self-righteousness of judging others while in the same condemnation.

3. What should lead man to repentance? V. 4: God's kindness expressed in patience and forbearance.

4. Will there be a day of reckoning and judgment before God? V. 5: Yes; mankind will have to give account for their continued impenitent rebellion against God in the final judgment that earns them his wrath.

5. On what basis will mankind be judged on the final day? Vv. 5–10: On the basis of God's righteous judgment as revealed in the perfect righteousness of a life lived in perfect obedience, submission, and delight to the truth of God's will.

6. How will this perfect life of obedience to God judge the world as a standard of righteousness on judgment day? Vv. 6–11: By holding everyone's works to scrutiny in light of that perfect life of obedience serving as the standard of righteousness.

7. Who will be righteous before God? Vv. 12–13: The doers of the law; they who have perfectly lived the life of obedience before God demanded by the law.

8. Does being in possession and hearing God's law, as in the case of the Jews, count for righteousness? Vv. 9–13: No; a Jew must be a doer of the law, namely, one who lives in the perfect life of obedience it demands.

9. Does not being in possession and hearing of God's law, as in the case of the Gentiles, count as an exemption from judgment? Vv. 9–13: No; a Gentile must also be a doer of the law, namely, one who lives in the perfect obedience it demands.

10. How can Gentiles be held to account for righteousness without knowing the law? V. 14–16: Because the Gentiles have the testimony of that law written in their hearts informing their consciences for right and wrong, as evidenced by the rational and moral judgments they also pass.

11. Are the Jews any better than the Gentiles for possessing the revealed instruction of the law? Vv. 17–25: No; although possessing the Scriptures and everything else as a chosen nation was a great privilege, it all amounts to condemnation, even more so for their boasting in judging themselves better than others while not actually living out the obedience the law demands.

12. Does having the outward conformity to the law such as circumcision make you a Jew or a true member of God's people? Vv. 25–29: No; outward conformity to the law means nothing except if there is inward/

heart conformity to the law, namely, being a doer and keeper of the law from the heart.

13. What is this inward/heart conformity to the law called? Vv. 26–29: It is regarded as circumcision, namely, circumcision of the heart to obey the law by the Spirit.

14. What does obedience to the law by the Spirit mean? Vv. 26–29: It means not just outwardly conforming to God's standards in his law, but inward conformity to and keeping of it from the heart.

15. What deserves the person who is a Jew from the heart, namely, one that conforms inwardly and in every aspect and demand of the law to do and to keep? V. 29: That person deserves praise from God who is a true doer and keeper of the law from the heart, perfectly conformed to it in every aspect.

Romans 3

1. What advantage has the Jew? Vv. 1–2: The privilege of having first received the Word of God, namely, the Old Testament Scriptures.

2. Does their not keeping God's Word reflect a failure on God's faithfulness or plan? Vv. 3–4: No; it highlights God's true and righteous judgment over sinful man.

3. What is implicit in the phrase of verse 4, "That you may be justified in your words, and prevail when you are judged," cited from Psalm 51:4? That sinful man resists God's righteous verdict in self-righteousness.

4. What does God want to uphold over against man's self-righteousness? Vv. 5–8: God wants to uphold his justice in condemning man for his failure to conform to his righteousness, including their evil attempts at justifying themselves in their failure by accusing and condemning God instead.

5. What lies at the root of man's unrighteousness? Vv. 5–8: Man's attempts to vindicate or justify themselves when their failure to trust and obey God meets God's true and righteous condemning verdict.

6. What is unrighteous man's attitude and treatment of God in his true condemning verdict? Vv. 5–8: Man proudly and foolishly accuse,

condemn, and contend with God in order to clear, justify, and vindicate themselves.

7. Is there anyone from among either Jews or Gentiles that can claim to be a doer or keeper of God's law in full conformity to it as God demands from the heart? Vv. 9–18: No; all mankind, whether Jews or Gentiles, have equally failed to do and keep God's law from the heart in full conformity to it. There is no one who can claim righteousness by their doing or keeping of the law.

8. What does the law do to what lies at the root of man's unrighteousness? V. 19: The law silences or stops mankind's boasting and self-righteous attempts at justifying, vindicating, and affirming themselves contrary to God's righteous and true condemning judgment. In short, the law holds everyone accountable before God as guilty and condemned.

9. Can the works of the law then justify any human being, namely, by keeping or doing the law? V. 20: No, by the works of the law, namely, by keeping or doing the law, no one will be justified.

10. Then, what is the purpose of the law according to this text? V. 20b: Through the law comes the knowledge of sin.

11. If one cannot be justified by doing or keeping the righteousness of the law because we all fail to do so, is there another righteousness by which we can be justified? Vv. 21–22: Yes; the righteousness of God in Christ Jesus.

12. How can one possess this righteousness? Vv. 21–23: One can only possess this righteousness by faith alone in the person and the work of Christ for sinners, namely, the gospel.

13. Can a sinner obtain this righteousness by faith alone without any works or obedience of the law? Vv. 21–25: Yes; in fact, whoever wants to mix their law obedience with faith in order to be justified falls back on the condemnation verdict they were before under the law. So, they must be justified freely, namely, without the works of the law by faith alone.

14. Where is this righteousness revealed? Vv. 21–26: This righteousness is revealed in the Scriptures, first in OT writings witnessing or announcing it, and then fulfilled in Christ and recorded in the NT Scriptures. In short, all Scripture as a whole testifies or witnesses to this

righteousness in Christ's person and work for the salvation of sinners, namely, the gospel.

15. Do both Jews and Gentiles obtain this righteousness the same way—by faith alone in Christ's person and work? Vv. 22–24: Yes; both are justified for salvation by faith alone in Christ alone. They both have failed to do and keep the law and can never attain to righteousness except through faith in the righteousness God reveals in Christ by the proclamation of the gospel for all sinners without difference.

16. What about the person and work of Christ qualifies him as the righteousness of God for all sinners? Vv. 23–26: Christ's perfect life and death as the substitute for sinners fully and perfectly satisfies the wrath of God for sinners who fail to keep the law. The law demanded the perfect doing or keeping of God's commands as well as death for failing to do so. Christ satisfies both requirements before the righteous demands and verdict of God's law on behalf of sinners who put their trust in him.

17. Is it righteous of God to justify sinners by faith alone without the works or obedience of the law? Vv. 23–26: Yes because in the person and the work of Christ, namely, his perfect life and death under the law on behalf of sinners, God upholds his justice while at the same time justifying those who put their faith on Christ's redemption. Christ's satisfaction under the law allows God to deliver sinners from their guilt, death, and bondage under the law by offering Christ in their place for everything God's law demands. In short, Christ lives the perfect life they should live and dies the death they deserve to die.

18. What about those before the time of Christ—did they die in their sins? Vv. 25–26: The person and the work of Christ satisfies the righteousness requirements of God's law for everyone who has lived, whether before or after Christ, provided they trusted in God's promise as either announced in OT times or fulfilled in NT times.

19. Can anyone boast of this righteousness they obtain by faith, whether Jew or Gentile, or on the basis of any other distinction in themselves? No; no one can boast of anything in themselves because the righteousness of faith only exalts the person and the work of Christ, namely, the righteousness of another, not our own.

20. Is the law cast aside as irrelevant and no longer mattering because the righteousness of God is obtained by faith? By no means; the law is affirmed and upheld by faith because those who seek after righteousness confess under the law their lack of it in themselves but its fulfillment and gift in Christ. They are justified and thus saved by the keeping, doing, and upholding of the law by Christ in their favor.

Counseling Vignette 1

Sally and Robert are an interracial couple in their mid-twenties. They have been dating for a year with plans to get married but have had opposition from family as well as financial hurdles that keep getting in their way. They have both had a strong Christian upbringing and lived very conservative lives. They present in counseling deeply shaken by the family turmoil regarding their marriage as well as shamed by the fact that they have engaged in sexual intercourse prior to marriage being consummated.

Robert (R), Sally (S), Pastor (P)

R: Pastor, we have been told by some family members and even some clergy that our relationship has to end. (Sally holds back tears and Robert looks deeply anguished as he says this.)

P: I can see how painful this is for you! (Pause) Tell me more about the reasons both family and clergy are saying this. (Active listening reflecting on feelings and seeking better understanding)

R: Our parents don't believe we belong together given our racial differences and the clergy believe our marriage won't be blessed because of our fornication.

P: Okay, let me say first that it must be really hard to feel rejected on the basis of your skin color or ethnicity. What do you think about that from the spiritual standpoint? (Empathic understanding and active listening for further rapport and strengthening of therapeutic alliance; the redemptive stance of the pastor is also at work in addition to a Cognitive-Relational [CR] question that seeks for rational and moral understanding in this relational challenge.)

S: (Almost sobbing) It is so unfair . . . and wrong . . . (can't say anything else)

P: (Allows for silence as no one else is saying anything in a moment charged with Sally's pain. The Pastor nods soberly and reverently in the presence of Sally's vulnerable display of emotions joined by Robert's visible struggle to hold back some tears himself. The pastor's silence and sober nodding communicates a non-judgmental stance and support for the couple's emotional distress without yet speaking to the moral dilemma presented.) (All three factors [ALL3]—1. non-judgment [NJ], 2. active listening [AL], and 3. empathic understanding [EU]—are profoundly at work here even in the silence fostered by the pastor's posture and body language.)

R: But maybe we deserve all of this and we should end this relationship . . . Maybe all this conflict and turmoil is a sign that this is all wrong! I feel so wrong!

P: Indeed, Robert, a lot of conflict you are facing; it is not easy to be going through this ordeal you are living. All of us at times get that 'I feel so wrong' kind of feeling when we get our good share of conflict and turmoil . . . and when we do, yes, it feels wrong, and we feel wrong too, as you say. Most everyone that comes into this office feels that wrong you are talking about when burdened with great pain. (All three factors [ALL3] at work in addition to the principle of Universality [U] being introduced; the pastor continues to work a CR angle of trying to make sense of suffering, priming it for engaging with a Redemptive Narrative approach.)

P: Sally expressed that it was wrong to be discriminated against and she is feeling the injury of such an offense. We know that God is not a respecter of persons when it comes to salvation and calls us through the gospel to offer the same welcome to all men without distinction in love. I'm sorry that hasn't been the case with you guys from the folks you love most, but, as I have already mentioned, God does not regard you that way and there's no reason why God would disapprove of your marriage on that basis; you know that, right? (Instillation of Hope [H] through gospel grace and Imparting Information [I] for cognitive-relational assurance about God and themselves; this brings a powerful Corrective Interpersonal Relationship [CI] by reframing the family relational challenge in view of how God relates to them.)

R: We believe that, Pastor, but . . . what about our fornication? Maybe . . . it's true that we don't belong together and we deserve all this heartache and turmoil!

P: What do you think about that, Sally? You feel the same way? (ALL3 at work here as I try to elicit more information about the stance of the couple on the issue while showing my concern about the matter in an empathic way)

S: Yes, I'm afraid that we have sinned and must pay for it. Maybe, we must end this relationship as some people have told us.

P: I can see that you are both conscious of having sinned and seem pretty broken up and bothered about it. I also agree with you that you have sinned by your premarital intercourse, but I'm not sure about the connection you see with the end of your relationship. Can you help me understand that part?

R: Pastor, how will God bless a relationship that started wrong? There has to be a consequence for our sin, right?

S: That's what I think, too. (Sally holds back tears.)

P: Folks, I agree you have sinned, but it seems by your own admission that you are confessing it and seem to hate the fact you have fallen for it. Is that an accurate description of how you feel? (reflecting back to them what they have said and their attitude about it)

R: (Joined by Sally) Yes.

S: But we must pay the price for what we have done.

P: Guys, have you ever considered that God does want you to stop fornicating but without interrupting your plans for marriage? (Instillation of Hope through CR reframing in a redemptive intervention)

S: How can that be?

P: In other words, can you believe that God is not out just to simply punish you, but he's out to restore and correct you in love?

R: But he's also a God of wrath and judgment and we deserve that judgment, don't we?

P: Yes, you do . . . actually, we all do! But God in Christ absorbed that wrath to treat his children with mercy and compassion, right? Why would he just punish without seeking our benefit if we are now his beloved children through Christ? What about repenting and living in the fruit of such repentance through faith in Christ by going through with your marriage may not be an option that your loving and forgiving Father has before you? Have you considered that in light of God's mercy to you in Christ as his beloved children? (The redemptive narrative of the gospel is brought to bear into the situation with the power to reframe their personal story into the grand gospel story where their lives are cognitive-relationally reframed through grace; ALL4 also apply.)

R: Pastor, that sounds amazing, and awesome, right Sally? Can it be so?

P: Yes, it can, Robert and Sally. Your sins are forgiven and you may go and live for his glory every time your fellowship with God is renewed by faith and repentance in God's gospel through Christ. Leave the correcting consequences of God's love to him and rise up to live in obedience once again through his forgiving love . . . and that can definitely look like marriage! (The Corrective Interpersonal Relationship [CI] factor is brought to bear here by both helping the couple relate to God through his mercy and grace in Christ, but also with the ALL4 and redemptive reframing gift of the pastor to the couple in pursuing them within a Cognitive-Relational Redemptive Narrative. The couple has been reoriented to fit their lives within the healing and transformative gospel grace giving story.)

(to be continued)

Romans 4

1. Can Abraham or any believer boast in their flesh before God? V. 1–3: No; they have nothing in their flesh or in what they do to provide reason for boasting.

2. What can be understood by "boasting in the flesh"? V. 1–3: It means to boast in one's works of the law, obedience, or anything else in ourselves rather than in the object of our faith, namely, the promises of God in Christ.

3. Why was Abraham counted as righteous? V. 3: Because he believed God.

4. What is the opposite of faith or believing? V. 4: The opposite of faith or believing is works or working.

5. If righteousness came by works or working, can it be called a gift or grace? Vv. 4–5: No; if righteousness was acquired by working for it, it would have to be called a payment, namely, meritorious payment or reward on account of working for it.

6. What can be considered works or working for the merit of reward or payment? Vv. 1–5: Any works of obedience, anything performed or achieved by the person, namely, anything done in or by them for God to reward.

7. What is the opposite of works or working for payment or merit? Vv. 3–6: Faith, meaning not working at all, not anything done by or in us to constitute grounds in ourselves for payment or merit.

8. What is faith? Vv. 3–6: Faith is the opposite of works or working for merit or reward; faith is only believing or trusting in another's word, promise, work, and/or person.

9. Can faith be defined to include works of any kind? No; that would be a contradiction and antithetical to the biblical concept of not working, faith is believing or trusting in the person and work of another as in the promises of God in Christ for salvation. Hence, believing for righteousness excludes working of any kind for it.

10. What blessings come to the believing or trusting one? Vv. 5–8: The blessings of salvation, namely, righteousness and forgiveness before God without our works, without anything in and by ourselves done to deserve it, a forgiven and righteous standing before God without

works in and by us of any kind. Hence, it is salvation by grace alone through faith alone.

11. Do these blessings come to us on account of our faith or believing? Is faith then meritorious before God? Vv. 5–8: No; faith has no merit whatsoever; it only receives the works, merits, obedience, holiness, and righteousness of another person, namely Christ, imputed, credited, or counted to our account without us really having them in ourselves.

12. Is this blessing for both Jew and Gentile without distinction? Vv. 9–12: Yes, this blessing of salvation in forgiveness and righteousness before God without our works is for all mankind without distinction.

13. Why can Abraham be considered the father of all who believe? Vv. 9–12: Because he believed unto righteousness before the law and circumcision. He is the father of all those who believe and are forgiven as well as counted as righteous without any of the works, obedience, signs, or any achievements described and demanded by the law in them.

14. What benefits accompany the forgiveness and righteousness of faith for salvation before God? Vv. 16–21: All the inheritance of the believer comes by this faith unto righteousness, or the righteousness of faith; namely, all the benefits that go with becoming an heir of the world, a new creation in Christ, a salvation that now imperfectly and progressively, but at the end finally and ultimately perfectly, will be demonstrated and vindicated in receiving all the promises of God for the righteous in and through Christ.

15. What does the barrenness of Sarah and Abraham's old age represent when it comes to the righteousness of faith and its inheritance? Vv. 19–21: It highlights that the inheritance of the saints only comes to us by believing or trusting alone, namely, without anything at all in ourselves to commend us with any kind of merit of works before God for such glorious inheritance.

16. Why are believers like Abraham considered worthy of such a glorious inheritance? (full chapter) Because Christ inherited all things for them through his meritorious personal righteousness and perfect obedience under the law. Christ lived the perfect life they ought to have lived but fail at daily, as well as dying the death they deserve to die for their failure to live perfectly as the law demands.

17. So, can one believe to be justified and then add works to faith in order to receive their inheritance? (full chapter) No; one must be righteous before God to receive their inheritance, and no one is ever righteous as God demands in themselves but only by having their sins forgiven and the righteousness of Christ imputed to their account.

18. Who is then rewarded with eternal inheritance? (full chapter) Only the righteous are rewarded with eternal inheritance, and we are righteous in and through Christ by the righteousness of faith, namely, Christ's righteousness.

19. Is our justification in Christ, namely, being forgiven on account of Christ's work and person and having his righteousness imputed to our account, the legal grounds and the full saving acceptance of our persons before God in order to receive everything else that accompanies such salvation? (full chapter) Yes; salvation, in an ultimate but narrow sense, can be spoken of as our justification before God because everything else that accompanies salvation in this narrow sense is the fruit, consequence, or result of our legal ground or status in justification by faith alone or the righteousness of faith. However, salvation can be spoken of, in the broad sense, to include with justification the inheritance that results from it or all the benefits that accompany such righteousness of faith—including our good works in progressive sanctification and the world to come in glorification, as long as this broad sense is never construed as conditioned to works but always received in and through Christ by faith alone.

Romans 5

1. Are we justified by faith alone? V. 1: Yes; we are justified by faith alone.

2. What can we be certain that exists between us and God upon being justified by faith alone? V. 1: We can be certain that we have been reconciled with God and no further enmity or hostility remains.

3. What benefits flow from being justified by faith alone? Vv. 2–5: We have the peace of reconciliation, access to the throne of grace, joyful assurance, suffering perseverance, confirming proofs, sustaining hope, and emboldening encouraging love by the Holy Spirit.

4. How can be we sure that such benefits are not conditioned upon my works or righteousness? Vv. 6–11: Because the promises of God in the narrow sense of the gospel, namely, final acceptance before God through his forgiveness and righteousness in Christ, speak such benefits for the ungodly through the righteousness of faith, not for the godly or those who work to merit, deserve, or obtain such blessings.

5. Is assurance of the essence of faith? Can assurance be conveyed by faith alone? Vv. 1–2, 6–11: Yes; because the promises of God in the gospel, in its narrow proper sense of being justified, accepted, and reconciled with God, speak of such benefits without our works, namely, by faith in the person and work of Christ alone for the ungodly, for those without righteousness of their own.

6. Can assurance be further conveyed or strengthened by other means including our works? Vv. 3–5: Yes; our good works of love in gratitude and obedience to our Savior are further evidence of grace received in our lives but are *not* to be trusted or sought after apart from the direct evidence of faith on gospel promises in its narrow and proper sense.

7. Does God provide for *both* ways of assurance, namely, the direct by faith alone on the gospel narrow and proper or definitive promises in justification, as well as the indirect or reflective evidence of love and transformation in sanctification unto glory in the broad general fruitful sense of our salvation? Vv. 1–5, 6–11: Yes; God assures his children directly by gospel promises in the narrow sense of justification of the ungodly, as well as indirectly and reflectively through the broad sense of salvation in the gospel fruits of sanctification unto glory.

8. Is there a dynamic of relationship between these two ways of assurance, namely, the direct through faith alone in the gospel narrow sense, and the indirect or reflective through the fruits of sanctification unto glory or salvation in the broad sense? Yes; there exists such a dynamic where the indirect assurance always depends and flows out of the direct assurance in the same way that love and good works proceed from faith. In short, a believer finds assurance by looking to Christ alone and the promises of God to save without works, and only insofar as anyone looks to Christ, keeping their eyes on him—his forgiveness and righteousness—will they see fruits of love and good works push against the selfish fear and boastful pride of the flesh.

9. What connection is there between Adam and Christ? Vv. 12–14: Adam is a type of Christ in several respects. For one, as Adam acts in a federal or representative position for many, so does Christ for the many who believe. They are public heads that stand in the place of many in their respective roles and positions.

10. How is Adam a representative or federal head for many? Vv. 12–21: He is a representative or federal head for mankind since by his sin death entered the world; consequently, all were constituted sinners and died on account of the guilt and corruption they inherit in Adam. By the actions of one, the many are affected unto death.

11. How is Christ a representative or federal head for many? Vv. 12–21: He is a representative or federal head for all who believe in him since by his perfect obedience and sacrificial death they are justified; thus, they are all forgiven and imputed the righteousness of Christ, becoming heirs of eternal life with all the benefits thereof on account of Christ's virtue and merit on their behalf. By the actions of one, the many are affected unto salvation.

12. Why does Paul talk about these two heads in the context of talking about our sin and our salvation from it? Because our spiritual health and growth requires placing our personal story of salvation within the larger story of redemption.

13. What are the benefits of a proper understanding of such a grand metanarrative for the Christian life? Firstly, it is the proper understanding of Scripture because all of it testifies to Christ as the second/last Adam, being faithful and obedient where the first Adam failed in order to rescue those affected by the curse of the fall. Secondly, our personal stories can never deeply and permanently be impacted by the transforming power and hope of the gospel except we live our personal stories in light of God's grand story. Our personal stories are always being reframed, redirected, and re-storied by the metanarrative of the gospel.

14. What can this framework of interpreting and living our Christian lives by the redemptive narrative of Christ be called? It can be called a redemptive covenantal framework whereby we interpret the Word and live our Christian lives by the redemptive narrative of another for us, wherein everything is provided for my salvation in both its narrow

and broad sense in the actions of a saving representative, Christ, to deliver us from the clutches of our damning representative, Adam.

15. What happens when we see our sin in Adam and the corruption we have inherited from the fall? Vv. 18–21: We see the depth of our sinfulness and ruin as well as the need for a Savior, someone to deliver us from that first story affecting our lives daily.

16. What happens when we see our righteousness in the obedience of Christ and the life we can have in him? Vv. 18–21: We can readily confess the magnitude of our sin and condemnation as well as delight in the abundance of our deliverance through grace in Christ.

Romans 6

1. Are we excused by the righteousness of faith in grace to live in sin? Vv. 1–2: Absolutely not; actually, grace works against sin and unto holiness of life.

2. What is it about grace that works in opposition to our sin? Vv. 1–3: Grace works in us our union with Christ through faith.

3. How does grace work in us our union with Christ? Vv. 1–4: Our union with Christ speaks of our union by faith with his death and resurrection; grace is God's unprovoked gifted favor in Christ of the merits and virtues of his person and work on our behalf, namely, his life, death, and resurrection. By grace we are united with Christ, namely, with his death and resurrection.

4. Why does Paul refer to our being baptized into Christ as our being baptized and buried into his death? Vv. 1–4: Because by his story of death on the cross for our sins, God puts our story of sin unto death, namely, it passes the sentence of death upon our flesh with its sinful desires and actions; it condemns all of our story in the first Adam to curse and death, so we may not boast in the flesh, in ourselves, but actually condemn it, or condemn ourselves.

5. Why does Paul say that we are also united with Christ's resurrection? Vv. 4–7: Because Christ's resurrection from death guarantees our walk in newness of life, having defeated sin, death, and condemnation for us. His resurrection story gives new life out of the grave of death and

condemnation of the first Adam that we used to live in; we now begin to live by faith in Christ's life raised to God from death forever.

6. Is there a dynamic of relationship between the death and resurrection of Christ as applied to our story? Yes; the redemptive story of the cross of Christ puts our first Adam story, the flesh with its sinful desires and deeds, unto death so we may not boast in our own ways and works, in order to confess our new life in Christ's resurrection as the righteous one who has satisfied all of God's righteous demands for us. We, through repentance and faith, daily confess and live in death and resurrection in Christ's redemptive story for us.

7. How does God view our body of sin in Christ? V. 6: Our body of sin, the old Adam, has been crucified with Christ. God considers our old nature, the old story in Adam, to have been put to death by Christ's death.

8. What does that mean practically for our lives? Vv. 6–10: It means that although sin is still present in us, it no longer rules us. We are no longer subject to the bondage of sin although it is present and active in our members.

9. Why does sin no longer rule us in bondage to it? Vv. 6–10: Because believers have already died the curse, condemnation, and death of sin as well as risen in righteousness in Christ. Sin has lost its grip because it no longer condemns us who have been forgiven and accounted righteous before God through Christ's death and resurrection. The story of Christ for us, namely, the gospel, overthrows the old story of the first Adam in us, causing us to bear the fruit of Christlikeness.

10. Is the newness of life in Christ the termination or elimination of sin in our flesh? Vv.11–14: No; sin continues to be present with us and we continue to sin, but now there is an opposite operation against our flesh and its works through the new fruits of obedience empowered by faith.

11. Does this operation against sin from our new life in Christ by faith produce real and increasing changes unto holiness in our lives? Vv. 11–14: Yes, it does. We are empowered to increasingly stop gratifying our sinful desires as well as to repent and turn from those we actually commit. This is a real sanctification in our lives that takes place progressively.

12. Does progressive sanctification mean that we are always growing and improving? Vv. 11–14: No, it does not mean that. Actually, believers may experience many setbacks and falls as well as be assaulted by many temptations and weaknesses, regardless of what stage in the process of sanctification they find themselves in. But God continues to work in them the grace and power of their real sanctification.

13. To what extent will believers grow in progressive sanctification? Vv. 11–14: To the extent that they are strengthened by faith to consider themselves dead to sin and alive to God in Christ Jesus. Growing in sanctification is the continual path of the believer who lives by faith in the person and work of Christ for him or in union with his death and resurrection.

14. Is this walk of personal sanctification empowered by the law or by grace? V. 14: It is not empowered by the law as a covenant of works—meaning one has to obey in order to be blessed if not cursed; rather, it is empowered in obedience to the law under the covenant of grace by the preaching of the gospel, where Christ's obedience to the law for the sinner becomes the grounds, motivation, and power to obey God's commands.

15. Does the covenant of grace, namely, being delivered from condemnation by Christ's person and work by faith, provide a license or incentive for sin? Vv. 15–19: Absolutely not; living under grace produces the contrary impulse unto holiness in sanctification because it provides an identity of belonging to God as his servants, which leads to presenting our members to obey righteousness out of gratitude and praise for what God has done.

16. What is the blessing or motivation for living in righteousness pursuing the fruit of sanctification? Vv. 20–23: The blessing or motivation, in addition to the joy, gratitude, and praise for already being saved in the narrow gospel sense of being accepted before God through forgiveness and imputation in Christ, is righteousness or the fruit of sanctification itself. It is love out of being loved in Christ.

17. Why is righteousness in sanctification, or love, a motivation in itself rather than the means to greater blessings? Because the fruit of sanctification consists in participation or sharing in the life of God with others in and through Christ, and such life is man's ultimate and greatest

blessing, namely, eternal life, or an abundant life of loving out of the love received in Christ.

Counseling Vignette 1 Continued

R: Pastor, we would like to believe that we could possibly marry and find God's blessing, but we have been too weak and sinful. We have continued to relapse into fornication even though we have tried to stay away from each other . . . How can God bless our marriage?

S: I even wonder if we are truly the Christians we claim to be when sin continues to master us like that? We are displaying the works of the flesh, not the fruits of saints . . . Aren't we supposed to see victory in our lives over habitual sin if we are truly believers?

P: So, you have kept relapsing back into your sexual sin and you are both questioning whether God can bless your marriage, and even more, your very own salvation, right?

R: Yes, that pretty much sums it all up. Right, honey?

S: I agree.

P: And can you help me understand better why you think this way?

R: Pastor, the Bible says the unrighteous shall not inherit the kingdom of God, and without holiness no one will see the Lord . . . is that not clear? We hear other preachers talk about these things for assuring evidence of our salvation. One of them even said that if we don't stop fornicating and separate to get all this right, we might not go to heaven . . . that was the import of his words.

S: We are very confused and scared!

P: I hear you . . . I think I get from what you have shared what thinking yourself accursed both in your relationship and your personal lives before God may look like. Does that describe your view of things; you see yourself cut off and forsaken of God in the midst of these thoughts and suspicions you have?

S: Yes, and . . . (sobs again) it feels horrible.

P: (Pastor again allows for a pause and nods several times in acknowledgment to confirm the message, both verbal and emotional, has been received.)

P: I know the feeling . . . I have been there too. (Another pause after this expression of solidarity)

R: Have you . . . really? How come?

P: Well, suffice it to say you are not the only repeat offending sinners in the room. Believers will always feel terrible about their sins. I know the feeling. But let me ask you: what do you do with those thoughts and feelings?

R: Sally and I repent again and ask the Lord to forgive us; we try to see the seriousness of sin and the threat of damnation that hangs over those who can't master it. I mean, we know we don't lose our salvation but we are afraid we may not have it and would like to make our calling and election sure by our resolve not to fall again, but . . . (holding back tears) we have continued to fail, Pastor!

P: So, you are trying to get away from fornication to ensure you are one of the elect, right? And it's hard to believe that based on what you guys keep doing. Is that an accurate assessment?

R: Yes, it is.

P: Now, when you see your sin, what is it that you desire more than anything else to do about it?

S: To stop sinning, of course.

P: You are right about wanting that, as every child of God does, but you seem to lack the power. Let me ask you: you want to stop sinning so badly because you love the Lord and are so grateful for his love and kindness? Are you so overcome by his forgiving love and assurance of his salvation that you want to serve him? Or do you really lack assurance and a sense of wonder and peace about his forgiving love and care of you until you get things right? Which one is it?

S: I have no peace, no joy until I obey. It's always been that way.

P: And you, Robert?

R: Well, I think I should have peace when I have fellowship with God, and sin hinders that, right?

P: You re both right that sin hinders our fellowship with God and that joy goes hand in hand with obedience. But both fellowship with God and obedience are lived out in joy, namely, the joy of forgiveness in the reconciling love of the Father. The elder John says that we love God because he loved us first and that perfect love drives out fear, namely, the fear of punishment. It seems to me you are working out of a punishment-based motivation rather than one of love.

S: How can we love him when we continue to sin? How can he accept us like that?

P: Guys, you recognize sin in your fornication, right? And, furthermore, you are stricken with grief about it, right? That means you are cut to the heart about the sin you commit; now, do you see a Savior for sinners like you? Have you trusted that he is able to save repeat offenders like you?

R: But what about repentance . . . forsaking sin?

P: Folks, repentance can never be divorced from ongoing faith in the Savior. We repent when convicted of our sins and, holding ourselves guilty and worthy of condemnation before God, we turn to the kindness of a Savior for real ongoing sinners. In other words, repentance must be done in faith that all sins are truly and finally forgiven as opposed to sins being forgiven only if and when we stop sinning.

S: You are saying that our salvation does not depend on our obedience . . . that we can sin and still be saved?

P: Yes and no. Let me explain. Our salvation is freely given as a gift, meaning without our works of obedience on account of the obedience of Christ. He obeyed perfectly the law that we fail to obey daily. He lived and died for us. This is why we are saved; because he lived to die under the law for us sinners, who will never live like that here, and actually deserve to die here and forever. It is Christ's story, namely, the gospel that accomplishes and announces your salvation. Do you believe it?

(to be continued)

Romans 7

1. Are believers still under the obligations of the law for blessing or cursing depending on their obedience or lack thereof? No; believers are no longer under such a covenant of works under the law.

2. Why are believers not under the law as a covenant of works, cursed for disobedience and blessing for obedience? They are not under the law because they have already died to the law. The law is no longer a legal obligation over them for either blessing or cursing by obedience or disobedience, respectively.

3. What analogy does Paul use to teach this truth of believers no longer bound under the law? The analogy of marriage where a spouse is legally free to remarry once the other spouse has died. We who have died to the law are no longer bound to it but are now free to marry another.

4. How did believers come to be free from the law's demands? Because they have died to the law in the dying of Christ under the law. They who are united to Christ by faith have satisfied the righteous requirements of the law and can no longer die because Jesus died in their place as if they had themselves died.

5. Why does the death of Christ deliver believers from being bound to the law? Because Jesus died the death that the law demanded so the law cannot accurse those who have already died the law's death in Christ.

6. Why was Jesus not bound by the law's death? Because he was without sin and only died as a substitute for sinners. Thus, he rose from the dead and lives forevermore to intercede for believers so they may also live forever with him.

7. Who are believers married to now, using Paul's analogy? Believers now are married to Christ and belong to him forever.

8. What are believers able to do now that they are bound to Christ as in a marriage, united by faith to his death and resurrection? Believers are now able to bear fruit of obedience unto God through their union by faith with Christ's death and resurrection.

9. Who is at work in believers for this new obedience or fruit of union with Christ's death and resurrection by faith? God, the Holy Spirit, is at work in believers for this new obedience or fruit of newness of life.

10. Why does the Holy Spirit now empower believers with such new obedience by faith? Because believers are now considered righteous in Christ, and as righteous in union with Christ's death and resurrection, they possess the Holy Spirit of Christ and of the Father.

11. Why could the law or the letter, namely, obey for blessing or be accursed by disobedience, not provide for the indwelling of the Holy Spirit? Because sinners remained under the curse and death of the law, not being able to work and do the law for righteousness as God demands. The Spirit does not live with and in the unrighteous but with and in the righteous; and believers are considered righteous in Christ and thereby receive the Spirit in and through him by faith.

12. Are believers then righteous in their own persons and deeds by virtue of their new obedience? No; believers are never righteous in themselves, but guilty of sin and worthy of condemnation and death in their own persons and deeds. But they are, nonetheless, considered righteous and indwelt by the Spirit unto new fruits of new obedience by union with Christ's death and resurrection through faith.

13. Does being under the law help provide power against the sinful passions of the flesh? No; being under the law as a covenant of works, meaning obey for blessing or accursed by disobedience, actually exacerbates the sinful passions of the flesh, producing much more works or fruit unto death.

14. Why does serving under the law as a covenant of works stimulate and produce fruits unto death? Because the more one works to try and earn God's favor, the more one either sinks further into self-delusion that they are accomplishing such self-righteousness or departs in despair from the living God who always accuses and holds the transgressor guilty.

15. Are believers susceptible to this deception of trying to be found acceptable before God, to earn or maintain his blessings by obedience to the law? Yes; we are because our sinful flesh always desires and strives for self-justification and validation in one's own person and work rather than in the person and work of Christ.

16. What is it about the sinful flesh that always desires and strives for self-justification and validation? The problem lies with the flesh or the old Adam not trusting the good word and works of God, as happened at the fall with creation, and as continues to be the temptation after new creation in redemption. The old Adam's essential sin is that of not trusting the word and the works of God that reveal his goodness, power, and deity, namely, unbelief in God and, ultimately, unbelief in the person and work of God in Christ for salvation.

17. What is God's definitive final word against the unbelief and disobedience of the old Adam? The word of the gospel in Christ, which reveals the ultimate goodness and righteousness of God to redeem sinners and creation in and through the person and the work of Christ.

18. Is the law evil because it cannot help sinners unto righteousness? No, it is not. Mankind is evil and condemned under the good, righteous, and perfect law of God. The law cannot help humanity because of the sinfulness of their flesh, not because of any defect or evil in the law or in God.

19. What is then the chief purpose of the law? Vv. 7–8: The chief purpose of the law consists in revealing our sin, guilt, death, and condemnation by explaining God's moral will in detail, thus showing how far we fall from it into the misery, ruin, and condemnation we deserve before such a holy, righteous, and perfect God.

20. What specific action does the law do in the sinner? Vv. 9–10: The law specifically kills the sinner, namely, it humbles us by pronouncing death upon all our works, both good and bad, outside of Christ.

21. What purpose does this killing of the sinner by the law serve? Vv. 24–25: It's the only way that sinners will live by grace, namely, not by their own works or anything in them, but by the works, sacrifice, and righteousness of Christ for them by faith alone.

22. What specific commandment is listed as killing the sinner? Vv. 7–13: The tenth commandment, "You shall not covet." This is the commandment against lust or concupiscence, namely, the sinful desires or passions of the flesh.

23. Does the tenth commandment prohibit the mere desiring of sin, namely, the mere inclination toward it in desire, lust, or passion? Vv. 7–13: Yes; the tenth commandment prohibits desiring to kill, desiring to commit adultery, desiring to steal, to lie, etc. Hence, sin is not just an outward action or internal thought but also the desiring, the impulse or inclination toward sin.

24. Does having sinful desires and inclinations make us culpable before God and liable to death and condemnation? Vv. 7–13: Yes; sinful desires and inclinations as experienced in the corruption of our sinful nature in our members deserve the wrath of God. Hence, sin is not just an action but also a condition or a state of corruption in which we are born liable to God's justice.

25. Does every Christian, even the most mature among us like Paul, carry these sinful desires and corruption with them daily? Vv. 14–23: Yes; we all do carry such a sinful corruption with us, expressed or experienced in sinful desires and inclinations to sin even without and before committing any sinful acts per se.

26. Does having these sinful desires and inclinations mean that believers have to follow or obey them every time and carry them to their ultimate consequences? Vv. 21–25: Absolutely not; our union with Christ's death and resurrection enable believers to not gratify the sinful and deceptive desires of the flesh, though our abiding flesh gets in the way of full and perfect conformance to God's moral will.

27. Does having these sinful desires mean that believers find themselves in the midst of a struggle against the sinfulness and sin within themselves? Vv. 21–25: Yes; it's a constant battle or conflict where believers daily confess those sinful desires or concupiscence that afflict them,

revealing the corruption and death of their old nature in Adam and the need for newness of life in and through Christ.

Counseling Vignette 1 Continued

R: So, Pastor, I hear a yes to continuing in our sin and being saved at the same time. Is that so?

P: My answer was yes and no, and let me explain. There will always be sin on your life even in your best day. So, being saved is the need of sinners, that is, of those who continue to be sinful and struggle with their sins daily. And the no comes from the believer now desiring to stop sinning, being bothered by the presence of sin in their lives so that we don't just go on happily sinning like before. We have acquired both a conscience of forgiveness and holiness. In other words, we live daily in the forgiveness of Christ for our daily sinfulness and sinful actions and we also live daily desiring to overcome sin, bothered and convicted by it as well as looking forward to the day it will be no more.

S: But don't you have to turn from sin in repentance to be forgiven . . . we need to repent, don't we?

R: Yes, Sally, but turning from sin is the fruit of repentance, and the fruit is never the condition for God's acceptance but the consequence of it. In other words, we bear fruits of repentance when we know ourselves forgiven and accepted before God.

S: So, if obedience is the fruit of repentance, what is repentance then?

R: Yes, Pastor; if you don't change you haven't repented, right?

P: True repentance will bring about change, but not perfect change, not even perfect repentance; but we are not saved by either, but by the perfect person and the work of Christ even with imperfect repentance and less than perfect change. Our change and our repentance is not the basis of our salvation but Christ's perfect person and work.

R: What does that mean, Pastor, for us, for our situation?

P: To have conviction of sins and sorrow for them as you do and to trust in the Savior for pardon and reconciliation is repentance. You are saved as you with conviction and sorrow for sin turn to the Savior's mercy to receive his forgiving grace. It seems that you have done that; you have great sorrow and conviction of sin. But the question is: do you believe the Savior who died for your sins so that all of your sins, including your remaining and continuing sin can be forgiven and not counted against you?

S: Yes, Pastor, we believe that, but now that we are believers we must be holy and walk in obedience as evidence of such a grace.

P: Yes, Sally, but that obedience and the repentance from which it springs will not be perfect. It may look like someone who struggles and falls into the area of sexual sin or any other area. As long as you have begun to love the Lord and desire to please him through faith. And that is the question: are you trying to please or obey him because you know yourself secure and kept safe in the Father's love?

S: I'm afraid not; I don't feel secure. Do you, Robert?

R: Me neither, but it sounds like we should. Are you saying, Pastor, we should seek assurance or make an effort to believe that we are secured and then things will turn around for us?

P: That's kind of right, but not exactly. You will gain assurance by seeking Christ, by dwelling in his promise for sinners, by trusting his gospel word for you. You seek Christ, and you will grow in assurance as well as in obedience. It is Christ you must seek since every good and perfect gift lies with him. When you seek Christ, his gospel promise speaks assurance for sinners as they are without works; and the result of believing or trusting in that saving word daily will be the reflective additional evidence of salvation in the fruits of a measure of love for God and neighbor, as imperfect as that may be.

R: So, trust and believe God's word—you mean the gospel or, like you said, the story of Christ for us? You are saying: don't look at your works, your story, your own person and work, but the person and work of Christ? This will bring assurance and obedience? It works like that?

S: Can God . . . ? (Tears well up again.)

P: (Pause) Can God accept you like that? Forgive you and bless you? Yes; he can and he wants to.

S: How can you be so sure? You never doubt?

P: Of course I do. I am very weak also and often, like you, struggle to believe and repent—less than perfect faith and repentance, remember? But then I hear the gospel word and remember that God's love for me does not depend or is not conditional on any of my failures; his is perfect love. As a matter of fact, it's precisely because my sin is deeper than just my actions that his love speaks so deeply and truly into my life—I desperately need such forgiving and reconciling love because I'm always flawed and corrupt at my deepest level.

R: Pastor, I think I was getting it but that last statement is perplexing. What do you mean you are always corrupt deep down?

P: Folks, your sin is not just the sexual fornicating acts you have committed, but it extends to the sinful desires of your heart. Sin is not just the external acts or even the thoughts you indulge in but the mere presence of the desires and inclinations that bend you in a sinful direction. We are sinners not because we sin; rather, we sin because we are sinners. We carry sinful corruption within us affecting all areas of our lives.

R: And how can we be rid of them? How can we be saved from them? When do they stop?

P: They don't; they don't ever go away until glory. (Pause)

(to be continued)

Romans 8

1. Are Christians who experience the sinful desires of the flesh and the sin they commit following those desires ever to conclude that they are condemned even though they have trusted in Christ for their forgiveness and reconciliation? V. 1: No; they are never to conclude they are condemned or separated from Christ because of the sins they see in themselves, because there is absolutely no condemnation for them who have trusted in Christ and are thus united to his death and resurrection by faith.

2. Can anyone profess faith and not be saved? V. 1: Yes; profession of faith may not be true faith, since a person may say they believe with their lips but lack a genuine trust and assurance on the promises of God in Christ for sinners who believe.

3. Why is there no condemnation whatsoever for those who truly believe in Christ? Vv. 1–4: Because they who believe have a substitute under the law before God, who has satisfied that law completely in both its death as well as its righteous perfect living requirement.

4. What is the law of the Spirit of life that sets believers free? Vv. 1–4: The law of the Spirit of life that sets believers free is the operation of the Spirit that constantly illumines, reminds, and applies the person and the work of the substitute to the believer by faith, namely, the gospel by which the believer's union with Christ is further nourished and strengthened.

5. What is the law of sin and death from which we have been set free? Vv. 1–4: The law of sin and death consists in the deceptive and sinful operations of the flesh under the condemnation of the law, namely, the sinner whose sinful flesh is exacerbated under the righteous demands and condemnation of the law, which binds them under a guilty record and verdict.

6. What did God do in Christ that the sinner could not do in their sinful flesh? Vv. 1–4: He satisfied the demands of the law completely in the flesh of Christ, thus obtaining perfect righteousness for the believer; namely, Christ was condemned in the flesh so that we could be set free from the condemnation of our own flesh and live for God in righteousness.

7. How can the believer live for God in righteousness? Vv. 1–4: Because they have the legal grounds before God of forgiveness and the imputation of Christ's righteousness. They are no longer under the law, bound by a guilty record and verdict before God that exacerbates their sinful flesh; rather, they have been set free from such condemnation by the law of the Spirit of life in Christ (see 4 above).

8. Is there a relationship between their legal ground on the basis of imputation and their real walk of obedience in righteousness or progressive sanctification? Vv. 1–4: Yes; the legal ground of imputation produces in them the real effect of participation in the fruits of Christlikeness; namely, the gospel, in its narrow sense of imputation, is the motivating and enabling power for their transformation or progressive sanctification.

9. How does God translate this verdict of justification into the working power of progressive transformation or sanctification in the believer? Vv. 1–4: By the Spirit at work in the believer through the granting, testing, refining, and increasing of faith; to walk according to the Spirit means to walk by faith, whose object is the person and the work of Christ in his death and resurrection for our union with him.

10. Where do believers set their minds as enabled by the Spirit? Vv. 5–6: Believers set their minds on their union with Christ, namely, their being united by faith to the person and the work of Christ, namely, his death and resurrection and thereby every benefit and blessing assured by such a union. They keep their minds by the Spirit on their legal union with Christ (gospel in narrow sense), which translates into their real access and participation (gospel in broad sense) in personal fruits of righteousness progressively.

11. Where do unbelievers set their minds? Vv. 5–6: Unbelievers set their minds on the sinful and deceptive desires of the flesh, being convinced that God is not good but rather evil and judges them worthy of death and condemnation under the law. Their sins are exacerbated by their guilt and death under the law, whether of conscience or in Scripture, in rebellion against God's truth. Furthermore, they ultimately reject God's righteousness and goodness displayed in Christ at the cross in obstinate unbelief.

12. How is setting one's mind on the things of the Spirit life? Vv. 5–8: It is life because the Spirit testifies through faith of union with Christ's

death and resurrection for forgiveness and the imputation of righteousness before God, as well as access and participation in Christ's virtues in progressive sanctification.

13. How is setting one's mind on the things of the flesh death? Vv. 5–8: It is death because it obstinately holds hostility against God through unbelief, rejecting his good works, verdict, and judgment in both creation and ultimately in Scripture. The flesh does not receive the righteous verdict of condemnation in the law, thereby also not receiving the ultimate verdict of death and life through the cross of Christ in his death and resurrection.

14. What does the unbelief of the flesh consist of? Vv. 1–8: The unbelief of the flesh consists of trust, acceptance, and dependence on one's own goodness, wisdom, justice, and ways at the exclusion or rejection of trust, acceptance, and dependence on God's goodness and righteousness in all his works and ways as revealed in both creation and Scripture.

15. Are Christians in the flesh? No; Christians are no longer in the flesh; although the flesh is still in them, which is why they are affected by its works. They are rather in the Spirit and are called to walk according to the Spirit in opposition to the works of the flesh.

16. Why is the Spirit of God also called the Spirit of Christ? Vv. 9–10: The Spirit of God is also called the Spirit of Christ because of the righteousness of Christ, which the Spirit illuminates and communicates to our spirits even though our bodies will die because of sin. The Spirit of God always testifies to the person and the work of Christ for the salvation of sinners.

17. What will the Spirit of Christ do to our mortal bodies now and in the future? Vv. 9–11: The Spirit of Christ applies the death and resurrection of Christ to sinners for their justification, sanctification, and glorification. The Spirit, by communicating Christ in his whole atoning and justifying work, applies the life of Christ in resurrection power to our bodies now for progressive sanctification, and our bodies in the final day for resurrection unto glory.

18. What is the main motivation to live according to the Spirit? Vv. 12–17: That we are no longer debtors or obligated to live according to the flesh since we belong to Christ. We are mainly motivated by

gratitude and the new identity of belonging and being in union with Christ as his children.

19. What does it mean to live according to the Spirit? Vv. 12–17: It means to live by faith in union with the death and resurrection of Christ in a legal union of being justified, as well as the familial and participatory aspect of such union in being transformed into Christlikeness through such faith.

20. How does the believer by the Spirit put to death or mortify the deeds of the flesh? Vv. 12–17: The believer by the Spirit mortifies the deeds of the flesh by reckoning, through faith, those deeds of the flesh, their sinfulness, sins, and the old Adam, dead in Christ and presenting themselves to God alive in Christ's resurrection for the legal ground and participatory access of the their new life in Christ.

21. Is mortifying or killing sin an external endeavor of stopping or forsaking sin by the Christian through their own will, resolve, and/or commitment? Vv. 12–17: Absolutely not; killing or mortifying sin is a walk of faith that looks to their legal union with Christ's death and resurrection as the fact upon which the believer depends in daily faith and repentance to ask and pursue their inheritance of Christlikeness. It is first an internal move to Christ by faith and then an external sharing of Christ also in faith, where the latter depends and flows from the former. In short, the gospel in its narrow sense (justification) is daily depended upon by faith for the gospel in its broader sense of its fruits of progressive sanctification unto glory in perseverance also by faith.

22. What is the fruit of living according to the Spirit by faith? The fruit is our sanctification or progressive path of growth in holiness and obedience, namely, the fruit of the Spirit.

23. What does it mean to live according to the flesh? Vv. 12–17: It is a reference mainly to unbelievers, who lacking faith or trust in the person and work of Christ and are not united to him, and thus always follow the evil and deceptive desires of the flesh in unrestrained unbelief and wickedness. However, believers may also walk according to the flesh or carnally insofar as they may be affected by the works of the flesh in unbelief and hardness of heart, but only temporarily and partially.

24. What is the most essential and direct testimony of the Spirit for our assurance of salvation? Vv. 15–17: The Spirit, illuminating the person

and the work of Christ in our union with him through faith, speaks the direct assurance of the promise of God for adoption as sons to everyone who simply believes in Christ. Through such direct testimony of God's promise in Christ for those who believe, the Spirit drives away fear of condemnation and continues to stimulate and grow believers in the assuring freedom of children who cry out, "Abba! Father!"

25. Can fear of condemnation be a motivator for obedience and described as godly fear? Absolutely not; godly fear exists in those who are no longer slaves of sin because they have been delivered from the fear of condemnation or death under the law. They who truly fear or reverence God do so in the increasing assurance of the promise of being adopted and secure as children through faith in the person and work of Christ on their behalf.

26. Does the direct assurance of faith mean that believers will no longer suffer, endure, or make efforts in their salvation? Vv. 16–17: Of course not; believers' path unto glory will be marked by much suffering, endurance, and effort. Firstly, because their faith will be tested in many trials; secondly, because their flesh, the world, and the enemy will oppose the use of the means of grace God has established for their growth; and thirdly, because the remaining sinful weakness or infirmity of their flesh will be daily confronted and killed by the cross for the fruits of new life in them.

27. Is this path of suffering a condition or consequence and further evidence of their salvation? It is definitely *not* a condition to be accepted or saved before God in the gospel's narrow sense; but in the gospel's broad fruitful sense, without good works, holiness, or some progress in sanctification, no one will enter their glorification because such is the path of the believer unto glory. This path entails much suffering and further confirms our faith as genuine and true. Thus, it is not a condition but public demonstration and evidence.

28. Is such suffering only a cause of pain and groaning for the believer? Vv. 18–25: No; although it is a cause of pain and groaning for the believer, it is also a cause for joy in hope and assurance of things not seen but believed and awaited in tested hope and patience.

29. How does the Spirit intercede for the saints in their weakness? Vv. 26–27: The Spirit reveals and works according to the will of God for

the saints in ways they cannot fully or visibly grasp. He accommodates every prayer of God's children to his good sovereign purposes.

30. What is God's purpose for his children even in the midst of trials and sufferings? Vv. 26–29: God's good purpose for his children is always to conform them to the image of his Son in love.

31. Do we have to love God as the condition to be called for his good purpose? Vv. 28–30: No; it's the other way around: God calls us through the gospel by faith and, believing, we are called into his good purposes in Christ. Love follows upon faith, which unites us to the love of God in Christ.

32. How is the love of God preeminently manifested in Christ? Vv. 28–30: The love of God is preeminently manifested in Christ in that all that he has done and will do in our lives from before the foundation of the world to future glorification has reference to exalting Christ in his redeeming person and work on behalf of sinners.

33. Is God's calling and work in believers contingent upon their works, response, or merits? No; it is God who always works first to effectively draw unto salvation and perfect whom he calls; these only respond from the beginning to the end to God's effective calling and work in them through Christ, being enabled to do so by the gift of faith granted in regeneration, which faith is also sustained, refined, and increased throughout sanctification in perseverance unto glory.

34. Is salvation then from beginning to end the work of God? Yes, it is. From election before the foundation of the world, to being predestined unto conformity to Christ, to then being called and justified in time as well as preserved in faith unto glory, this is all God's work. God's children always work in response to and together with God's effective ways and means of producing in them to will and to do according to his purposes.

35. Is this work of God in his elect ever separated from the person and work of Christ as a reference and basis for what God does? No; all of God's work must always be spoken of in light of, on account of, and with a view to the person and the work of Christ, namely, the lamb slain before the foundation of the world for his glory.

36. What are then three strong pillars of assurance for the believer? One, that they have been elected in and for Christ before the foundation of

the world; two, that they have been granted faith in regeneration for union with the death and resurrection of Christ as promised in the gospel without works of righteousness; and third, that they through the faith of regeneration are enabled to love God and neighbor being gradually transformed unto the image of Christ.

37. Should believers try to look to their election or their works first and foremost for assurance of salvation? Vv. 31–39: No,;they should always look first and foremost to Christ, namely, to the promise of the gospel that inherently speaks assurance to those who without anything in themselves or knowing anything else can trust the word of promise in Christ for their salvation assurance. The other two pillars, election and good works, may be said to constitute derivative and supporting grounds for assurance accessed only in and through the message of the cross, namely, the gospel.

38. What does that assurance of faith in the gospel promise enable believers to increasingly know and trust? Vv. 31–39: Through faith, believers come to increasingly know and trust the unchangeable and unshakable love of God for them in and through Christ, with whom they have been inseparably united by the same faith and continue to grow in the confidence, closeness, and communion of such union by the same faith.

Counseling Vignette 1 Continued

R: What do you mean our sinful desires don't go away? Are we then doomed by slavery to our sins? Can we not change?

P: I see you are following this, Paul . . . let me explain. Ours is a daily constant battle against or in opposition to the sinful and deceptive desires that rage in our flesh. Insofar as we focus on what God has done for us and live daily out of the humble reminder of his forgiving and justifying grace and mercy, we shall experience a new set of desires and inclinations, namely, holy desires or affections that do change our lives.

S: So, wouldn't that mean the sinful desires disappear?

P: Sally, in a way, they sort of disappear, but the reality is they are still there . . . At the moment, they are just being eclipsed by more powerful desires and affections. These are the holy affections that result from bathing, basking, and abiding in God's unconditional love for us no matter what circumstances in our lives, that is, without regard to our works or obedience of any kind.

S: You mean one can have a sense of peace without working or obeying? Is that so?

P: Yes, the peace of forgiveness . . . (pause) which comes from a certain kind of obedience, namely, the obedience of faith . . . it's trusting that while my sins and even my best works deserve condemnation, we are loved and accepted in the person and the work of Christ for us. It's seeing and confessing the ugliness and death of our sin but trusting the beauty and virtue of God's power in Christ to forgive us, justifying us and adopting us as his beloved children.

R: Without any change on our part?

P: That's right! Without any change in terms of working righteousness or proving ourselves worthy before God, but actually confessing our utter unworthiness and death to trust and rest our case in Christ's person and work for us.

S: But isn't that somehow a change . . . I mean, that's a different attitude the way it sounds, right?

P: That's very perceptive, Sally. Indeed, it involves a change. It's the change in repentance and faith of trust and confidence in the Savior's promise, not the change of working or presenting some kind of virtue or obedience before God to be accepted.

R: Isn't that faith and repentance virtuous or somehow worthy of acceptation before God as humility, I guess?

P: No; the change of faith and repentance is nothing but an empty hand trusting to receive and be filled in the asking . . . or sort of like eating with a spoon where the spoon does not bring anything of value in itself but simply the instrument to receive what is valuable, in this case food.

R: That value is Christ in our case; we must trust him to be forgiving and loving unto us although we have been disobedient.

P: Exactly; you must exercise the spoon or reach out the empty hand in confession of your guilt and sinful desires by hearing and entering the richest banquet laid before you in Christ. You must believe his forgiving hand . . . trust him as the atoning sacrifice and righteousness for your sins. If you see your need as a sinner, knowing the deadly weight of your sins, do you then see and embrace Christ as your forgiveness and righteousness apart from or without your works of obedience? (pause) Do you both?

S: I want to . . . Yes, I do. Robert?

R: Of course, Sally, that's what we want and our only hope.

P: You are forgiven and blessed in Christ, folks! Let us begin to plan your wedding, shall we?

R: Pastor, but what about our dirty secret, our fornication?

P: What about it?

R: Yes, what do we do about it? We should stop that until marriage, right?

P: Of course you should!

R: Then, again, how?

P: You are forgiven and loved in Christ; you belong to him as beloved and holy children of God. Your sin is death but God is greater than your sin. Can you guys begin to dwell on that more?

S: How? We can't always be coming to you for that.

P: You guys have the church, the Word of God, the sacraments, prayer, the fellowship of the saints—in short, the means of grace. Avail yourself of them often again and again.

R: We try to practice those, Pastor, but always fall short.

P: How about coming into them to meet a God who, every time you enter through the door of one of these means of grace with your need, is there to say, "You've come to the right place; I've been awaiting you to forgive, cover, and provide for your failures." You meet with God passing through those doors and hear him say, "I love you no matter what and look not on your failures and sins when you come before me in need of my mercy. I live to offer it to you daily behind these doors." How's that for the means of grace? (Pause)

S: But what if that is not what we are hearing?

P: I trust God will help you find those good pastures and the leading of the shepherd with his gospel voice. And you don't just depend on the church for that, or any man for that matter, because you have the Scriptures and hopefully the support of a church where you get gospel truth and absolution.

R: But it's hard and confusing at times, even the many interpretations of Scripture.

P: Indeed, it is. And yes, many interpretations do abound, but the voice of the gospel where God speaks to you of judgment and mercy through the cross, with mercy triumphing over judgment for they who believe, will not fail to lead you in the right direction by his Spirit. That's the testimony of the Scriptures; they testify of Christ and the Spirit illumines his story for us to daily depend on it rather than our own, and such should be the witness of the church. Remember, it's about his story, not about ours . . . his story for our story . . . it's about Christ, not about us . . . Christ for us! Shall we begin to talk of marriage, please!

In the case above, we have focused on showing the redeeming power of the gospel to speak forgiveness and hope to sinners who are trapped in the despair of shame and guilt under their sin, unable to see the light of God's unconditional forgiveness and justifying story in Christ Jesus. We do not disavow the usefulness of other behavioral interventions, like establishing accountability partners and staying away from circumstances and places prone to strengthen the force and the occasion for their sin; however, we have tried to focus on the essence of using a Redemptive Cognitive-Relational Narrative framework to their treatment in their particular case. For other cases, the approach within the same framework may be rather different, as we shall proceed to show below in the following mini-cases.

Counseling Vignette 2

Johnny, a young adult, can't seem to stay long enough in fellowship before he relapses into a homosexual lifestyle. He has bought into the lie that this is who he is and has trouble connecting to healthy churches where his lifestyle is not accepted and exposed as a sin.

> Pastor (P): Hey, Johnny, it's good to see you and share this coffee with you. We have called you a couple of times but couldn't reach you. How have you been?
>
> J: Uhh, not too good, Pastor. I mean according to you guys . . . if you know what I mean.
>
> P: I'd rather hear what you have in mind, Johnny. How are you not doing so good, and, what do you mean by "according to us"?
>
> J: Pastor, it's no secret I'm gay. You know that right?
>
> P: Johnny, I didn't want to make any assumptions but I'm sure glad we can talk openly about it now. I'm guessing your unhappiness has to do with our stance on the issue. Let's talk about it.
>
> J: Let me be direct, Pastor: I don't think this is a sin. This is who I am.
>
> P: Johnny, it's hard for me to understand your claim, let alone your experience, and I can see the passion that you have in saying that. I respect your candor in sharing this and value your presence among us; however, at the end of the day, I trust what the Bible says about the issue, and it clearly calls it sinful.
>
> J: I was born this way, ever since I can remember. I can't fight it anymore. This is who I am.

P: Johnny, while, as I said, I can't deny your experience and view of things, it's all part of the old story.

J: What do you mean by "the old story"? I'm telling you this is my story and it's true!

P: Again, I don't dispute your story; as a matter of fact, I'm interested in hearing more about it. It must have been hard.

J: What do you know, Pastor?

P: Why don't you tell me, tell me what's been the most difficult or painful thing?

J: The pain of rejection and isolation, not to be able to say what I'm saying to you now for fear of rejection, reprisals, consequences. But not anymore; it's enough.

P: (pause) (Pastor nods a couple of times, confirming that the message has been received and the emotional content of it registered.) (leaning closer) I can only imagine the pain you have been through and the release you must be feeling at being able to share it openly and come out like that. That takes a lot of courage. I always suspected you were wrestling with that but didn't have the courage to address it. I'm sorry about that. Again, I'm really glad we are finally talking about it.

J: (More relaxed) Yes, that's good. So, what do you say now?

P: Johnny, what I have to say is what I say to all sinners who want to hold on to their sin, including me as well. There's a greater story to live by than your own. There's a better and new nature to embrace than the old one we all so strongly hold on to.

J: But my sexuality is part of my nature, part of who I am. What do you mean "a better nature"? There's no story or nature for me that does not include who I am as a gay man.

P: Johnny, I must disagree. Neither our gender nor our sexuality is ultimately part of our new nature in Christ. God wants to get us used to that idea by pointing to our eschatological existence without marriage and sexual expression. Even now, these are only subservient to God's call in Christ, where there is neither male nor female, neither Jew nor Greek, there is no slave or free; we are all one in Christ Jesus. Have you ever thought about this?

J: No . . . hmmm, not sure . . . I mean, I can't separate myself now from my sexuality even if that is true in heaven.

P: What do you mean by separate?

J: You know, stop feeling the way I do, attracted to other men rather than to women. I can't stop that. I have no command over this.

P: I know and I agree. I'm not saying you simply decide, command, and wish this to go away. As a matter of fact, it will always be part of your experience somehow.

J: Wow, you lost me now, Pastor. What are you talking about? You don't want to change me, make me into a different me with some type of moral resolution and decision?

P: No, I don't and I can't. Let me explain. I don't dispute your experience, feelings, attractions, and story since you were born as you claim. That's your story. I'm only saying there is the power and possibility of another story, another nature, which brings another path.

J: There you go; you do want me to change, don't you?

P: Listen, the issue here is not simply changing and all of a sudden feeling like a heterosexual and living happily ever after. That's not what I'm talking about; I'm talking about embracing, believing, trusting, being persuaded of another story greater than your own and any temporary identity, roles, work, and pursuits we have engaged up to now with ultimacy and finality.

J: Break it down, please; speak English.

P: Johnny, I'm talking about believing in a new story over the one you have believed in up to now and find it worth following and living by. Believing that in Christ you are a new creation and called to live out of the new identity of his death and resurrection for you; that you belong to him and his love and life defines who you are rather than anything else at all—not your homosexuality, not your sin, not your best accomplishments and life now. Does that make sense?

J: I'm not sure I'm following that, Pastor . . . what do I need to do?

P: You need to believe that your old life, your old story—homosexuality included, as well as your best works—is accursed before God. You need to confess the sinfulness of your old nature and its entire works spent living for yourself in rebellion against God, gratifying your wicked desires in unbelief and disobedience against the good works and law of God.

J: Why does that include my homosexuality? Does that include your heterosexuality; is that sinful for you? Do you repent of your heterosexuality?

P: Excellent question, Johnny. Firstly, let's establish that sexuality and gender are gifts from God for this age; secondly, that we are called to live in them to serve God and neighbor, testifying of God's righteousness and goodness; and, thirdly, that all humanity has corrupted the good gifts and works of God for us, using them in a sinful way, which essentially means without recognizing God as the good giver and not thanking him in worshipful service.

J: I take it you are saying your heterosexuality is not sinful in itself; did I hear that?

P: You heard right. God created us male and female for the gift of heterosexual marriage, procreation, and stewarding his creation in his name; homosexuality goes contrary by its own nature to God's original design.

J: I knew it; you had me sort of tricked for a moment.

P: No, wait, I didn't mean to trick you. You know we believe homosexuality is a sin corrupting God's original design and thwarting its original intended fruits. But what I'm trying to say to you is that given the nature of sin in everyone's life inherited from Adam, nothing, absolutely nothing we do is not tainted by sin.

Even the good we do as heterosexuals, we corrupt and pervert and continue to damage God's original design contrary to his law. We need a new birth, a new nature, a new story. And that story, nature, and birth we simply receive by believing Christ, who died for our sins and rose for our justification, our gift of a new life in Christ, no longer our own!

J: And what do I have to do for that—change my homosexuality, stop liking men?

P: No, you must believe you are a sinner, homosexuality included. You must confess your holding on to your identity in the old story, with all its perversions of God's good gifts, all the corruptions of God's good works, is worthy of nothing but condemnation. You must repent of such mindset and direction in life and agree with God that all of it deserves to die and believe that Christ died for all of it to give you forgiveness and a new life in his resurrection. You must condemn what the law condemns, and it condemns not just your homosexuality but also every way in which I have perverted my heterosexuality, such as: not loving my wife as I ought, pornography, adultery, lasciviousness, abuse of power, and the many ways that we fail to love the other in our God-given roles and relationships. I don't condemn my heterosexuality but I condemn the way I have corrupted it and misused it, not trusting God's good word, design, and works for my life.

J: So, go on, how does that look in my case?

P: Not much different from mine; you must condemn your homosexuality as a corruption in unbelief and rebellion from God's good gift and works for you in his original design. He created us male and female for heterosexual marriage, procreation, and stewardship for God's glory. You must agree with God and confess your condemnation and death in your first story, in order to come by faith to embrace and trust that he recreates you anew by trusting the dying of Christ for you to that first story and the rising of Christ for you to the new story. You must trust that by Christ's death and resurrection your sins are forgiven and the righteousness of Christ is yours to now live and serve before God as his child.

J: Of course; and that involves changing my disposition, because if I continue to desire after men I'm doomed, right?

P: No, that's the point. God does not save you because you change your desires and abandon your like for men. He forgives and covers your desires and attraction for men with his story. You begin to live now in the confession and gratitude of God not counting your sins against you and treating you as his beloved child in Christ; that forgiveness and merciful kindness of your Savior will create in you holy desires and affections that will battle your old desires, and you will begin to love God and want to obey him. Those desires and attraction will be now a source of groaning in the weakness of your flesh being tempted and possibly falling at times; but God will never abandon you and will always be rescuing you, and bringing you back to faith in his love for you in Christ.

J: Wow that would be a miracle . . . wouldn't it?

P: Yes, the miracle of grace!

Counseling Vignette 3

Ryan is a hard-working person with a good reputation in the community. However, he constantly humiliates his wife and points out all her faults, often in a brutal and demeaning way. He is very involved in his local church, where he enjoys the respect of the church and serves as a deacon with the utmost discipline and severity. This counseling session with Ryan takes place after several sessions with his wife, who has been battling depression and anger issues.

P: Ryan, your wife has been deeply distressed. I'm afraid she may be suffering from depression.

R: No, Pastor, she has always been like that, always complaining of something. She may be frustrated with her own ways, but it's her own doing. She doesn't do anything for herself.

P: Tell me more about what she does wrong and the nature of her complaints, please.

R: Well, to put it in a nutshell, she's always tired and shows no interest in really important things. It's like she lives with a very limited view. She could expand her life, do better.

P: What would you like to see her do?

R: Well, change the attitude at home, especially with me for starters. And then, you know, get more involved in church, study more, just widen her horizons and live a fuller life with me.

P: And how does that make you feel, Ryan?

R: Extremely frustrated.

P: I see. Your wife has expressed that your frustration causes you to say demeaning things to her often as if she was worth and contributed very little. That seems to match your assessment of her, right?

R: I'm just very honest, Pastor. I tell her the truth and pray in hope for a change.

P: The truth, to use your own words, that she is stupid, incompetent, carnal, and that without you she couldn't do much. Is that so?

R: Yeah, I can be blunt sometimes.

P: No, that is not being blunt, Ryan; that is downright mean and destructive . . . you realize that?

R: I beg to differ. I have put up with a lot from her. She needs a reality check. She could use some toughening up, some dose of what it takes to make it out there. I've been an exemplary provider and a man of integrity in my church and community.

P: Ryan, your wife, with whom you have raised three children, is a vessel that we are to treat with gentleness as we would treat our own flesh. As I understand it, she holds seasonal jobs to help with finances and has stayed home with the children all these years until now that they are almost ready to go to college. To any outside observer, it seems like you have mighty fine children and a very virtuous wife.

R: Things are not what they appear. You'd be surprised.

P: I hear you; we are not perfect and those closest to us get to see that firsthand. I'm sure that is true for your wife and you as well, right?

R: What are you implying?

P: I'm saying the way you talk about your wife confirms most of the things she has shared about your treatment of her. And I want to tell you, it is downright sinful. That is not the way God wants you to treat your wife.

R: I think I've done right by her. She lacks nothing. Yeah, I may be the kind of guy that doesn't embellish things and isn't too romantic, but I've done right by her.

P: Ryan, Christ came and died for us. He's been merciful and kind to you in spite of your many sins and repeated failures. You are called to bear with your wife and treat her with the same kindness, patience, and tenderness God has offered you. God continues to bear with you, love you, and forgive you in undeserved mercy. Do you see how God daily gifts you his mercy and goodness?

R: I know God is merciful, but he rewards those that keep his covenant in obedience. I believe God has blessed my obedient efforts and work. Laziness, ignorance, complaining, and complacency are not pleasing unto God. That is what I tell my wife. I'm trying to help her constantly. I've fought hard to rise above my weaknesses and God was there to help and reward me accordingly. She needs to do the same, Pastor.

P: Ryan, your wife is trying to face her own issues as well as her sins, but you have to do so as well. You are not treating her right; the law of God calls us to love our neighbor, and in the case of your wife it involves daily forgiving, forbearance, and especially tender care, encouragement, and support. You have been tearing her down with your words and demeaning attitude toward her. You need to repent from that. You are yourself a debtor to God's tender mercies and do not deserve his salvation and everything else he freely gives you, even as you continue to fall short daily. Do you see how great is your own sin in not caring with tenderness and compassion for your wife in light of God's tender and forgiving mercies for you?

R: Sir, I must tell you that you have it wrong. I'm no longer a sinner. That doesn't mean I don't sin, but I'm a new creation and striving daily to live in obedience before God. I'm not perfect but I have acted with integrity with my wife and know what is best for her. I love her with firmness, truth, and hard work. God is not a softie; he disciplines us so we can get our act straight and that is how I know his love. My wife needs to get her act straight, get herself back in church, and cultivating the spiritual disciplines. I'm sure that will go a long way to stop her complaining and begin to improve things between us.

P: Ryan, did you get your act together for God to love you and embrace you with his forgiving mercy?

R: Yes, he gave me his mercy because I repented, I changed, and I cleaned up my act. I'm only asking the same of my wife for her to get better.

P: When one truly repents, indeed, there are changes, but the changes make us full of grace, mercy, and kindness for those broken and burdened by afflictions, weakness, and even sins. We reflect those changes in benevolent and tender service to those around us, beginning with those in our family. We combine truth and mercy in love as we begin to seek the good of our neighbor.

R: Well, maybe that's what she needs. I'm okay, Pastor. Don't worry about me; believe me.

P: No, Ryan, you are not okay. This is for you. You are guilty of not loving your wife as you should. You need to repent, to see your sins with her as worthy of death and condemnation. You need to confess your sin and turn to Christ for forgiveness. You need to acknowledge Jesus as the gift from the Father's kind and loving mercy to you as a sinner. Until you do, you have not repented. This is your issue!

CHAPTER 10

Concluding Thoughts to Keep the "Package" Going

THE GRACE OF GOD in Christ is free; we are called to gift living, namely, to approach God through Christ without merit and without our works. We are totally accepted by God through faith without our works, which means through grace without our merits. This, in a nutshell, is the word of promise contained in the gospel for sinners, and it is the word that gives us life, not just for justification and adoption as children but also for sanctification and good works unto glorification. This is gift living because we receive life from God both legally as well as practically through the gift of Christ's person and work, his righteous perfect living, atoning death, and vindicating resurrection for sinners freely. We must emphasize *freely* because no conditions whatsoever must be placed to receiving Christ through the gospel promise. He saves sinners, the ungodly, to wit, transgressors of the law without their works. Whoever comes does not have to bring anything of worth; rather, on the contrary, their unworthiness, their sins and offenses, their need and weakness, their ruin and misery qualify them for the kindness of the Savior of sinners.

Jesus Christ saves sinners without any works of righteousness; not their own works, not works in cooperation with God, not works inspired or produced in them by any virtue wrought in them, not by obedient loving repentance or faithful deeds of faith, not by any sin-forsaking virtue produced of the Spirit. No, Christ alone saves them by his redeeming representation, by his person and work, which is proclaimed and announced in the gospel for all sinners to receive through faith alone; and for all sinners who, receiving through faith alone and being declared forgiven and righteous in Christ alone, now ever feed on the same gospel promise for growth and nurturing of our faith, which now freely works through love. Christ is indeed the free gift for all of life. But many are the hindrances on the road to this blessed truth and life of gift living, obstacles through history, roadblocks in the interpretive task of Scripture, and lastly, hazards and dangers in the pastoral counseling and shepherding of souls.

We have traveled through history, especially early history and throughout the Middle Ages until the Reformation, perhaps an unpopular, not-much-traveled road because we have traveled looking for this free gospel and grace, not just looking to magnify other virtues and highlight contributions in the historical record. If we just travel through history looking for good contributions, we shall discover many that others have amply and sufficiently documented and can be clearly seen in the first few ecumenical councils of the church. But our hypothesis in traveling or tracking the gospel "shipment" has been to discover clear enunciations of the free gospel promise as announced by the biblical NT record, especially by Paul. More specifically, we have tracked looking for the gospel of forgiveness without works and righteousness imputed, namely, by grace without merits and faith without works. It is our conclusion that such doctrine and gift living is eminently scarce, if not altogether missing in fullness of clarity and splendor a la Romans or Galatians. Generally, the early fathers and the subsequent landscape unto the Reformation are strewn by a doctrine of righteousness conceived as infused and wrought within the sinner. Such seems to be the overwhelming verdict of the history that culminated in the Reformation. Now, this work does not claim an absolutely exhaustive study of the historical witnesses but only a significant representation, where the Pauline gospel grace should be radiantly shining through but appears glaringly absent or distorted.

We also admit and concur with the opinion that early witnesses were focused on other pressing matters impressed upon them by their contextual circumstances. Such a reality provides cause for our premise that no matter what other important battles are fought, if gospel proclamation is assumed, taken for granted, or relegated to a secondary plane, gospel truth has begun to be corroded because gospel truth proclamation is always a necessity and is always under attack. Thus, we claim that the enemy will often busy the church with very important fights as long as they can get their mouths and tongues to cease from clearly repeating the same gospel things. We can get the Trinity right, the two natures of Christ, the hypostatic union, the divinity of Christ and the Spirit, the virgin birth, the inerrancy of Scripture, the fundamentals, etc., but in the filling of our mouths with other very important truths we often let go of the cardinal truth of gospel salvation by grace without merits and faith without works. We have advanced the premise and recommend the dual burden and practice of fighting any important battles that come our way without ever ceasing to articulate gospel truth as if it is the most disputed and contested truth of the battle; and we must do so because even though it may seem that such is not the point in question, it is! The gospel is always the point in question and under attack as Christianity's capital. We must never stop defending it even when it seems like it needs no defense. That the enemy is always gunning for it we must always keep in mind. Thus, we commend the study of the early fathers and pre-Reformation contributions, but simply call attention to and encourage further study on what clarity they had on the gospel of forensic imputation through grace without merit and faith without works. Studies highlighting some precursors in this direction should be encouraged with more precision and clarity on the foregoing gospel criteria, which could be a follow-up work to this study. We also must reiterate that our sampling of the fathers is not at all comprehensive and remains open to reevaluations and reappraisals of the views expressed here, either on the topic generally or on any specific figure of the time. We will definitely be engaging in further and more in-depth studies on this period and would welcome more definitive and conclusive evidence as would change the conclusions and/or hypothesis provided herein.

We have also advanced an intramural criticism of the Reformed tradition in terms of the concepts of faith and repentance, the nature of the covenant and the necessity of works, the lack of clarity in distinction and use of law and gospel, as well as assurance. We believe that Calvin, whose admirable contributions cannot be overemphasized, however, laid a singular "muddy" seed in his treatment of faith and repentance. Calvin assigns for repentance the meaning of regeneration or the fruits of faith. He rightly defines faith, the instrument by which we are united to Christ, as persuasion and confidence in the mercy and love of God in Christ as announced in the promise of the gospel for sinners, and rightly affirms that such promise speaks assurance of itself for the sinner, who is thus called to come to Christ without their works. Hence, assurance, for Calvin, is of the essence of faith given the free nature of the grace and mercy of God in the gospel promise through which sinners are called to salvation. But in separating faith from repentance and loading the latter with the freight of obedient fruit or sanctification, Calvin now has provided for a widely known statement with its nefarious implications: "Yes, we are saved by faith, but you must also repent." The implication is that faith alone is not enough to be accepted before God unless you have also the working obedient repentance part of your faith as necessary for salvation, even if it is in in some ultimate sense of final or future salvation, as Piper, among others, is fond of saying.

We have commended the Augsburg Confession language of repentance as worthy of full acceptance over Calvin's, who may have been familiar with it, even tacitly acknowledging and somewhat agreeing that others have spoken differently on the issue with some degree of faithfulness, in his estimation. If repentance is loaded with the freight of obedience, and the biblical record demands repentance together with faith for salvation as instruments thereunto, then the obvious conclusion is that the works of repentance must be considered as part of the instrumental cause of salvation, which many among the Reformed accept, but we flatly denounce and reject as confusion on the nature of the covenant of grace and the lack of proper distinction between law and gospel. If a proper and classical distinction between the covenant of works—do this and you shall live in your righteousness—versus the covenant of grace—believe in the one who lived and died for you for righteousness—is maintained, no works, obedience, or righteousness wrought in us can be mixed to the basis for acceptance before God. Only if God demands of those he will justify both faith and obedience for acceptance before him can they be maintained, since the covenant of grace is then to be construed as conditional on both faith as well as works.

We must maintain that the only "condition" to be "instated" in the covenant of grace, to use Marrow theology language, is repentant belief or believing repentance, which does not involve any virtue value of works and righteousness obedience wrought or renewed within to be accepted before God. We commend then that repentance, though distinguished, cannot be separated in its definition from faith and vice versa. We must repent, that is, we must acknowledge ourselves guilty and worthy of death or condemnation, believing that Christ Jesus alone lived and died to save us, thus turning to God through his promise in Christ to save such who bring nothing of value in themselves to be saved but the sin that necessitates such a Savior. We must believe such promise in repentance, namely, turning to God as worthy of death and condemnation to be saved with empty hands bereft of any personal righteousness or virtue within to be accepted. This is true repentance and faith; God does not demand our law-keeping/righteousness/obedience to save us, except to lead us to the gospel promise through faith and repentance, where we are definitely and finally saved now and forever in and through Christ!

Our catechetical instruction in the book of Romans aims at supporting biblically the assertions, arguments, issues, and conclusions raised in the historical portion. Among some of the most important implications in this biblical piece are the following. Firstly, Paul aims in the first couple of chapters to accuse the whole world of their transgression and failure before God, as specially demonstrated or reckoned against them in the law. Paul is not, in chapter 2, advancing a positive note of being justified as a doer of the law, but rather accuses and holds everyone guilty of not being conformed to such righteous demands. Secondly, Paul goes on to advance the gospel promise in chapters 3–5 of salvation through "redemptive representation" or the mediating and substituting person and work of Christ. This is the righteousness of God for those who believe without merit and works, or by grace alone through faith alone. We highly commend the classical forensic view of justification with Luther's alien righteousness as according with the biblical way to be saved before God, rather than the transformational view afoot in the scholarly and doctrinal currents that have challenged Luther and the classical positions on Paul and justification. We, however, do not discount the transformational blessed implications of the classical view but affirm them.

Thus, thirdly and lastly, we wish to advance a path of sanctification through faith in the gospel promise, highlighting that Paul, when talking about union with Christ, makes reference to union with his dying and rising for us. Mortification and vivification takes place through ongoing active faith and repentance as provided for through the means of grace; the Christian walk consists in daily dying and rising with Christ or growing more deeply in the assurance of our union with his death and resurrection for us in love. Before mortification and vivification becomes a dynamic of obedient work, it is essentially a dynamic of faith and repentance without works, namely, gift living. This makes the preaching of the gospel central to feed and nourish believers unto progressive or practical sanctification. We must reject and get away from the notion and practice that preaching for the growth of believers can only involve the law and its commandments, and affirm that it is necessary to develop and practice a preaching that involves both law and gospel in their correct distinction, function, and application. Furthermore, we reject that the law in its third use (you must do this as a believer) is enough as content and application of the Christian sermon, while affirming that the preaching of the law, in addition to showing what ought to be done as a moral guide, always accuses; hence, it is always necessary to apply the grace and mercy of God in Christ, namely, the gospel—explicitly—in the Christian sermon for edification and growth by faith.

Our pastoral counseling sections aims at several important goals. One, to apply law and gospel to our interactions where conviction and guidance on God's moral will can be established, while also providing an empathic and merciful presence that may act and speak redemption for counselees through gospel truth and its manifold applications. Two, to steer away from a mere relationship of hostility and rejection of everything in modern psychology by providing an appropriate biblical framework that may offer the necessary gospel centrifugal and centripetal forces that help us filter whatever may be untrue and destructive from both theology as well as psychology. And three, to demonstrate through real-life cases the application of the two goals above in what we have called the Redemptive Cognitive-Relational Narrative framework (RCRN) for pastoral counseling. We consider it important to always reflect on our pastoral counseling endeavors within the bounds of a well-defined theoretical framework. Pastoral counseling, like preaching, should not proceed on a haphazard course. The gospel redemptive story provides the metanarrative to engage counselees with the kind of cognitive and relational appraisals that may help people embark on healthier paths within a Christ-centered perspective.

We believe these times, as always, have their share of gospel threats. Several winds of doctrine abound today that require careful thinking and discernment by the church. It is our belief that unless a clear and healthy law and gospel approach to our theology, preaching, and pastoral counseling emerges, the church will suffer greatly from very sophisticated attacks on the gospel. Among these we would name Lordship Salvation (LS), Federal Vision, New Perspective, and Final or Future Justification (FJ). What all of these have in common is a blurring of the lines between law and gospel that ends up conditioning the gospel to some kind of law obedience, thus compromising the faith-alone, grace-alone, Christ-alone gospel of our salvation. While excellent work has been done on Federal Vision and New Perspective lately, not enough reflection and engagement has been done with LS and FJ as of late.[1] We recommend more specific engagement with

---

1. For an excellent critique of Lordship Salvation as espoused by John MacArthur see Horton, *Christ the Lord*. We thoroughly identify with Horton's critique of both Hodges and MacArthur. We are not aware of any thorough critique of Piper's position in print and encourage further critical interaction with it.

these two currents that seem to have been given a pass in some circles and continue to claim many adherents nationally as well as internationally, especially among the Reformed. We are aware that such doctrinal positions may claim some historical backing within the Reformed, as it can be observed that such controversies about free grace or unconditional covenant versus a conditional covenant in varying degrees have always existed, e.g., the Marrow controversy and Seceder tradition in Scotland. Undoubtedly, the gospel of the free and unconditional grace of God in Christ will also suffer at the hands of libertine and graceless people who use it for their own means of perverse living and gain. There is no end to the corruption of gospel truth and grace; however, we have wanted to highlight the arguably most insidiously popular, especially among the Reformed, given their high admixture of truth with error.

In the hopes of continuing to stimulate inquiry, dialogue, and reflection, we wish to close with the following theses based on the law and gospel understanding we have historically, biblically, and pastorally sought to advance in this work. We hope that these can be used as a tool for instruction as well as a challenge for further interaction with the topic by other authors, students, and believers seeking to discern and embrace gift living as opposed to works living! While the insights and practical living that may result from law and gospel applications may originate from Lutheran teachings, we are not promoting here a wholesale embrace of Lutheranism. We must always remember the biblical mandate to "examine everything and retain what is good," and such also applies to whatever tradition we come from, own, and prefer. Let us then send the "package" off for further transit with the following theses:

1. We reject that repentance for salvation is to give up sin or any other surrender, resolution and/or commitment to obey the law of God or of Christ; and we affirm that

    It is the conviction or knowledge of our sin before God as guilty and worthy of condemnation, leading us to the confession of sin with faith in Christ Jesus for salvation, from which the obedient fruits of repentance result.

2. We reject the call to repentance for salvation to be a call to discipleship, although everyone who truly repents becomes a disciple; and we affirm that discipleship is a call to grow in obedience to Christ and the commandments of the law through him for those who have *already*

been called to salvation and become disciples *without* obedience or works of the law.

3. We reject that faith saves or counts before God for salvation only if it has works of obedience; and we affirm that faith *alone*, that is, without obedience to the law, is sufficient to be accepted before God because it simply trusts in Christ; although such faith will always be accompanied by obedience as its fruit.

4. We reject that the call of the gospel consists in a call that includes obeying the law, or the commandments of God or of Christ, as a condition for salvation; and we affirm that obedience to the commandments of God or of Christ according to the law are *fruits* and *consequences* of having been saved *already*, without any works or obedience to the law.

5. We reject that the believer must seek in his works and/or fruits of obedience to the law the primary evidence and assurance of salvation; and we affirm that these should be sought only as secondary/reflective evidence after seeking and finding our own assurance primarily in the direct promise of salvation for sinners *without* their works.

6. We reject that the works and the fruits of obedience are the essential characteristic of faith for salvation; and we affirm that the essential characteristic of faith for salvation is that it trusts and rests in the person and work of Christ for salvation, *without* works of righteousness despite being affected by diverse sins, weaknesses, and temptations.

7. We reject that the works and obedience of believers are necessary to justify them before God in the final judgment and thus be finally accepted for salvation; and we affirm that the believer is justified or accepted by God *without* any works, through faith alone, at all times during their past as a believer, at present, and also in the future including the final judgment; although good works do serve an evidentiary or demonstrative role before the world.

8. We reject that the believer is sanctified by the mere teaching of the law and practices or disciplines of obedience to the law; and we affirm that the constant preaching of the gospel is absolutely necessary, that is, of the grace, mercy, and love of God without our works, through the means of grace, for a progressive sanctification by faith; only in light of such gospel indicatives should the imperatives of the law be used for the believer's edification.

9. We reject that the believer cannot fall and remain in great sins and/or spiritual aridity even unto death; and we affirm that the believer can be carnal and/or disobedient and immature for a long period of time, or until death, without losing his faith and eternal salvation but bringing upon himself the severe discipline of the Lord; this, however, does not mean such a person will be utterly bereft of love, faith, and hope in Christ, as diminished or obscured as these may be, or that they are in the flesh.

10. We reject that progressive sanctification in obedience to God is promoted and advanced merely by the fear of punishment or torment, whether temporary or eternal; and we affirm that the goodness, mercy, and love of God are the essential, primary, and most effective motivators of the Christian life.

11. We reject that there is a true faith where there is an absolute lack of good works and/or love of God; and we affirm that true faith that trusts in Christ without works in order to be thus accepted by God will have some fruit of love and obedience, which must be cultivated and increased during the Christian life.

12. We reject that the Christian can grow spiritually without striving to remain in the constant use of the means of grace; and we affirm that these are necessary for growth in spiritual maturity as they communicate the promise of the gospel for sinners without works, namely, the free gospel promise for all who believe.

13. We reject that preaching for the growth of believers can only involve the law and its commandments; and we affirm that it is necessary to develop and practice a preaching that involves *both* the law and the gospel, in their correct distinction, function, and application.

14. We reject that the law in its third use (you must do this as a believer) is enough as content and application of the Christian sermon; and we affirm that the preaching of the law, in addition to showing what ought to be done as a moral guide, always accuses and gives conviction of sin, hence, it is always necessary to apply the grace and mercy of God in Christ, namely, the gospel, *explicitly* in the Christian sermon for edification and growth by faith.

15. We reject that Scripture can be understood or preached without an *explicit* reference to Christ; and we affirm that all of Scripture, in each

CONCLUDING THOUGHTS TO KEEP THE "PACKAGE" GOING

of its parts as well as in its totality, testifies to Christ, *who* must be *explicitly* proclaimed and applied to the church in all the comfort and splendor of his person and work.

Admittedly, these theses may sound very provocative and even radical, but we trust that for those accustomed to a law and gospel perspective, the biblical truths and practices they seek to advance may be readily apparent. And for those who would disagree, we would only hope for a chance for dialogue and debate to be had on them in such a way that the topics and perspective presented in this book can have a true and engaged hearing. The gospel mail must go on; Godspeed!

Bibliography

Aristotle. *Nicomachean Ethics*. Book 2.1. Translated by W. D. Ross. Internet Classics Archive. http://classics.mit.edu/Aristotle/nicomachaen.html.
Allison, C. Fitzsimons. *The Rise of Moralism: The Proclamation of the Gospel from Hooker to Baxter*. Vancouver: Regent College Publishing, 1966.
Barclay, John M. G. *Paul and the Gift*. Grand Rapids: Eerdmans, 2015.
Beeke, John R., and Mark Jones. *A Puritan Theology: Doctrine for Life*. Grand Rapids: Reformation Heritage, 2012.
Bridges, Jerry. *The Disciplines of Grace: God's Role and Our Role in the Pursuit of Holiness*. Colorado Springs: NavPress, 2006.
Calvin, John. *Institutes of the Christian Religion*. Translated by Henry Beveridge. Peabody, MA: Hendrickson, 2008.
Duffy, Eamon. *The Stripping of the Altars: Traditional Religion in England, c. 1400–c. 1580*. New Haven, CT: Yale University Press, 1992.
Fisher, Edward. *The Marrow of Modern Divinity*. N.p.: n.p., 2014. Originally published in two parts, London: E.F., 1645, 1649.
Forde, Gerhard O. *On Being a Theologian of the Cross: Reflections on Luther's Heidelberg Disputation, 1518*. Grand Rapids: Eerdmans, 1997.
Gathercole, Simon J. *Where Is Boasting?: Early Jewish Soteriology and Paul's Response in Romans 1–5*. Grand Rapids: Eerdmans, 2002.
Gonzalez, Justo L. *A History of Christian Thought: From the Beginnings to the Council of Chalcedon*. Nashville: Abingdon, 1970.
Horton, Michael S. *Christ the Lord: The Reformation and Lordship Salvation*. Eugene, OR: Wipf and Stock, 1992.
Jurgens, William A. *The Faith of the Early Fathers*. 3 vols. Collegeville, MN: Liturgical, 1970–1979.
Johnson, Eric L. *Foundations for Soul Care: A Christian Psychology Proposal*. Downers Grove, IL: InterVarsity, 2007.
Johnson, Gary L. W., and Guy Prentiss Waters. *By Faith Alone: Answering the Challenges to the Doctrine of Justification*. Wheaton, IL: Crossway, 2006.
Kendall, R. T. *Calvin and English Calvinism to 1649*. Eugene, OR: Wipf and Stock, 1997.
Kolb, Robert, and Timothy J. Wengert, editors. *The Book of Concord: The Confessions of the Evangelical Lutheran Church*. Minneapolis: Fortress, 2000.
Lane, Timothy S., and Paul David Tripp. *How People Change: How Christ Changes Us by His Grace*. Greensboro, NC: New Growth, 2008.

Linebaugh, J. A. *God, Grace, and Righteousness in Wisdom of Solomon and Paul's Letter to the Romans: Texts in Conversation*. Leiden, Netherlands: Brill, 2013.
Lull, Timothy, F. editor. *Martin Luther's Basic Theological Writings*. Minneapolis: Fortress Press, 1989.
Luther, Martin. *Commentary on Romans*. Translated by J. Theodore Mueller. Grand Rapids: Zondervan, 1954.
———. *Lectures on Galatians (1535), Chapters 1–4*. Translated by Jaroslav Pelikan. Luther's Works 26. Saint Louis: Concordia, 1964.
———. *Lectures on Galatians (1535), Chapters 5–6; Lectures on Galatians (1519), Chapters 1–6*. Translated by Jaroslav Pelikan. Luther's Works 27. Saint Louis: Concordia, 1964.
MacArthur, John F. *The Gospel According to Jesus*. Grand Rapids: Zondervan, 2008.
Magill, Frank N., and Ian P. McGreal, editors. *Christian Spirituality: The Essential Guide to the Most Influential Spiritual Writings of the Christian Tradition*. New York: HarperCollins, 1988.
McCormack, Bruce L., editor. *Justification in Perspective: Historical Developments and Contemporary Challenges*. Grand Rapids: Baker Academic, 2006.
McGrath, Alister. E. *Iustitia Dei: A History of the Christian Doctrine of Justification*. Cambridge: Cambridge University Press, 1986.
———. *The Intellectual Origins of the European Reformation*. 2nd ed. Oxford: Blackwell, 2004.
———. *Luther's Theology of the Cross: Martin Luther's Theological Breakthrough*. Oxford: Blackwell, 1985.
McGiffert, Arthur Cushman. *A History of Christian Thought*. Vol. 1: *Early and Eastern*. New York: Scribner, 1960.
McMinn, Mark R. *Sin and Grace in Christian Counseling: An Integrative Paradigm*. Downers Grove, IL: IVP Academic, 2008.
McMinn, Mark R., and Clark D. Campbell. *Integrative Psychotherapy: Toward a Comprehensive Christian Approach*. Downers Grove, IL: IVP Academic, 2007.
Null, Ashley. *Thomas Cranmer's Doctrine of Repentance: Renewing the Power to Love*. Oxford: Oxford University Press, 2006.
Piper, John. *Future Grace: The Purifying Power of the Promises of God*. Colorado Springs, CO: Multnomah, 2012.
Rolle, Richard. *The Fire of Love and the Mending of Life*. Translated by M. L. del Mastro. New York: Doubleday, 1981.
Seneca, Lucius Annaeus. *Seneca: Moral Essays*. Vol. 3. Translated by John W. Basore. Cambridge, MA: Harvard University Press, 1989.
Vandoodeward, William. *The Marrow Controversy and Seceder Tradition: Marrow Theology in the Associate Presbytery and Associate Synod Secession Churches of Scotland (1733–1799)*. Grand Rapids: Reformation Heritage, 2011.
Walther, C. F. W., editor. *Law and Gospel: How to Read and Apply the Bible*. Saint Louis: Concordia, 2010.
Waters, Guy Prentiss. *Justification and the New Perspectives on Paul: A Review and Response*. New Jersey: P & R, 2006.
———. *The Federal Vision and Covenant Theology: A Comparative Analysis*. New Jersey: P & R, 2006.
Watson, Francis. *Paul, Judaism, and the Gentiles: A Sociological Approach*. Cambridge: Cambridge University Press, 1986.

Westerholm, Stephen. *Justification Reconsidered: Rethinking a Pauline Theme*. Grand Rapids: Eerdmans, 2013.
Winston, David S. *The Wisdom of Solomon*. Anchor Bible 43. Garden City, NY: Doubleday, 1979.
Yalom, Irvin D. with Molyn Leszcz. *The Theory and Practice of Group Psychotherapy*. New York: Basic, 2005.
Zahl, Paul F. M. *Grace in Practice: A Theology of Everyday Life*. Grand Rapids: Eerdmans, 2007.
———. *2000 Years of Amazing Grace: The Story and Meaning of the Christian Faith: the Christianity Primer*. Lanham, MD: Rowman & LittleField, 2007.

Vita

DAVID MENENDEZ WAS BORN and raised in Cuba where he learned English from an early age as well as acquiring a love for the Lord and freedom in his formative years. He would later immigrate to America. He married Aurora 20 years ago, his best friend and companion, and with whom he has been blessed to parent a son and a daughter.

In America he pursued undergraduate studies in English and concentration in American History. He would further go on to pursue graduate degrees in Social Studies, Counseling Psychology, and Divinity, as well as a Doctor of Ministry from Knox Theological Seminary, amid his growing passion for the humanities and ministry with a strong gospel/grace emphasis.

He has been a pastor now for almost 20 years years with a bilingual ministry that pursues both Spanish and English speaking people with the passion of knowing and sharing the amazing grace of God proclaimed through the gospel. He shares with all his lifetime passion for learning as well as the supreme delightful blessing of loving and being loved by God in Christ.

www.ingramcontent.com/pod-product-compliance
Lightning Source LLC
Chambersburg PA
CBHW062042220426
43662CB00010B/1608